The
Schleswig-Holstein War 1864

TWO VOLUMES IN ONE SPECIAL EDITION

The
Schleswig-Holstein War 1864
Between Denmark and Prussia & Austria

TWO VOLUMES IN ONE SPECIAL EDITION

Edward Dicey

The Redoubts of Düppel

Charles Lowe

LEONAUR

The Schleswig-Holstein War 1864
Between Denmark and Prussia & Austria
TWO VOLUMES IN ONE SPECIAL EDITION
by Edward Dicey
The Redoubts of Düppel
by Charles Lowe

FIRST EDITION

Leonaur is an imprint
of Oakpast Ltd

ISBN: 978-1-78282-521-0 (hardcover)
ISBN: 978-1-78282-522-7 (softcover)

http://www.leonaur.com

Publisher's Notes

The views expressed in this book are not necessarily
those of the publisher.

Contents

The Redoubts of Düppel

Charles Lowe

Schleswig-Holstein, the cradle of the Anglo-Saxon race, was the beautiful and interesting province which formed the bone of bloody contention between the Prussians and the Danes in the year 1864, just a year after the Prince of Wales had wedded the Danish "sea-king's daughter from over the sea," and made all Englishmen take the very deepest interest in the hopeless struggle of her undaunted countrymen against an overwhelming foe.

The cause of quarrel was one of the most complicated questions which ever vexed the minds of statesmen, and seemed so incapable of solution that an irreverent Frenchman once declared it would remain after the heavens and the earth had passed away. But on the death of Frederick VII. of Denmark, in November, 1863, Herr von Bismarck, who had the year before become Prussian Premier, determined that the difficulty should now be settled by "blood and iron." Briefly put, the new King of Denmark, Christian IX., father of the Princess of Wales, wanted to rule over the Elbe Duchies, as Schleswig-Holstein was called, in a way, as was thought at Berlin, unfavourable to the rights and aspirations of their German population; while, on the other hand, the Germanic *Diet*, or Council of German Sovereigns at Frankfort, was resolved that this should not be so. And rather than that this should be so, it decreed "execution" on the King of Denmark, who had a seat in the *diet* as for the duchies, and selected two of its members, Hanover and Saxony, to enforce its decision.

But not content with this, Austria and Prussia, the leading members of the *diet*, also resolved to take the field, as executive bailiffs, so to speak, of the judgment of the German Court; and this they did at the beginning of 1864 with a united force of about 45.000 men. That

7

was not so very large a force, considering the size of modern armies, but it was much larger than that opposed to it by the valiant Danes, about 36,000 in number, who were commanded by General de Meza. The Austrians were commanded by Field-Marshal von Gablenz, and the Prussians by their own Prince Frederick Charles, surnamed the "Red Prince," from the scarlet uniform of his favourite regiment, the Zieten Hussars.

The commander of the combined Austro-Prussian Army was the Prussian Field-Marshal von Wrangel—"old Papa Wrangel," as he was fondly called—who looked, and spoke, and acted like a survival from the time of the Thirty Years' or the Seven Years' War. He was a grim old *beau sabreur*, who, in his later days, used to grind his teeth (what of them were left) and scatter *groschen* among the street arabs of Berlin, under the impression that he was sowing a crop of bullets that would yet spring up and prove the death of all democrats and other nefarious characters dangerous to military monarchy and the rule of the sword in the civil state.

"*In Gottes Namen drauf!*"—"Forward in God's name!"—"Papa" Wrangel had wired to the various contingents of his forces on the 1st February, when at last the Danes had replied to his demands with an emphatic "No!" and then the combined Austro-Prussian Army swept over the Eider amid a blinding storm of snow.

The Prussians took the right, the Austrians the left of the advance into the duchies; and after one or two preliminary actions of no great moment, the invaders reached the Danewerk, a very strong line of earthworks which had taken the place of the bulwark thrown up by the Danes in ancient times against the incursions of the Germans. Here the Prussians prepared for a stubborn resistance, but what was their surprise and their delight, on the morning of the 6th February, to find that the Danes had evacuated overnight this first bulwark line of theirs, leaving 154 guns and large quantities of stores and ammunition a prey to their enemies! Caution, not cowardice, had been the motive of this retreat of theirs, for they saw that, if they had remained, they would have run the risk of being outflanked and outnumbered; so they determined, from reasons of military policy, to retire further northward and take up their dogged stand behind their second line of entrenchments at Düppel, there to await the assault of their overwhelming foes.

Sending on the Austrians on the left into Jutland to dispose of the Danes in that quarter, "Papa" Wrangel selected the "Red Prince" and

FIELD-MARSHAL VON WRANGEL

his Prussians to crack the nuts which had been thrown in their way in the shape of the redoubts of Düppel. Prince Frederick Charles was one of the best and bravest soldiers that had been produced by the fighting family of the Hohenzollerns since the time of Frederick the Great. A man about the middle height, strongly built, broad-shouldered, florid-faced, sandy- bearded, bull-necked, rough in manner and speech, and homely in all his ways—he was just the sort of leader to command the affections and stimulate the courage of the Prussian soldier. There was much of the bulldog in the "Red Prince," so he was the very man to entrust with such a task as that of hanging on to the Danes at Düppel.

Yet this task was one of exceeding difficulty, for the redoubts of Düppel formed such a formidable line of defence as had rarely, if ever, before opposed the advance of an invading army in the open field. All the natural advantages of ground, with its happy configuration of land and water, were on the side of the Danes, whose main object it was to prevent their foes from setting foot on the Schleswig island of Alsen, forming a stepping-stone, so to speak, to Denmark itself, much in the same way as the island of Anglesey does to Ireland. To continue the comparison, the Menai Strait corresponds to the Alsen-Sund which separates the mainland of Schleswig from the island of Alsen. Of this island the chief town is Sonderburg, which was connected by the mainland, into which it looks over, by two pontoon bridges, at the end of which the Danes threw up a *tête-du-pont*, or bridge-head entrenchment, to defend the approach and passage; while about a couple of miles further inland they had constructed a chain of no fewer than ten heavy forts, or redoubts, all connected by lesser earthworks and entrenchments.

This line of redoubts, about three miles long, ran right across the neck of a peninsula of the mainland, called the Sundewitt, one end resting on the Alsen-Sund and the other on a gulf, or bay, of the Baltic, called the Wenningbund. The redoubts were placed along the brow of a ridge which overlooked and commanded all the undulating country for miles in front, while in the rear again the ground dipped away gently down towards the Alsen-Sund and its bridge-head, affording fine shelter and camping-ground to the Danes. A lovelier or more romantic-looking region, with its winding bays and silver-glancing straits, its picturesque blending of wood and water, could scarcely be imagined.

Such a position as that which the Danes had taken up would have been of no value whatever against foes like the English, seeing that the latter might have gone with their warships and shelled the Danes clean out of their line of redoubts without ever so much as landing a single man, for, as already explained, the line of forts rested on the sea at both ends. But at this time, fortunately for the Danes, the Prussians had little or nothing of a navy, so that they must needs essay on land what they could not attempt by sea; while the Danes, on the other hand, though weaker on land, were decidedly superior to their foes on water. In particular, they had one warship, or monitor, the *Rolf Krake*, which gained immortal fame by the bold and devil-may-care manner in which it worried, and harassed, and damaged, and kept the Prussians perpetually awake. It lurked like a corsair in the corners of the bays, and creeks, and winding sea-arms of that amphibious region, and darted out upon occasion to shell and molest the Prussians in their trenches before the Düppel lines.

For the Prussians had soon come to see that it would be quite impossible for them to capture the Düppel redoubts save by regular process of sap and siege. The redoubts proved to be far more formidable than they ever fancied; and it would have involved an enormous sacrifice of life on the part of the Prussians to rush for them at once. The pretty certain result of such impetuosity would have been that not a soul almost of the stormers would have lived to tell the tale. For three whole years the Danes had been at work on these redoubts, and what it takes three years to construct cannot by any possibility be captured in as many days. Much had to be done by the Prussians, then, before sitting down before the redoubts.

If a simile may be borrowed from the game of football, the "forwards" of the Danes had first to be disposed of. For not only did they occupy the redoubts, but likewise all the strong points in the country for two or three miles in front of them, just as modern ironclads hang out nets to guard their hulls from the impact of torpedoes. In a similar manner the Danes had thrown out a network of men to fend off all hostile approach to their forts and prevent the Prussians from settling down near enough to them for the purposes of sap and siege.

While, therefore, the Prussians were busy bringing to the front their heavy guns and other siege-material, others of them were set to the work of sweeping clean, as with a broom of bayonets, the open positions in front of the redoubts held by their defenders. But this sweeping process was by no means either an easy or a bloodless task. For while the Danes numbered 22,000 troops, the "Red Prince" in front of them disposed at this time (though later he was reinforced) of no more than 16,000 men, and there was always the danger that the Danes, assuming the offensive, would sally out of their lines and seek to overwhelm their numerically weaker foes. Consequently the Prussians had recourse to the spade in order to supplement the defensive power of their rifles, and thus they first of all took up an entrenched position running in a long semicircle from Broacker on their right to Satrup on the left, at a distance of about three miles or more from the real object of their ambition—the line of Danish redoubts.

Two positions in front of these redoubts—the villages of Düppel and Rackebüll—were fiercely contested by the Danes; but on the 17th of March, after fighting in a manner which gave their foes a very high opinion of their courage, they retired behind their earthworks with the loss of 676 men, while the Prussians, on their part, had to pay for their victory by only 138 lives. This disparity in loss was doubtless due to the fact that, while the Danes were only armed with the old smooth-bore muzzle-loading musket, the Prussians had adopted the new Zündnadelgewehr, or needle-gun, the parent of all modern breech-loading and repeating rifles, which gave them a tremendous advantage over their opponents.

In one of the preliminary encounters above referred to, a party of Danes, against whom a superior force of Prussian light-infantry (*Jäger*) was advancing, threw down their arms in token of submission; but as the Prussians came forward, they snatched them up again, fired a volley, and rushed on with the bayonet. The Prussians let them come to within twenty-yards' distance, and then, raising their deadly needle-guns, shot them down to a man. The treacherous conduct of the Danes above referred to caused great bitterness among the Prussians; but, even after death, the latter showed their foes the respect which brave men owe to one another, and in West Düppel they raised a cross with this inscription:—

Here lie twenty-five brave Danes, who died the hero's death, 17th February, 1864.

The result of these preliminary tussles was that the Danes attempted no more outfalls, and from the 17th to the 28th of March one might almost have concluded that an armistice had been agreed to but for an occasional sputtering and spitting of rifle-fire between the foreposts, who thus employed their time when not exchanging other courtesies in the form of pipe-lights, tobacco-pouches, and spirit-flasks. But now the time was come when it behoved the Prussians to get as close to the redoubts as possible, for the purpose of opening their siege-trenches, and General von Raven's Brigade was selected to sweep the ground in front of the Danish position of ail its outposts. It was an early Easter this year, and just when the preachers were proclaiming to their congregations that the season of peace and goodwill to all men had now again come round, the Danes and Prussians were fighting like fiends under cover of the darkness.

The 18th Prussian Fusiliers had crept forward as far nearly as the wire-fencing and palisades in front of the redoubts, when the dawn suddenly revealed them to the Danes; and just at this moment, too, what should appear upon the scene but the ubiquitous *Rolf Krake*, which, at a distance of about five hundred yards, opened upon the advancing Prussians such a shower of shell and grape-shot as forced them to retire, causing these baffled fusiliers to curse the very name of the ship-builder who had ever laid the keel of such a bold and bothersome vessel.

At length, during the night of the 30th March, the Prussians managed to open their first parallel at a distance of about eight hundred paces from the line of the redoubts, and now, so to speak, they had reached the beginning of the end. The men on duty in this parallel, or shelter-trench (about eight feet deep), were relieved at first every forty-eight hours, and then every twenty-four, the former period having been found to be too great a strain on the soldiers, who, in consequence, had soon as many as ten per cent, on the sick list. For nothing could have been more trying to the constitution than this trench-life, with its cold nights, and rain, and mud, and manifold wretchedness.

Yet the Prussian soldiers, who were all very young fellows—mere boys some of them—kept up their spirits in the most wonderful manner, and indulged in all kinds of fun—mounting a gas-pipe on a couple of cart-wheels, and thus drawing the fire of the Danes, who imagined it to be a cannon; making sentries out of clay, and otherwise indulging in the thousand-and-one humours of a camp. They were also cheered by frequent visits from their commander, the "Red Prince," who—although housed in most comfortable, not to say luxurious, quarters at the *schloss*, or *château*, of Gravenstein, about six miles to the rear—failed not to ride to the front every day and acquaint himself with all that was going on. With such a commander soldiers will do anything, and hence the whole Prussian force in front of the Danish redoubts began to burn with a fighting ardour which neither cold, nor wet, nor

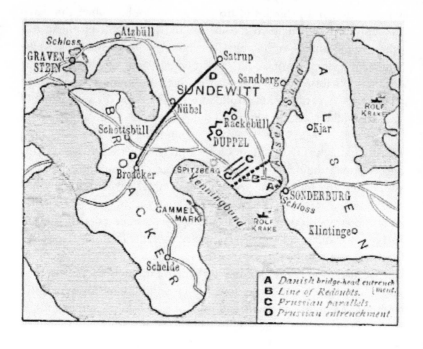

Schloss

GRAVEN
STEIN

Atzbüll

Satrup

D

Sandberg

SUNDEWITT

Nübel

Räckebüll

DÜPPEL

Schöttsbüll

B
R
Ö
D

D

Brodcker

SPITZBERG

C

C

A

A
L
S
E
N

ALSEN SUND

Kjar

ROLF
KRAKE

SONDERBURG
Schloss

A
C
K
E
R

Venningbund

GAMMEL
MARK

ROLF
KRAKE

S
E
N
Z

Klintingeo

Schelde

A	*Danish bridge-head entrench-* [ment.
B	*Line of Redoubts.*
C	*Prussian parallels.*
D	*Prussian entrenchment.*

knee-deep mud could in the least degree damp or depress.

On the other hand, the Danes, though better off for shelter in their block-houses, wooden barracks, and casemates, were not in such good spirits. One of the few things, apparently, that cheered their hearts was the sight of the numerous English tourists—"T. G's," or "travelling gents," as they used to be called in the Crimea, and *kriegs-bummler*, or war-loafers, as they are dubbed in Germany—who, arrayed in suits of a most fearful and wonderful make, streamed over to the Cimbrian Peninsula in quest of sensation and adventure, exposing themselves on parapet and sky-line to the shells of the Prussians with a devil-me-care coolness which proved a source of new inspiration to the Danskes.

Simultaneously with the pushing on of their parallel work, the Prussians kept up a tremendous fire on the forts, but the Danes showed their good sense by lying quietly in their case- mates and scarcely noticing the storm of missiles directed against them. These missiles did them and their earthworks very little harm, and they were not to be terrified by mere noise. Before the Prussians had settled down to their trench-work, their batteries over the bay at Gammelmark firing day and night had in the course of a fortnight thrown about 7,500 shot and shell into the Danish redoubts, yet not more than seventy-five officers and men had been killed or disabled by all this roaring volcano of heavy guns; and, indeed, it was computed about this time that the Prussians were purchasing the lives of their enemies at about 500 cannon-shots per head. "The huge earthen mounds or humps (of forts)," wrote a correspondent, "might have marked the graves of an extinct race, or been the result of some gigantic mole's obscure toil," for all the signs of life which the Prussian bombardment drew from the redoubts.

One night a curious thing happened to a company of the 60th Prussian regiment. In the course of some skirmishing it got too far forward, and, when day broke, it found itself in a slight hollow of the ground so near to Forts 1 and 2 that, had it tried to return to its own lines, it must have been annihilated by the grape-shot of the Danes. The shelter afforded it by the nature of the ground was so trifling that the men were forced to lie down flat upon their bellies to avoid being shot. In this unpleasant position they lay the whole day, for the Danes, strange to say, did not seek to sally out and capture them; and it was not till late in the evening that the company, under cover of the darkness, was able to rejoin their friends. They had eaten nothing in the interval, for, though they had provisions in their pockets, or haver-

PRINCE FREDERICK CHARLES

sacks, the least movement they made to get at this provender exposed them to the enemy's fire.

The first parallel had been opened on the 30th of March, and the second was accomplished in the night of the 10th of April. It was now expected that the "Red Prince," without more ado, would make a rush for the forts and be done with them—the more so as there now began to be whisperings of a political conference of the Powers which might meet and baulk the Prussian soldier of the final reward of all his toil. But still Prince Frederick Charles gave not the signal for the assault, and then it oozed out that this delay was simply due to the command of his royal uncle, King (afterward *Kaiser*) William, a very humane monarch, who, wishing to spare as much as possible the blood of his brave soldiers, had directed that still another—a third—parallel should be made, so as to shorten the distance across which the stormers would have to rush before reaching the redoubts.

Meanwhile the Prussians prepared themselves for the assault, among other things by getting up sham works in imitation of those they had to attack, where the battalions destined for the purpose were practised in breaking down palisades and using scaling-ladders, as well as in disposing of *chevaux de frise* and other impediments usual in the defence of forts. The Danish redoubts were known to the Prussians as Nos. 1, 2, 3, 4, 5, 6, 7, 8, 9, and 10, beginning from their—the Prussian—right on the sea, and their foremost parallel fronted this line of forts from 1 to 6. Against these forts the Prussians had thrown up twenty-four batteries mounting ninety-four guns, and now at last these guns were to give voice in a chorus such as had not rent the sky since the fall of Sebastopol.

But just as every storm is preceded by a strange delusive silence, so the day before the assault on the Düppel redoubts—the 17th of April—was a beautifully calm, sunny Sunday, with earth and sky embracing in a common joy over the birth of spring, and the encircling sea smooth as glass—a lovely day, and the last but one that many a brave man was doomed to see. For the order had gone forth from Prince Frederick Charles that at 10 o'clock precisely on the following (Monday) morning the redoubts should at last be stormed. At dawn of day the whole line of Prussian batteries should open fire on the forts, pouring upon them one continuous cataract of shot and shell till 10 o'clock, when the storming columns would start out of their trenches and "go for" the redoubts with might and main.

At 2 o'clock a.m. these columns—six in number, drawn by lot

from the various brigades so that all might have an impartial share in the honour of the day—emerged from the Büffell-Koppel wood well in the rear, and silently marched in the darkness to the parallels. Each of these six columns was thus composed:—First of all a company of infantry with orders to take extended front about 150 paces from its particular redoubt, and open fire on the besieged. Following these sharpshooters, pioneers and engineers with spades, axes, ladders, and all other storming gear, including bags of blasting powder, and after them, at 100 paces distance, the storming column itself, followed at 150 paces by a reserve of equal strength, together with a score of artillerists for manning the captured guns of the Danes.

The Danes, in the darkness of the night, knew nothing whatever of all these preparations, and it was only when the first streaks of dawn began to chequer the eastern sky that they were aroused out of their sleep by such an infernal outburst of cannon-thunder all along their front as had never before, in lieu of the twittering and chirping of birds, greeted the advent of a beautiful day in spring. For six long mortal hours did the Prussians continue this terrific cannonade, of which the violence and intensity may be inferred from the fact that during this time no fewer than 11,500 shot and shell were hurled at and into the Danish redoubts. The material damage done to these redoubts was less, perhaps, than the demoralisation thereby caused to their defenders; but the latter was the result which the Prussians, perhaps, aimed at and valued most.

Shortly before ten the awful cannonade suddenly ceased, and was followed by a few minutes' painful silence. During this brief interval the field-preachers, who had given the Sacrament to all the stormers the night before, now again addressed to them a few fervid words of religious encouragement, and then at the "*Nun, Kinder, in Gottes Namen!*" ("Now, my children, away with you in God's name!") of their commanders, the six storming columns, raising a loud and simultaneous cheer, dashed out of their trenches and across to their respective redoubts to the stirring music of the *Preussenlied* played by the bands of three regiments—"*Ich bin ein Preuss; kennt Ihr meine Färbe?*" ("I am a Prussian: know ye then my colours?")

For a few seconds the Danes seem to be taken aback by this sudden onrush of their foes, and then they recognise that this is no mere outpost affair such as caused them some time before to boast that they had repulsed a Prussian attack all along their line. They look and comprehend; and by the time their Prussian assailants have half covered the

THE GERMAN SOLDIERS MAKING SENTRIES OUT OF CLAY

distance between the trenches and the forts, their parapets are fringed with the smoke of sharp-crackling volleys of musketry, for, strange to say, they do not use their guns and dose their assailants with destructive rounds of grape. The Prussians rush forward, and many of them fall. Their pioneers cut down the wires, hack and blow up the palisades, tug, strain, and open up a passage for the stormers, who swarm down into the ditch and up the formidable face of the breastwork.

The crown prince, at the side of "Papa" Wrangel, is looking on from the Gammelmark height on the opposite side of the bay, while his cousin, the "Red Prince," and his staff have taken their stand on the Spitzberg, well to the rear of the line of zigzags. The stormers swarm up the breastworks like ants, and some of them fall back upon the heads of their comrades mortally struck by Danish bullets. At last they reach the top of the parapets and see the whites of their enemies' eyes, and a short but desperate hand-to-hand encounter ensues. Many of the Danes, seeing the foe thus upon them, throw down their arms and surrender, but many will not give in, and are shot or struck down with bullet, bayonet, and butt.

At Fort 2 the Prussians cannot force their way through the palisades, and are consequently slaughtered as they stand. "Better one of us than ten!" cries a pioneer, Klinké by name (for a monument now stands to his memory on the exact scene of his heroism), who rushes forward with a bag of powder and blows at once the palisades and his own person into atoms—sacrificing himself to save his comrades, and thus secure himself a golden register in the annals of the Prussian Army. The stormers now dash on and up, and presently the black-and-white flag of Prussia is seen waving on the parapets of the redoubt. It sinks again, but is once more raised to remain, and in less than a quarter of an hour from the time that the stormers sprang out of their trenches they are masters of six redoubts. It was all done, so to speak, in the twinkling of an eye—short, sharp, and decisive. From the six redoubts thus so swiftly rushed, the Prussians made a sweep to the rear of the others, and captured them in much the same manner, though one fort spared them the necessity of fighting for it by surrendering.

As it was at Fort 2 where the highest act of individual heroism had been performed on the side of the Prussians by brave pioneer Klinké, so it was also within this redoubt that Danish courage found its most brilliant exponent in the person of Lieutenant Anker. The Prussians were quite aware that a man of more than usual bravery was posted here, for they had admired the stubborn valour with which the redoubt had always been defended. And when at last they had stormed their way behind its parapets, they beheld the man himself whose acts had hitherto moved their admiration. He had spiked some of his guns, and was in the act of firing another when a Prussian officer sprang upon him, and, clapping a revolver to his breast, cried, "If you fire, I fire!" Anker hesitated, and finally desisted. But just afterwards he took up a lighted match and was making for the powder magazine, when the Prussian officer cut him over the head with his sword, only just in time to prevent him from blowing up himself and a considerable number of his foes. He was then taken prisoner, and his lifelike figure may now be seen on the fine bronze bas-relief of the Storming of the Düppel Redoubts, which adorns the Victory Column in Berlin.

The Danes had been defeated—not so much because the Prussians were braver men, which they were not, as because the latter were armed with better guns and rifles, and more expert at handling them; but, above all things, because they had taken their foes by surprise. For it cannot be doubted that this was the fact. Said a Danish officer who was taken prisoner:—

> We waited all morning, thinking the assault might still be given, although we had expected that it would take place still sooner; we waited under the terrific cannonade kept up against us, while hour after hour passed slowly away. At last we said to ourselves that we must have been misinformed, or that the Prussians had changed their minds, and the reserves were withdrawn. It was past nine o'clock when I left the forts and went back to breakfast. While thus engaged, I heard somebody utter an exclamation of dismay. 'What is that? The Prussian flag floats over Fort 4!' And so it was—the forts were lost.

But there was still another and a better reason for concluding that the Danes had not yet awhile expected the Prussian assault, and that was the circumstance that the *Rolf Krake*, most daring and deviceful of warships, did not immediately appear upon the scene to pour its volleys of shell and shrapnel into the flanks of the storming columns. True, it was lying at the entrance to the bay (Wenningbund), like an ever-vigilant watch-dog; but by the time it had got its steam up and come to where it was most wanted, the Prussians were already within the Danish redoubts, and, after firing a few ineffectual rounds, the monitor had to retire again well battered with Prussian cannon-balls, but by no means beaten yet like the battalions which had held the forts.

Yet even these battalions, when beaten out of the redoubts, continued to cling tenaciously to the ground behind them, and once or twice they even made a counter-attack with the object of recovering their lost positions. But Prussian ardour proved too much for Danish obstinacy; and at last the Danes in the country behind the forts, after several hours' fighting, were all swept back to the bridge-head in their rear, and then over into the island of Alsen, leaving their foes undisputed masters of all the field.

This latter phase of the fight was well described by a correspondent with the Danes, who wrote:—

> Düppel was lost, but the battle was by no means at an end. Indeed, as we watched the terrible cannonade from 12 at noon till 3 or 4 p.m., the violence of the fire seemed to increase at every moment. Anything more sublime than that sight and sound no effort of imagination can conjure up, and we stood spellbound, entranced, rooted to the spot, in a state that partook of wild excitement and dumb amazement — a state of being which spread equally to the dull hinds, ploughmen, woodmen, and the foresters, and their families of wives and children, as they emerged from fields, woods, and huts, and clustered in awestruck, dumbfounded groups around us. The flashes of the heavy artillery outsped the rapidity of the glance that strove to watch them; the reports were far more frequent than the pulsations in our arteries, and the reverberation of the thunder throughout the vast spreading forest lengthened out and perpetuated the roar with a solemn cadence that was the grandest of all music to the dullest ear.
>
> The air seemed all alive with these angry shells. I have witnessed fearful thunder- storms in my day in southern and in tropical climates; but here the crash and rattle of all the tempests that ever were seemed to be summed up in the tornado of an hour. Nor was all that noise by any means deafening or stunning. It came to us lingering far and wide in the still air, softened and mellowed by the vastness of space, every note blending admirably and harmonising with the general concert—the greatest treat that the most consummate pyrotechnic art could possibly contrive for the delight of the eye and ear.
>
> Many of the Danes surrendered, but many more were taken pris-

oners; and as they came along the Prussian soldiers shook them good-naturedly by the hand and tried to cheer them up. Few of the men seemed to want cheering up, being only too glad, apparently, to have escaped with their lives, though their officers looked gloomy enough over their defeat. The Prussians found these captive Danes "sturdy fellows, but by no means soldierly-looking," with their "rich sandy hair reaching far below the nape of their necks." And, to tell the truth, their victors, no less than their admirers throughout Europe, expected that they would have made a far more vigorous defence; for desperate a defence could scarcely have been called which resulted in the capture of their chief redoubts within the brief space of about ten minutes.

The Prussians had won a glorious victory, but a dear one; for in dead they had lost 16 officers and 213 men, and in wounded 54 officers and 1,118 men. Among the officers who were wounded—mortally, as afterwards proved—was the brave General von Raven, who, as he was being borne to the rear, exclaimed:—

It is high time that a Prussian general should again show how to die for his king.

On the other side General du Plat was also killed, while in dead and wounded officers and men and prisoners the Danish loss otherwise amounted to about 5,500. Among the trophies of victory which fell into the hands of the Prussians were 118 guns and 40 colours.

On being informed of all this. King William telegraphed from Berlin—

To Prince Frederick Charles. Next to the Lord of Hosts. I have to thank my splendid army under thy leadership for today's glorious victory. Pray convey to the troops the expression of my highest acknowledgment and my kingly thanks for what they have done."

On seeing that victory was his, the "Red Prince" had bared his head and muttered a prayer of thanksgiving to the Lord of Hosts, while some massed bands played a kind of *Te Deum*.

Dr. Russell wrote:—

In the broad ditch to the rear of Fort No. 4 the bands of four regiments had established themselves, and while the cannon were firing close behind them, they played a chorale, or song of thanksgiving, for the day's success. The effect was striking, and the grouping of the troops and of the musicians, with their

23

The Prussians attacking the Danish breastworks.

smart uniforms and bright instruments, standing in the deep trench against the shell-battered earthwork, and by palisades riven and shattered and shivered by shot, was most picturesque.'

But King William was not content with telegraphing to his troops, through his nephew Prince Frederick Charles, his acknowledgment of their bravery. Following hard on his telegram his Majesty himself hurried to the seat of war, with his "blood-and-iron" Minister, Bismarck, at his side, and passed in review the troops who had so stoutly stormed the redoubts of the Danes. These troops appeared on parade in the dress and equipment they had worn on the day of their great feat, and in the course of their march past jumped a broad drain to show his Majesty how nimbly they had stormed in upon the Danes. A fortnight later a select number of the Düppel stormers escorted into Berlin the guns more than a hundred in number which they had captured from the Danes, and were received with tremendous enthusiasm.

But this popular jubilation grew louder still when a few weeks later the war was ended altogether by the storming of the island of Alsen, into which the Danes had retired after their defeat at Düppel and entrenched themselves down to the water's edge. In the deep darkness of a summer night (June 29th) the Prussians, in 160 boats, crossed the channel—about eight hundred yards broad—between the mainland and the island, though not without the usual amount of harassing opposition from the *Rolf Krake,* and under a murderous fire jumped ashore and made themselves master of the position in a manner which made some observers describe the affair as a mere "skirmish and a scamper."

But all the same it was a feat which recalled the "Island of the Scots," as sung by Ayton, and will always live in military history as a splendid feat of arms.

Lieutenant Anker taken prisoner

Preface

The letters of which this book is mainly composed were written, all of them, on the spur of the moment, many of them under circumstances of extreme haste and difficulty. In revising them, however, I have thought it best to leave them much as I originally wrote them, omitting only such portions as had, if any, solely a passing interest I trust that these pages, faulty as they are in many ways, will be found to represent fairly the momentous struggle which it was my lot to witness.

I know that there is much in these letters with which both Danes and Germans will disagree. I can only say that I sought to write the truth, as I saw it. As far as intention goes, I have done justice to what little amount of reason and fairness there was on the side of the Danes, while I have also appreciated at its full value the gallantry and honesty shown by their opponents in that too unequal struggle.

Writing as I do, at the commencement of another chapter in this unhappy war, it would be idle for me to express prognostications as to its final issue. The end must come shortly; and my only prayer is that that end may be favourable to a country I have learnt to know and esteem so highly.

Oxford and Cambridge Club;
27th June, 1864.

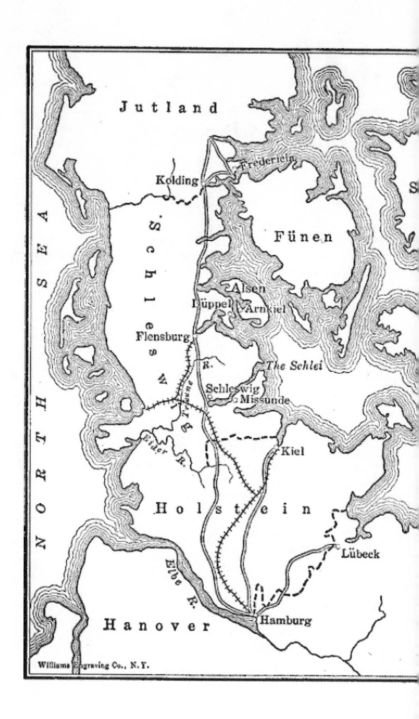

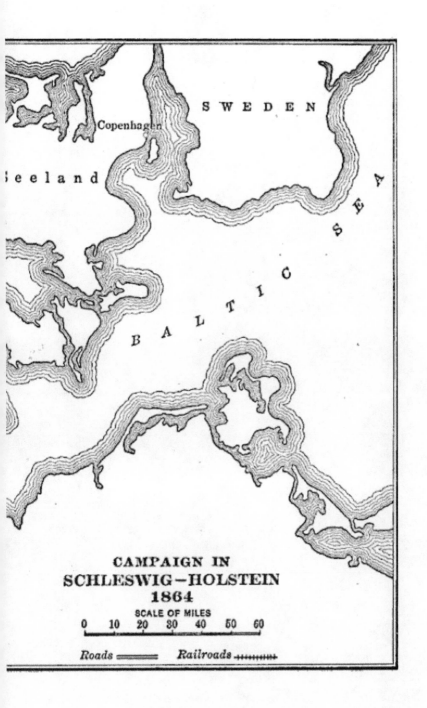

CAMPAIGN IN
SCHLESWIG—HOLSTEIN
1864
SCALE OF MILES
0   10   20   30   40   50   60

Roads ════   Railroads ++++++++

CHAPTER 1

The Schleswig-Holstein War

On Sunday, the last day of January in the present year, the war between Denmark on the one hand, and Prussia and Austria on the other, commenced in earnest by the skirmish of Missunde. On the news reaching London, I was at once commissioned to start for the Duchies. I remained at or near the scene of action as correspondent of the *Daily Telegraph* till the armistice was finally concluded. Thus my correspondence during that period forms a sort of diary of the war, and as such I present it to the public. Before, however, I enter on the narrative of my adventures, let me say something as to the rights and wrongs of the subject-matter of this unhappy war.

Gibbon says:

The profane of every age have derided the furious contests which the difference of a single diphthong excited between the Homoousians and the Homoiousians.

I am afraid that the profane of future generations will find equal grounds for satire in the fact, that the peace of Europe was disturbed for years by the question whether the name of an obscure principality should be spelt with or without two additional consonants. When the whole Schleswig-Holstein dispute is narrowed down to the real points of issue, everything will be found to depend on whether the twin Duchy of Holstein should be described as Schleswig or Sleswig. To insert the consonants at Copenhagen, or to omit them at Gotha, is to commit the unpardonable sin against the respective causes of Scandinavian or Teutonic nationality. Correct orthography in the matter of the Duchies is the Shibboleth by which Danes and Germans recognise their friends or foes. Taken by itself, apart from all accidental issues, the sole point in dispute is, whether Schleswig is German or

31

Danish? to be spelt with the *ch* or without it?

At the death of the late King of Denmark, the European dominions over which he ruled belonged to three categories—Jutland and the isles of the Baltic Archipelago, forming what may be called Denmark Proper, the Duchy of Lauenburg, and the States of Schleswig-Holstein. From time immemorial, as far as modern history is concerned, Denmark Proper has been one country; and—except that its sovereigns have had a perpetual mania for intermarrying with their relations, dying childless, getting divorced, abdicating, and committing every act which can possibly complicate a royal pedigree—there is nothing that need be said as to the nature of the tenure by which the House of Oldenburg has ruled over Denmark for the last four centuries. The question of Lauenburg is also comparatively simple.

Half a century ago, (as at 1864), we were at war with Denmark on account of her adherence to the fortunes of Napoleon; and, with that sublime indifference to the wishes of nationalities which characterised the era of the great European coalition against France, we forced Denmark to cede Norway to Sweden, in reward of Bernadotte's services, and to take Pomerania in exchange. This acquisition was found to be something like the gift of a white elephant, and was very soon surrendered to Prussia in return for a considerable sum of money and the little Duchy of Lauenburg. In fact, the Duchy was annexed to Denmark, and it is as completely part of that country, by law, as Corsica is of France.

The difficulty, as usual, arises with regard to Schleswig-Holstein. These Duchies belong to Denmark, not by right of conquest, or by European settlement, or by hereditary descent, but by mutual agreement. Schleswig was a fief of the Danish crown, while Holstein was a fief of the Holy Roman Empire. In 1440, Christopher III., the last Danish king of the line of Waldemar, bestowed the fief of Schleswig on Adolph, Count of Holstein, "to be held for ever by hereditary right." On the death of Christopher, he was succeeded on the throne of Denmark by Christian of Oldenburg, a nephew of Count Adolph of Schleswig-Holstein.

This count himself died shortly afterwards, and, in 1460, Christian of Demark—the ancestor of the late King Frederick VII.—was elected Duke of Schleswig and Holstein. At this period, as at the present, there was a rival claimant to the throne of the Duchies. In order to paralyze all opposition, Christian consented to refer the matter of the succession, not to the Emperor of Germany, but to the local Estates of

Schleswig and Holstein, who had assembled at Rendsburg, and there passed a resolution:

> Never to follow separate interests, but in all things to act as if they were component parts of the same political system.

Coming before the Estates as a suitor Christian was compelled to accept the throne on their own conditions, and these conditions are described as follows by an historian of Denmark:

> The king acknowledges that he has been elected Duke of Schleswig and Count of Holstein by the free choice of the States; not as King of Denmark, but purely through the good-will of the electors. He agrees that his descendants can only succeed in virtue of a similar election, and that the States shall for ever enjoy the right of choosing their princes. He promises to levy no tax without the sanction of the States, nor to compel any inhabitant to follow his banner beyond the confines of the two provinces.

Now I suppose even the most ardent of Danish sympathisers would not venture to assert, that these stipulations were literally observed by the Kings of Denmark. The answer would be, that no compact can be perpetually binding; that an arrangement made four centuries ago is inapplicable to the present day; and that all progress would be impossible, if the centralising tendencies of the nineteenth century were paralysed by regulations passed in conformity with the segregating spirit of the fifteenth. For a considerable period—in fact, for upwards of three centuries—the arrangement entered into between Christian and the Estates of Schleswig and Holstein appears to have worked well; but then, during that period, the connexion between the two countries was scarcely closer than that between England and Hanover. Gradually, however, Denmark became anxious to unite the Duchies by closer bonds of union; and with the progress of this change in Danish policy, disaffection sprang up in the Duchies. Englishmen are apt to forget that Schleswig-Holstein contains one million of the two millions and a half of inhabitants whom Denmark can reckon in Europe; and that, judging from the latest statistics of export and import, it owns almost half the wealth of the monarchy.

These States, forming the most important portion of the kingdom, were governed from the island of Zealand, separated from them by very nearly the distance of the Irish Channel. On the other hand, they were divided from Germany by a purely imaginary frontier; and the vast commercial metropolis of Hamburg, with its quarter of a million of inhabitants, is actually part of Holstein, as far as its territory is concerned. Given these data, it would be contrary to all the analogy of history, if there had not been a soreness, to say the least, between the provinces of the mainland, and the island which is the seat of empire.

The course of commerce tends constantly to bring Schleswig-Holstein closer to Germany, and to separate her more and more from Zealand. Hamburg, not Copenhagen, is her real capital. The only thing that could counteract this tendency would be a similarity of race between the Duchies and Denmark, and a dissimilarity between them and Germany. Unfortunately, the opposite was the fact. Somehow or other, the German element is more powerful than the Danish. The land throughout the Duchies has been falling for years more and more into the hands of German proprietors, and in consequence the Danes have lost ground. Holstein is as thoroughly and completely German as any part of the Fatherland, and the southern part of Schleswig is being very rapidly Germanised. In 1860, according to the "*Almanach de Gotha*"—whose official statements are generally to be relied upon—of the 400,000 inhabitants of Schleswig, 146,500 spoke German, 135,000 Danish, 85,000 used either language indifferently, and the remainder understood no language except the Frisian dialect.

On this view, and this view only, the nature of the issue between Denmark and the Duchies becomes intelligible. As Schleswig-Holstein became Germanized by the operation of natural causes, Denmark sought to strengthen the union by political regulations, and the result of this attempt was naturally to increase that very tendency towards disunion it was intended to remove.

It was a dynastic difficulty which brought this long simmering quarrel up to boiling point. During the wars of the First Napoleon, Frederick VI. of Denmark renounced all allegiance to the German Empire in respect of Holstein, and declared that the Duchies were integral portions of the monarchy. This high-handed decision had to be retracted when the fortunes of Denmark succumbed with the fall of Napoleon; and by the arrangement of the Congress of Vienna, the King of Denmark was declared a member of the Confederation, as Duke of Holstein and Lauenburg.

Then came quarrels about the delay in convoking the Estates of the Duchies, complaints about the introduction of Danish as the official language, and proposals in the provincial assemblies for separation from Denmark, and union with Germany. At last, in 1848, this ill-feeling culminated in open insurrection. The insurgents, supported by the Princes of Augustenburg, were finally defeated, and though Danish supremacy was restored, the ill-will between the Duchies and Denmark was increased by the memories of an unsuccessful struggle for independence.

To complicate matters, it became apparent that the House of Old-enburg was dying out In 1852 the late king, Frederick VII., was in his forty-fourth year; he had been twice married, and twice divorced, and had formed a morganatic marriage with a third lady, the famous Countess Danner. Having had no children as yet, it was not likely that he would have any in future; and his only male heir was his uncle, a childless man of sixty. Whenever the time should come that the king and his uncle were gathered to their fathers, it was evident that there would be a dispute about the Danish succession. The Salic law pre-vailed in the Duchies, but was not binding on Denmark.

The point is one that has been very hotly contested; but this much is certain, that the Danes did not feel certain whether a woman could legally reign over the Duchies, and were therefore anxious not to give the Schleswig-Holstein malcontents any legal ground for disput-ing the succession. Every person connected with the Royal family of Denmark sacrificed all personal considerations to the wish of main-taining the integrity of the monarchy.

The heir to the throne of Denmark Proper was an aunt of the late king, a certain Princess of Hesse Cassel. This lady, however, consented to waive her rights and those of her children to facilitate the reten-tion of Schleswig-Holstein. In order to find the nearest male heir to the House of Oldenburg, it was necessary to go back to the collateral branches which had split off at different periods during the four cen-turies that had elapsed since Christian became Duke of Schleswig and Count of Holstein.

Nobody has ever ventured to try and explain exactly what were the relationships of the princely Houses of Sonderborg-Augusten-burg and Sonderborg-Glucksburg to the reigning House of Holstein-Denmark. When everybody's father, after his first divorce, marries his nephew's divorced wife, *en secondes noces*, relationships become too complicated for any man to attempt to disentangle, with the fear of Bedlam before his eyes. However, the proper authorities appear to have agreed that the House of Augustenburg came first in the suc-cession, the House of Glucksburg (I drop the supernumerary titles) second, and the House of Holstein-Gottorp third.

According to this hypothesis—which nobody has had the audacity to dispute—the head of the Augustenburg family would have been the nearest heir to the throne, in default of the Princess of Hesse Cassel and her descendants. Unfortunately, there were two objections to this potentate. In the first place, he had married a lady, a countess of Daneskiold Samsöe, not of princely origin, and there was some doubt as to whether his children could inherit his throne; in the second—and this was the most important consideration—he had taken an active part in favour of the Schleswig-Holstein insurrection, and was therefore bitterly unacceptable to the Danish monarch and still more to the Danish people.

It was resolved, in consequence, to pass him over; and the duke was partly bullied and partly cajoled into surrendering his claims in return for some £40,000 or £50,000, of which he was sadly in need. His eldest son, however, Prince Frederick, never formally abandoned his claims, and maintains to the present day that, as the neatest male heir of the late Duke of Schleswig and Count of Holstein, he is entitled to succeed to his honours. Next in rank came the House of Sonderborg-Glucksburg, the head of which, by-the-way, had married one of the divorced wives of the then King of Denmark,

It was an object to settle the succession for once and for all, and as this prince and his two next eldest brothers had at that time no male children, the fourth brother. Prince Christian, who was married to a daughter of the Princess of Hesse, the undoubted heiress to the throne of Denmark Proper, was fixed upon as the heir presumptive to the throne not only of Denmark but of the Duchies. This arrangement was sanctioned finally by the London Treaty of 1852. If there is anybody who still believes in the divine right of kings, there is nothing to be said, as far as he is concerned, in favour of this settlement

According to the strict laws of descent, Christian had no more right to be the successor of Frederick VII. than the writer or reader of these lines. If, on the contrary, rulers are selected for the interest of the governed, there was no objection in itself to be made against this alteration in the succession. It had but a single flaw, though this was rather a fatal one. The proposal was submitted to the sanction of the Danish assemblies, and—though vehemently objected to on account of the advantages supposed to be conferred by it on the Russian branch of the family, the Holstein-Gottorps—was finally ratified. Schleswig-Holstein, however, whose succession was quite as much interfered with as that of Denmark Proper, had never been consulted as to the change in the line of her sovereigns.

The Danish plea in defence of this omission was, that the Estates of Schleswig and Holstein are in the hands of the landed proprietors, who are chiefly Germans, and that therefore they would have objected to the arrangement simply and solely because it was favourable to the interests of Denmark. This plea may be sound, but the awkward fact still remains, that Denmark was united to the Duchies by a compact which stipulates that the States of Schleswig-Holstein shall enjoy for ever the right of choosing their own sovereigns; and that these States were not consulted about a change by which they were transferred from the dominion of one princely House to another.

Now, I am not disposed to consider this a great grievance. Whether a constitutional sovereign belongs to one branch of an insignificant family or another; whether his name is Christian IX. or Frederick VIII., are scarcely matters to make a revolution about at the present day; and, moreover, the Schleswig-Holsteiners had no very serious cause of complaint against the Government of Copenhagen. The wrongs of Schleswig-Holstein, whatever they may have been, are not to be mentioned in the same category with those of Poland or Italy, or other oppressed nationalities. On the contrary, the Duchies, compared with most continental countries, were well-governed throughout their connexion with Denmark.

The misfortune is, that the bulk of the population was German, and the ruling minority Danish, and the two races are—what the Italians call—antipathetic to each other. According to the orthodox Copenhagen point of view, Holstein may possibly be German in feeling and race, but Schleswig is Danish and wishes to belong to Denmark. The theory is plausible rather than sound. The two Duchies had been united in interests for centuries, just as they are united by natural position, and it is natural enough that Schleswig should value more highly its connexion with the adjoining territory of Holstein than with the distant Island of Zealand.

The cause would have been one, I think, very susceptible of compromise, if it were not for the complications introduced into it by the attitude of Germany. The position of the German Confederation with regard to the Duchies of Holstein and Lauenburg is a very awkward one at all times. The object of the Federative Diet may be defined as the maintenance of external security and of internal peace. This definition, which is the most intelligible that can be formed, is at the best very vague, and is capable of the most various interpretations, according to the sense in which the interpreter wishes to explain it.

As a rule, this general power of interference in the internal affairs of the States which compose the Bund, has been exercised by that most cumbrous of governing powers, in the interests of despotic rule. Soon after the foundation of the Diet, Holstein requested that its authority might be exercised in order to induce the King of Denmark to convoke the Estates of the Duchy, but this application was disregarded. However, it is pretty clear that, if a small State, like Holstein, under the rule of a non-German potentate, suffers injustice, it is the duty of the Federal Government to see the injustice righted.

And supposing that Denmark had proposed to overthrow the constitution of Holstein, the Diet would have been justified in interfering. The mere fact that it had allowed grosser violations of popular rights to pass unnoticed on previous occasions, could not debar it from the power of upholding the law upon the present one. However, the Diet failed to bring forward any act—if we except the question of the succession—which could be regarded as a distinct violation of the internal rights of Holstein, and therefore—in order to justify the action of the Confederation—an hypothesis was started, more remarkable for its ingenuity than for its honesty. Holstein—so the argument runs—is indissolubly connected with Schleswig; Holstein will not consent to share a common constitution with Schleswig and Denmark; the attempt to unite Schleswig with Denmark apart from Holstein is an infraction of the rights of Holstein; and therefore the Diet is bound to forbid the enactment of any regulations which tend to separate Schleswig from Holstein.

Any advocate of this decision would find considerable difficulty in defending it Legally, it remained a question, whether the Bund had not exceeded its power; and it is impossible to believe that the sovereigns of Germany were actuated by any sincere regard for popular freedom and independence. The cause, and at the same time, the justification of their conduct, lay in the fact that for once they represented the wishes and aspirations of their peoples. The German princes rose in arms against Denmark, not because they cared for the wrongs of Schleswig-Holstein, or because they had any keen sympathy with the idea of Teutonic nationality, but because they were afraid of their own subjects.

Their thrones would not have been safe if they had deserted again the cause of "Schleswig-Holstein, the sea-surrounded;" and the reason of the intense popular enthusiasm on this subject which spread through the length and breadth of the Fatherland—reminding old men of the excitement preceding the war of liberation— is that the question at issue was one of race.

That this should be so, is not so strange as it appeared to us at first sight. We Englishmen are apt to be forgetful of the fact that, alone among the nations of the world, we have no kindred population subject to a foreign power. There is not a country in the globe where our countrymen are not to be found, and yet there is no instance where an English-speaking community is governed by an alien race. We do not therefore make sufficient allowance for the irritation which a nation naturally feels at seeing men of its own blood and lineage and language governed by foreigners. If we can conceive the case of an independent Ireland in which the Northern Counties, with their Anglo-Saxon Protestant population, were ruled by a Celtic Government, we shall understand something of the jealousy with which the Germans regarded any oppression, however slight, on the part of the Danes, towards German Holstein and half-German Schleswig.

Moreover, Germans are susceptible about any slight on their nationality to a degree we hardly give them credit for. The outer world declares that we English are the most self-worshipping people in the universe. Whether we are so or not it is hard for an Englishman to say; but this I am certain of, that—putting ourselves out of the question— the Germans have a higher collective opinion of their own merits, than any people I have ever come across. The idea that any portion of the Fatherland should be under the dominion of what in their own opinion is an inferior race, is gall and bitterness to every true German, *burgher*, noble, or professor, or whatever he may be. Moreover, the passion for German unity is involved in this Schleswig-Holstein question.

To us it may seem that unity, like charity, should begin at home; and that Berlin and Vienna should have arranged their own quarrels before they interfered with Denmark. I am not sure, however, that this view is correct. A war for Schleswig-Holstein—that is, a war in vindication of the principle that Germany belonged to the Germans—was likely to do more for establishing a real unity than old inland reforms and progress. Such, at least, was the belief of the German world; and on this belief Count Bismarck speculated with an acuteness, for which he has scarcely yet received due credit.

There is no good arguing philosophically about the absurdity of the quarrel. All wars about questions of race, viewed philosophically, are absurd in themselves. As long as a nation is well ruled, it matters very little abstractedly whether it is ruled by foreigners or its own people. Abstract principles, however, have never governed the world yet, and are not likely to become the rules of popular action even in these days of international congresses. Schleswig or Sleswig, that was all the question; but it was one which the sword alone could decide.

Having said thus much as to the origin of the war it was my lot to witness, I proceed to the narrative of my journeyings.

CHAPTER 2

The Duchies

Hamburg, February 5.

A close omnibus, packed with some fourteen human beings, is not a pleasant conveyance at the best of times. Its pleasantness is not increased when your fellow-travellers are stout, and out of temper; when the hour is late at night; and when the air is so piercing cold outside that not a window can be opened. Nor can it be considered an additional attraction if the omnibus in which you sit is placed upon a ferryboat, and that ferryboat is locked in the ice in the middle of a broad river. Yet it was after this fashion that I made my first entrance into the domain of the Schleswig-Holstein question.

The ice on the Elbe is breaking fast, and the river is blocked up with dense masses of floating drift, through which a passage has to be forced each time that the steam-ferry ploughs its way between Hamburg and Harburg. It was a wild weird scene enough. As we gazed through the windows of our floating prison we looked out on a dreary waste of ice, and snow, and water. The snorting of the engine, the crunching of the ice, and the shouts of the bargemen, as they shoved away with their long poles the blocks we came into contact with, were enough to terrify the nerves of passengers worn out with a journey of some two-score hours.

Every now and then we came to a dead lock, and—like the Schleswig-Holstein difficulty—were unable to move either forwards or backwards. One dolorous long-faced German began a narrative of how, some years ago, a ferry-boat had been lost on such a night, with every soul on board; while a stout lady, of more cheerful disposition, seized the opportunity of distributing addresses of her boarding-house in Hamburg. However, there is an end even to Elbe steam-ferries, and at last, in the early morning, we were landed in the free city of the North.

Forthwith I found myself in an atmosphere of war. My journey through Germany had been too helter-skelter a one for me to catch much glimpse of the excitement prevailing throughout the Fatherland. The armies had all passed on before; and a few batches of soldiers waiting at the road-side stations, accompanied by an admiring crowd of sympathizers, alone showed that something unusual was stirring. Throughout a long day's journey from daybreak to midnight, over some hundreds of miles of German territory, I did not see one paper offered for sale, containing late intelligence from the scene of war. It was not that people were not anxious to learn the news, but that the idea of special correspondence has not yet familiarised itself to the German mind.

However, all along the road every second word seemed to be Schleswig-Holstein; and at Hamburg, the first news I heard was a report that the Austrians had occupied the fort of Bostorf, in front of the town of Schleswig. I tried to prove to my informant, from the position the two armies were known to have occupied on the previous day, that the report could not be true; but I found at once that my assertion laid me open to a suspicion of anti-German proclivities, and therefore I made up my mind to listen in future, and not to argue.

Let me say a few words of the plan on which the Germans have commenced this campaign. The Schlei forms a great inland lake on the frontiers of Schleswig, at the western extremity of which is the town of that ilk; while at the eastern, the lake contracts to a narrow strait, called the Missunde Enge. When once the Federal troops had obtained possession of Eckernförde, there was nothing to stop their march northwards till they reached the Schlei. It was resolved, therefore, that the Prussian Army should attempt to force the passage of the river at the narrowest point, while the Austrians should march directly upon Schleswig from Herdsburg. In the one case the passage of the Germans was barred by the fortifications at Missunde; in the other, by the Dannewerke.

If the Prussians could have forced the Danish position at Missunde, they could have marched easily to the north of Schleswig, and thus have taken the Danish Army in the rear, while it was attacked by the Austrians in front. This plan, however, failed, in consequence of the resistance of the Danes being more obstinate than was expected. The Prussian artillery was found not to be of sufficiently powerful calibre, and the attack on Missunde ended in what, if the truth is to be spoken, must be regarded as a repulse. Meanwhile the Austrians drove in several of the Danish outposts, captured some small works near Ober Selk, at the south-west comer of the lake, and advanced till they came within the range of the guns of the Dannewerke. In spite, however, of these partial successes the combined movement was a failure. Such, at least, was the opinion at Hamburg up to a late hour last night.

The impression which this intelligence produced in the metropolis of Northern Germany was, as far as I could gather, of a very mixed character. The mercantile section of the community regretted, of course, any delay which might prolong the wars and, in consequence, everything, to use a commercial expression, was very flat indeed. On the other hand, the German party—much as they disliked the Danes assuming any success whatever—were consoled by the consideration that a too easy victory would be fatal to the cause of Schleswig-Holstein. The belief in Hamburg was that, if the allied powers overran Schleswig speedily, without any serious resistance, they would surrender it again to Danish rule, subject to certain stipulations in behalf of the inhabitants. If, however, the conquest of Schleswig should prove a work of time, only to be achieved after serious losses, then Austria and Prussia would never consent to surrender what they had won at so heavy a cost.

On this view, therefore, a partial defeat of the Austro-Prussian Army was a boon rather than a misfortune; and as with the Hamburg merchants the German element, at the present moment, is even stronger than the mercantile one, the news of this temporary check was received with very qualified dissatisfaction. Moreover, the citizens have, as yet, no serious apprehension of being personally involved in the conflict. The state of the ice must hinder the Danes from blockading the Elbe for some time to come; and, even if the coast were clear, it is doubtful whether any blockade could be legally instituted, as Hamburg is not an Austrian or a Prussian city, but a member of the Confederation, and there is no absolute war between Denmark and the Diet.

However, the role of Hamburg, on the present crisis, is that of a spectator, not of an actor. The other day, when the Prussian troops were marching through the territory of the Free State, a meeting of the Senate was held to consider whether their passage should be allowed; but the meeting was not summoned till the evening of the day, when two thousand Prussian troops had passed through the town.

Meanwhile, my first care in Hamburg was not to look after political opinions, but to provide myself with a horse. Every animal in Holstein that could crawl on four legs had been bought up by the invading armies for purposes of transport, and I was assured my only chance was to obtain a horse in Hamburg itself. To any one not blessed with boundless confidence in his own acuteness, a search after horse-flesh is always, I think, a humiliating process. More especially is this the case when you have to carry on your negotiations in a foreign language, wherein terms are employed with reference to equine manners and customs, of whose meaning you have not the remotest conception.

However, if you answer "So" to every remark made, you can put on an appearance of profound acquaintance with that, or any other conceivable subject. The stable-keepers kept on informing me, with ominous sameness of diction, that they had sold a very jewel of a horse only the week before to some field-officer, who, with his horse, had already fallen a victim to the war. At last, after many searches, my choice was reduced to three. The first had some mysterious malady, either the glanders or the staggers, or both; the next had a cough, more closely resembling a dog's bark than any other sound I ever heard; and the last had the one fault of having attained to miserable old age. However, the groom assured me that she would carry me over hill and valley, and as she had no palpable and patent defect, I agreed to have her on trial.

When this arrangement was made at last, after many consultations, my difficulties were only half over. Having caught my mare, I had to convey her to the scene of action. I do not wish my worst enemy a more cruel punishment than having to arrange any matters with German railway officials. In order to obtain a horsebox for Kiel, I had to see about a dozen different *employés*, and to get a score of signatures. And when at last I had obtained my permission, and exhibited my steed for the gratification of a clerk, who felt bound to see it in the flesh before he signed an order for its conveyance, I had to spend about an hour in hunting after the horsebox, for whose use I had bargained and paid. Patience, however, and perseverance, as copybooks used to tell me, overcame every difficulty, and at last I found myself *en route* for Kiel and the Prussian camp.

Kiel, February 6.

I remember, amidst a collection of old French caricatures of *Le Sport*, there was one which always tickled my fancy. A sportsman fresh from behind a counter in Paris is out shooting, when a daring snipe perches upon the muzzle of his gun, which he is holding out at full length in the attitude appropriate to the occasion. Astonished at the event, the Frenchman pulls out the sportsman's hand-book to see how he ought to shoot a bird which has disregarded every rule of propriety, and closes it with a sigh, saying, "*Cas non prévu dans le manuel des chasseurs.*" So it has been with me. I have fallen upon a contingency not contemplated in the manual of our correspondents. I am brought to face—if Kiel is to be believed—with an eventuality I had never counted on as possible. Visitors at Naples, in the days of the Garibaldian dictatorship must remember how a certain American major-general—now of the Confederate States Army—used to tell everybody he met, with a variety of strange oaths, that:

> He had come four thousand miles, sir, to see a free people, and he had only seen them swap kings.

My plight, it seems, is very like that of my quondam acquaintance. I have come hundreds of miles to see two brave nations fighting gallantly for victory or death, and I have just arrived in time to see a sham fight, followed by a precipitate retreat. Such, at least, is the faith of the place from whence I write.

However, it is too early to assume that all is over. This morning there seemed every reason to suppose that the struggle would be a long and a bloody one. Everything breathed war. Last night, in Hamburg, there were rumours of severe fighting on the left wing of the allied armies, where the Austrians were drawn up in front of the Dannewerke; and the impression was, that the result of the day's fighting had been, if not actually favourable to the Danes, decidedly less so to their opponents. The Hamburg newsboys were shrieking out second editions with important intelligence from the war. It is not only in our own happy country that second editions are sometimes a delusion and a snare, but still the fact that these catch-penny issues had so good news to report, implied that some such had been received.

It had snowed heavily all day, and the ice was melting fast, so that the weather itself appeared to be in favour of the Danes. As I drove in the dim grey morning light up the long straggling street which leads from Hamburg to the Altona Station, I passed scores of waggons laden with powder and biscuits, intended for the use of the army. The station was crowded with Austrian soldiers on their road to Rendsburg. The troops were in high spirits at the prospect of active service, and kept on singing the song of "Schleswig-Holstein, the sea-surrounded," on every conceivable occasion when there was the slightest, possibility of anybody hearing them. All the apparatus of war was there. Officers' horses were being sent up by rail to the front; half the ordinary trains had been suspended on this very day in order to facilitate the transport of troops; hospital beds were arranged in large packages, blocking up the entry' to the carriages; and hundreds of parcels of lint, collected from every part of the Fatherland, were being forwarded by the same train which was to carry me to my destination. Everything, in fact, told of war, near at hand and imminent.

At this season of the year the journey through: Holstein is not a lively one. The snow kept falling constantly in great heavy flakes, so that it was difficult to see anything except the hedges, which ran along the line, save on the rare occasions when the snowstorm ceased for a few minutes, and we had dim snatches of pale sunshine. Vast wide fields flat as an American prairie; swamps and morasses of peat, broken by dull sluggish streams; grey forests, whose leafless trees were clad in a foliage of snow-white icicles—these were the main features of the scenery through which our road lay.

Every now and then we came upon little villages, half buried in snow, where every house was built of dull-red brick, and looked as warm and snug within as it seemed dull and cheerless without. But the villages were few and far between, and isolated farmhouses were not very plentiful. Still, if you happened to be a German, and had no dislike to cold, I should say—judging from the look of the Holstein houses—that your lot could not well have fallen in pleasanter places. Everything and everybody, I should add, were German; and of Danish, you could see no trace, except in the superscription of the coins, which vendors of refreshments and newspapers along the road palmed off upon unsuspecting travellers.

At Kiel I found myself on the very outskirts of the war. Immense trains of artillery and provender waggons were passing constantly through the narrow streets of this picturesque little town, where Frederick VIII., Duke of Schleswig-Holstein, holds his puny court The streets were gay with colours. The white, green, and red tricolour of the Duchies floated from window and housetop, side by side with the long-concealed, if not long-forgotten, colours of the German nation—the yellow, black, and red of the old revolutionary era—the flag whose symbolic meaning, according to a democratic poet of that bygone era, now a prosperous merchant in New York, was that, "*powder is black, and blood is red, and fire glitters like gold.*"

Of the duke himself, or of his rule, there was no outward sign visible, as far as I could see; no proclamations bearing his royal signature were on the walls, and the town appeared to be entirely in the possession of the small Prussian force with which it is garrisoned. It was said that heavy firing had been heard in the direction of the Schlei, and intelligence was anxiously expected from the Prussian headquarters, which, on the night before, had been between Eckernförde and Missunde. Gradually a rumour came, no one knew whence, of some great German success; and, indeed, the first person from whom I heard it was an old peasant, whom, I am sorry to say, I looked upon as a lunatic. By little and little the report gained consistency, and at last, on finding that its truth was confirmed by a despatch received by Prince Frederick himself, I was enabled to telegraph the astounding intelligence that the Danes had abandoned their positions on the Dannewerke, and were in full retreat northwards. Since this message was sent off it has been published in a supplement to the official Kiel paper.

According to the received version of the story, the Danes evacuated the Dannewerke, under cover of the snowstorm on Friday night, or early on Saturday morning. As soon as it became daylight the absence of the enemy was observed by the German outposts, and the attacking armies were forthwith put in motion. By tonight, the Austrians are said to have reached Gettorf, a little village north of Schleswig, while the Prussians have pushed on as far as Koppel, a town some five miles beyond Missunde, on the left bank of the Schlei.

Now, supposing this news to be substantially true, it is believed by the best judges here, that it can be capable of only two explanations: one is, that the Danish retreat is due to strategic reasons; and that the Danes, finding their forces too weak to defend the straggling works of the Dannewerke, have retired to the much shorter line of fortifications which covers the narrowest point of the peninsula from Flensburg on the Baltic, to Husum on the North Sea.

The second explanation is, that this retreat, if true, is due to political motives. It is possible the Danes may have become convinced that any resistance, however gallant, could have no permanent chance of success against the overwhelming forces, of Germany, and that, therefore, the wisest policy was not to continue a resistance, whose only practical result could be to render any compromise impossible. The latter is the version which finds most supporters, and the Prussian officers here state confidently that, "the war is over." It this opinion is sound the retreat of the Danes is of doubtful benefit for the cause of the Duchies; and this fact may account for the utter absence of any outward enthusiasm with which the news has been received in Kiel. Certainly, the intelligence that the Danes are retreating was even received with extreme outward indifference in this the capital of Schleswig-Holsteinism.

Eckernförde, February 7.

This day week the Danes marched out of Eckernförde with colours flying, and prepared for a long and determined resistance. Their retreat was believed by the inhabitants and by the soldiers themselves to be simply a military movement, in order to place their army behind the impregnable line of works which go by the general name of the Dannewerke. Not a week has passed, and the Danes have surrendered their strongholds, evacuated the chief part of the province whose preservation they declared essential to their national existence, and have given up almost everything of which a long series of defeats could possibly have deprived them.

One thing is clear, that it is scarcely a case in which, the Danes have retired *pour mieux sauter*. Their object is thought to have been to place themselves in safety behind the frontier of Jutland, and even in that attempt they appear not to have succeeded. Up to Friday evening, the result of the various small engagements which had taken place had been decidedly not in favour of the attacking force. Very early on Saturday morning Schleswig peasants came in to the Austrian headquarters with tidings that the Danes had evacuated the Dannewerke. The intelligence was thought so incredible that the messengers were detained as spies, and no steps were taken till daybreak to ascertain the truth of their story. As soon as it was light scouts were sent out to investigate, and the enemy was found to have vanished. So rapid was the flight of the Danes, that they left a great portion of their artillery behind them.

According to the general report, the Austrians have captured some hundred cannon, many of them light fieldpieces, which the Danes had not even taken the time to spike. Nor, as far as I can learn, had they blown up any of the bridges, or placed any obstructions in the way of pursuit. Their notion obviously was that an advance of six hours would enable them to gain their strongholds north of Flensburg before the enemy could come up with them. The idea proved to be mistaken. The Austrian *jagers* pushed on with surprising energy, and came up with the rear of the retreating force near Idsted, and inflicted a severe defeat upon them.

In this engagement, however, an Austrian regiment got into a de-file, when they were subjected to a murderous fire from the Danish riflemen, who manned the heights on either side. Meanwhile, the Prussians followed up the enemy, though not with equal vigour. They crossed the Schlei somewhere near Kappeln, and then struck inwards, with the view of cutting off the retreat of the right wing of the Dan-ish Army, which had been engaged in the defence of Missunde, and which was retiring on Flensburg. For two days nothing whatever has been heard of them. How all this is to be accounted for I cannot hope to explain.

One never knows in this world "*where is the place of understand-ing*," and at Kiel, of all places in the globe, I met with a believer in Mr. David Urquhart, who accounted for the occurrence, in a man-ner perfectly satisfactory to himself by attributing it to a conspiracy between the *Czar* and Lord Palmerston for carrying out the will of Peter the Great. The more rational hypothesis—that the withdrawal of the Danes is due to a private understanding between the Courts of Copenhagen, Vienna, and Berlin—is rendered untenable by the en-ergy with which the Germans have pursued the Danes on their retreat Altogether, as a German friend remarked to me tonight—"*Es ist ganz unerklärlich.*" Let me say that, in all the conversations I have ever heard here, nobody has attributed this flight to personal cowardice on the part of the Danes. Everybody says now that the Danes must have been defeated if they had stood their ground; but everybody says, also, that they were expected to fight to the last.

And this brings me to the feeling entertained in Schleswig towards the Danes, of which I have now had some little opportunity of judg-ing. In the first place, this part of Schleswig is altogether and absolutely German. The names of the villages are the only evidences I can see of a Scandinavian population ever having ruled and reigned here. The streets are all designated by German names.

Everybody you meet upon the high road greets you with "*Guten Morgen*" or "*Guten Abend*," as the case may be. And this cannot be be-cause they see you are a stranger, as I was constantly addressed so, while riding alone, when it was so pitch dark that nobody could have told whether I was a Chinaman or a Maori chieftain. Every conversation I have overheard was in German, The inscriptions in the shop windows, the placards upon the walls, the performances at the theatre, are all in German. Moreover, it is impossible to shut your eyes to the fact that the population are heartily glad to see the last of their Danish rulers.

All along some twenty miles that I travelled over yesterday, there was scarcely a farmhouse on which the Schleswig-Holstein colours were not displayed. On the roadside, triumphal arches had been raised to welcome the Prussian soldiers as they marched into Schleswig. At all the taverns that I passed people were singing the national air of Schleswig-Holstein, and a drunken peasant I met reeling along homewards hiccupped out to me a question whether "I, too, did not love my Fatherland."

In this little town of Eckernförde there are very few houses indeed from whose windows the flag of Schleswig-Holstein is not suspended. There are enough without the flags to show that they are not hung out in obedience to dictation or terror; and, curiously, the few houses that remain undecorated have almost all of them names of Danish origin over their shop-windows. National rosettes and pictures of the duke are displayed everywhere; and a travelling pedlar whom I came across appears to be doing an enormous business in the sale of full-length portraits of the prince—who is now described as the reigning Duke of Schleswig-Holstein—and of Duke Ernest of Saxe-Gotha, who is very popular here, from the fact that he was the first to espouse the cause of Frederick VIII.

My landlady, when she was asked to purchase a portrait of the duke, replied, with a smile of patriotic pride, that she had had one hung up in her cellar for weeks past On the other hand, I should say fairly that I have heard no expressions of hatred used towards the Danes; I can see no traces of any animosity, like that which existed in Lombardy against the Austrians, or which exists in Poland against the Russians. It is obvious that in this part of Schleswig the inhabitants are not sorry to be quit of the Danes, and are very anxious to preserve their independence under a sovereign of their own; but they do not regard their former rulers as tyrants or oppressors. But of material grievances, the Schleswigers, I should think, can have had but little hitherto to complain.

If it is true that our forefathers came from Schleswig, and if , as I presume, they did not dislike the cold, I think when they got to the eastern counties of England they must have been inclined to say, as was said about the Forest of Ardennes, "when we were at home we were in a better place." Barring the climate, which is simply detestable, I never saw a more comfortable or prosperous looking country than Schleswig. The people are a fine, well-built, pleasant-spoken race, of much larger stature than ordinary Germans.

Poverty appears almost unknown; the farmhouses are all built of red brick, with high-perched slated roofs; and the cottages are all whitewashed and covered with thatch; the fields are large, and hedged in with a neatness rare upon the continent, and the roads are excellent. If anybody wishes to see a prosperous country he should take the ride I took last night from Kiel to Eckernförde. I should recommend him, however, to take it in summer, and when the roads are not blocked up with all the *matériel* of an enormous army. In a distance of twenty miles I passed, I should think, a thousand vehicles of different kinds—provender carts, artillery waggons, courier post carriages, and every description of four-wheeled conveyance.

On the roadside, at frequent intervals, there were vast encampments of artillery and cavalry—all Prussian—on their march northwards. A cavalry officer with whom I rode for some distance told me that his orders were to press on as fast as possible, and that that day his troops had ridden twenty odd miles—a distance which, in the present state of the roads, was enormous. If anybody has a fancy for a new sensation, I should advise him to ride, as I did, after dark, on a road as slippery as polished oak, in a country he does not know, with the waves of the Baltic breaking on the shore a stone's-throw from him, with an ice-cold storm of snow beating about his ears, in absolute uncertainty how far off his destination lies, and with a still greater uncertainty whether he will find shelter when he gets there.

P.S.—A rumour has come that the Danes are about to make a stand at Düppel, near the island of Alsen. If it is confirmed I shall make my way at once to the front.

Rendsburg, February 9.

I wish I could convey to you the aspect of the country through which I have ridden for the last three days. If it were possible to do so, I think the nature of this Schleswig-Holstein war would become better known to you than it would by any description of strategical operations. To the whole scene you must fancy one vast background of snow. There is snow everywhere, and on every side, as far as your eye can reach. The fields are covered so deep that the hedgerows are scarcely visible above the surface; great banks of snow are drifted up on either side the road; the air is full of snow; every now and then the great white flakes come falling silently; then, as the ice-cold winds blow in gusts from across the Baltic, the snow beats upon the ground like a shower of hailstones; and at the bright hours of the day, it comes in slowly succeeding drops, like a straggling fire of musketry.

But somehow or other the process of snowing is always going on. Snow appears the normal condition of the country. You cannot fancy that these bare, bleak fields can look anything but white, or that this dull sepia-coloured sky can ever by any possibility be blue. At rare intervals throughout the day you catch glimpses of a pale, sickly orb in the low horizon which the light of reason tells you is the sun, but the very idea that this luminary can ever warm anybody or anything is transparently absurd. It would be some comfort if the temperature were nominally colder.

There is a sort of morbid satisfaction in saying that you have experienced weather ever so many degrees below zero, but even this satisfaction is denied you. I very much doubt whether, except at night, the thermometer has ever been below zero, since I have been in the Duchies, but the suffering from cold has been intense. The east wind, which is always blowing here, appears to derive an additional keenness from passing over some thousands of miles of ice and snow. I cannot discover that this state of the weather is anything unusual, or that a life-long experience has hardened the inhabitants to its discomforts. In fact, the only drop of consolation I have in my sufferings is derived from the fact, that the natives appear to suffer as much as I do myself.

To complete the utter desolation of the aspect of Schleswig in winter oily one thing is wanted, and that is the absence of passengers along the road. To do the country justice, in ordinary tunes this requisite cannot be wanting. All farming operations are, of course, completely suspended, and the peasants—the whole population are either farmers or fishermen—keep within doors. Villages seem extremely rare anywhere but on the map, and isolated houses are still rarer. In a ride of twenty miles, from Eckernförde to Schleswig, I doubt if I passed as many dwellings of any kind, and throughout the whole distance there was not one single tavern or place of refreshment The roads are all made like the old-fashioned French *chaussées*, and therefore are admirably adapted for rendering travelling even more perilous in winter than it would be naturally.

Moreover, you are always going up or down hill. Schleswig in this part consists of a series of low round hills, just high enough to prevent you from ever getting a distant view of the country. It shows, by the way, the extraordinary ignorance which prevails even amongst Germans about the Duchies, that a very well-informed gentleman resident at Hamburg assured me that in the event of defeat, the Danes could flood the country behind the Dannewerke. You might as well talk of flooding Leicestershire, putting aside the fundamental difficulty that round about here there is no water wherewith to flood the country, even if it were capable of being flooded. The roads are as straight as if they had been made by the Romans, which very possibly they were; and the result is, that you seem always to be toiling up one low snow-clad hill to see from its summit another facing you of exactly the same aspect.

However, the roads are lively enough in themselves. An enormous traffic passes over them every hour of the four-and-twenty, though it is of an order bringing no profit to the turnpikes, which are as numerous as on the Great North Road of England. Let me try to recall the spectacle which passes constantly before your eyes as you jog on at a snail's pace, cold, shivering, and wretched; first there comes a company of Prussian infantry, with their dark-brown cloaks, wearing the white sash upon their left arm, which General von Wrangel has ordered them to wear, in memory of the campaign the Austrians and Prussians fought side by side half a century ago.

The officer in command is riding on in front, with his helmet buried beneath the hood of his cloak, in a vain attempt to keep out the cold, and the men stumble on in broken line, footsore, silent, and weary. There is no singing now, as on the rail; this is business, not pleasure; then follows a long straggling team of provender waggons, filled with bricks of coarse black bread, frozen over with a fine sprinkling of snow. The drivers are walking slowly by their horses' heads, smoking long large-bowled pipes, and swearing at their horses whenever they have time to take the pipes out of their mouths. Then, in the grey dim distance, you see a cloud of snow advancing, and out of the mist there comes a troop of Austrian cavalry, who gallop on in defiance of the roads, and without the fear of sudden death before their eyes.

Then a peasant's waggon jogs by, filled with farmers and civilians of every class, huddled together in a heap at the bottom of the cart, going on business to the army. Sledges are not unfrequent; the "*herrschaften*" sitting in front, wrapped up in rugs and furs, with little beyond their noses visible, and the driver sitting astride on a plank jutting out behind the car. Following the sleighs, there will be perhaps a train of artillery struggling its way onwards to the front. There are six horses to every gun—stout, stalwart nags, looking like our brewers' horses with the extra flesh pared down—but it is as much as they can do to keep the wheels rolling.

Then there are stray detachments of Hungarian infantry, with their grey coats and white pipe-clayed belts and close-fitting blue hose. Somehow or other, these non-German troops appear to suffer less from the weather than the Prussians, at any rate, they keep up their spirits better; and then upon the high roads there are scores and scores of well-dressed pedestrians, with long fair hair, and blue spectacles, and red caps, and all the other inseparable attributes of Teutonic studentom. Cover the whole of this long never-ending procession with a veil of snowdrift, and fancy it traversing a wilderness of snow, and you will have some idea of the spectacle that is passing before me daily.

But I own, of all its features, the one which has struck me as most significant is the presence of these youthful pedestrians. As a rule, foreigners are not actuated by that demon of curiosity which drives our countrymen to every place where there is the slightest chance of a disturbance. I was at Naples during the whole of the siege of Capua, and there were very few days when I was not at the Garibaldian camp. It was the easiest and cheapest journey in the world from Naples to Capua; but, during all my many ramblings about the camp, I never once met an Italian who had come out to see the war.

Now it is no joke walking some scores of miles along roads like those of Schleswig, and in weather such as we have at present. Yet hundreds of young German lads are encountering a labour to which they are utterly unused, simply to catch a glimpse of the war. Right or wrong, you may depend upon it, the heart of Germany is in this contest to an extent that Englishmen can hardly realise. There is one feature, too, in this sketch of the advance of a great army, whose omission must have struck military readers. I have made no mention of campfollowers, or of the heterogeneous vagabonds who attach themselves to most armies, because, in as far as I have seen here, they have no existence. Anything more orderly than the present state of the country cannot well be conceived. It is very hard to say what is the government of the Duchies at this moment, and yet there is not a symptom of disorganisation.

Vast armies are passing through the country in every direction, but nobody ever dreams of suggesting that it is not safe to travel along the most solitary of roads unarmed and alone. At the hotels the waiters are astonished if you hint that the public passages—in which hundreds of strangers are going in and out hourly—are not safe places in which to leave your luggage standing. The very ostlers themselves are honest; and, even in these war times, I have never been asked an exorbitant price for any article I wanted.

Of actual war news, the little that seems positive amounts to this. The great bulk of the Danish Army has succeeded in making good its retreat to the island of Alsen and South Jutland, as the Danes call the northern part of Schleswig. Here they are expected to make a last stand, and they will have the advantage of having a smaller area to defend, and of being in the midst of a friendly population, or at any rate a Danish-speaking one. On the other hand, their army must be demoralised by a hasty and disheartening retreat, and it is not expected that, as they surrendered the Dannewerke almost without a blow, they will make a steadfast resistance when they have lost the chief object for which they were about to fight However, Austria and Prussia are acting as if they expected Denmark to resist, and they are pushing on the war with a vigour which can hardly fail to command success. As far as Flensburg—that is, up to what is called the "*Sprach-grenze*"— they have no cause to dread the active hostility of the country in which their campaign lies. About this fact no honest observer can entertain a doubt.

Rendsburg, February 10,.

I am here on the confines of Schleswig and Holstein, on the banks of the Eider; and, as the stoppage of the rail by snow has delayed my journey northwards to the front, I cannot do better than write to you of the state of feeling in the countries which I have traversed for the last three days. Travelling, as I have done, on horseback, and mixing with wayfarers of all kinds, I think I have had some opportunity of judging what the tone of public conversation is, and that tone, I do not hesitate to say, is unfavourable to Denmark. In the first place, this much is certain, that as far north as the town of Schleswig, the population is altogether and entirely German.

According to all accounts, this statement holds true to the frontier of North Schleswig. At Flensburg, which lies close upon the frontier, there is a considerable Danish population; and one of the most candid Germans I have met with admitted to me that there, in all probability, his countrymen were in the minority. In fact, if the question of the Duchies were to be ultimately decided in accordance with the principle of nationalities, I entertain no doubt that Holstein and South Schleswig would be formed into a German State, while North Schleswig would be annexed to Denmark.

But it is doubtful whether this solution would give satisfaction eyen to the Duchies themselves. Between Denmark proper and the peninsula, of which Schleswig and Holstein are the chief portion, there exists that inevitable ill-will which always prevails, more or less, between two countries geographically separated, in one of which the seat of government is placed The normal relations between Denmark and the Duchies are similar to those between Sicily and Italy, or between England and Ireland, except that here the centre of empire is on the island, instead of on the mainland. The universal complaint of even the most moderate Schleswig-Holsteiner is, that the interests of the Duchies were invariably sacrificed to those of Denmark; that all the money drawn from the mainland was spent for the benefit of the islanders; and that they themselves were burdened with heavy taxes in order to lighten the imposts placed upon the inhabitants of Zealand. I am assured that a similar feeling of discontent exists in Jutland to what is found in either Schleswig or Holstein, and it seems to me probable enough, from the nature of the case, that this should be true.

To this normal sense of dissatisfaction there has been added, as far as the Duchies themselves are concerned, the antagonism of race. As I have before stated, the evidence of gross oppression seems to me to be wanting, but still every Schleswig-Holsteiner I have met has his own catalogue of grievances. Let me tell you some of those which I have had told me from different quarters within the last few days. I cannot vouch in any way for the truth of each individual statement. I only relate them as they were given to me, to show the condition of public sentiment which their narration indicates.

In one house I was informed that every official, down to the policeman, was a Dane, and made himself "a little king" in the circle over which he ruled. Another informant, a small tradesman in Eckernförde, assured me that the wives and daughters of his townspeople were constantly insulted by the Danish officials, and that they employed the influence of their power and position to debauch the women of the country. In one place I heard a complaint that a Danish officer had broken a large looking-glass to bits, simply because he conceived that the way in which the frame was decorated was intended to represent the national colours of Schleswig-Holstein, and that no redress could be obtained for the outrage.

A gentleman resident in Kiel complained to me bitterly that nobody had ever been able to know where the produce of the taxes collected in the Duchies went, and that a Danish collector had assured him there had been more than 800,000 *thalers* collected from

Schleswig and Holstein in the last few years, for which no account had ever been rendered, even in Denmark. Drivers and carmen have told me that they never had a civil word from a Dane; and the universal opinion of the Duchies is, that the Danes are knavish and dishonest, and untrustworthy.

I have always observed that, when two nations have a mutual dislike, they generally bring similar accusations against one another; and I only mention this statement as a proof that the German Schleswig-Holsteiners do dislike the Danes cordially. If you press them about specific national grievances, you are told that the constitutional Estates of the Duchies were not allowed to meet; that their armies were incorporated with the Danish; that their national language was suppressed; that their children were forced to learn a foreign tongue; that every post in the administration of their own country was given to foreigners; and that, finally, there was neither freedom of speech, nor of the press, nor of religious worship.

Now, I am not saying that these grievances are unexaggerated, or that even if they are true they are altogether intolerable, like the wrongs of Poland or Venetia. There is no doubt that if the inhabitants of the Duchies had been willing to throw in their fortunes heartily with the Danes, their lot would have been a very much better one. Unfortunately, there is no particular reason why they should sacrifice themselves for the good of Denmark. Constituting as they do much the largest and wealthiest portion of the disjointed dominions which form the Danish monarchy, they derived no benefit from belonging to a small Power, and they suffered much inconvenience from belonging to a country with different language and interests from their own.

If you add to these causes the animosities created by civil war, and the belief that their own advantage would be promoted by separation, you cannot wonder if the Schleswig-Holsteiners are anxious to seize the first opportunity of terminating their connection with Denmark. At any rate, the secession party has, for the moment, the immense upper-hand. In a crisis like this malcontents speak more openly to foreigners than they do to their own countrymen, and yet not one single person I have spoken to expressed anything but satisfaction at the overthrow of the Danish rule. If you could poll the country fairly by universal suffrage, I have no question you would find an overwhelming majority in flavour of independence under Duke Frederick.

Until within the last few years, (as at 1864), the people would have been perfectly contented with a dynastic union with Denmark; now their one desire is to part company with the Danes for once and for all. As far as Flensburg the invading armies have met with cordial sympathy and aid from the population, and this in spite of many actions on their part which have been discouraging to the national cause. The mere fact that the Schleswig-Holstein volunteers have not been allowed to take part in the war is a bitter mortification to the people. At the skirmish near Missunde young lads from Kiel mixed themselves in the Prussian ranks, saying that they wanted to be fighting for their fatherland, and had to be driven back by force. I have heard an old man complain, with tears in his eyes, that it was cruel he should not be allowed to serve against the enemies of his own country; and this feeling, doubtless, is very general.

With regard to the duke himself, I question if the public sentiment is strong. Personally he has gained considerable popularity, and the friendliness of his manners is certain to have considerable influence with a simple and kindly people, like that over whom he aspires to rule. But as yet he has shown singularly little energy, and I fancy much disappointment has been caused by the facility with which he has given way to the pressure exerted upon him by Prussia and Austria. His real claim to popular favour lies in the fact that he is the representative of Schleswig-Holsteinism, and any prince who represented the same principle would soon be equally popular.

Meanwhile the impression is certainly gaining ground that Austria and Prussia will not attempt to restore the Danish rule. Everybody declares that, if they should endeavour to do so, there will be a revolution in the Duchies. How far this is true I have little means as yet of judging. No doubt as long as the Governments of Vienna and Berlin keep their immense armies within Schleswig-Holstein, any attempt of the inhabitants to resist their will by force would be absolutely hopeless. Yet the Schleswig-Holsteiners may easily make resistance enough to afford the great German Powers sufficient excuse for not carrying out their avowed policy; and, if need comes, this resistance, I believe, will not be wanting.

Flensburg, February 12.

The tide of war has passed by the Dannewerke, and moved on northwards. At Rendsburg there is nobody left except a few regiments of Saxon soldiers. The position of these Bund troops, as they are called, is a very mortifying one. Having come north to carry out the orders of the Diet, they have been quietly shelved by the Austrian and Prussian commanders, and are simply allowed to perform a nominal duty. While they remain stationed at out-of-the-way places like Rendsburg or Itzenhoe, the whole glory and credit of the campaign devolve on the armies of the allied Powers; and, for the present, all that the Saxon contingent can do is to parade about the dull little town of Rendsburg, and drink beer at its numerous *cafés* and *bier-kellers*.

In gait and appearance the Saxon troops are remarkably fine; and it was no wonder to me to observe that their officers commented with extreme bitterness on the enforced idleness to which they were subjected. By some chain of argument which I could not exactly follow, the Saxons considered that the Western Powers, and especially England, were responsible for the slight passed upon the forces of the Bund by Austria and Prussia, and were, therefore, disposed to look on England with extreme disfavour.

However, the great subject of conversation was the probable fate of a certain Dr. Blumhardt, who had just been under trial as a spy. This gentleman, who had been long unpopular in Holstein for his supposed Danish sympathies, had acted as guide to an Austrian regiment. On their march he had informed them that a Prussian force they saw advancing consisted of Danes. In consequence of this information, the Austrians fired upon their allies, and only discovered their mistake after several lives had been lost The doctor was forthwith sent to Rendsburg under arrest, as a spy, and has been tried by a court-martial there, and condemned to death.

The sentence, however, has not been carried out, on one pretext or another, and the impression is that it will be commuted to some minor punishment. To do the German Powers justice, they have exhibited hitherto a very laudable desire to repress any measures of retaliation against the adherents of the Danes in the Duchies.

******

This gentleman, after being kept in prison for four months, was finally discharged, on the ground that there was no evidence to convict him of the crime for which he was condemned.

******

The flight of the Danish troops was too rapid to permit of their doing much injury to the railroads. They cut down the telegraph wires, and blew up two or three of the bridges, but otherwise they effected little damage. In truth, the only reason why the railroad to Flensburg could not be made available at once was that, owing to the absence of trains, the snow had collected upon the line to the depth of some two and three feet The Prussians set men to work as soon as the Danes had evacuated the town of Schleswig, and yesterday, for the first time, the line was thrown open. Nobody, of course, knew when the trains were going to start, or whether there was to be a train at all. Fortunately, the officials of the line—which belongs, I hear, to Messrs. Peto and Brassey—were all English, and, by appealing to them as a fellow-countryman, I got permission to accompany one of the first trains which started from Rendsburg for the north.

It was late last night when I reached the headquarters of the German Army, and the difficulty of finding shelter of any kind rendered my first impression a very unfavourable one. However, seen by daylight, and after a good night's rest, there are worse places in the world than Flensburg. It lies at the end of one of the numerous fiords which indent the coast of Schleswig. Like most of these small seaside Danish towns, it consists of one long street running parallel to the sea, and of a few short lanes at right angles to the main thoroughfare. If you look at a map of the country, you will find that between the Fiords of Flensburg and Apenrade there lies a straggling promontory, terminating in the Isle of Alsen. It is on this promontory that the Danish army has made its stand.

Opposite the channel, some quarter of a mile broad, which divides the island from the mainland, are the heights of Düppel. On these heights there are entrenchments, supposed to be of considerable strength. In order to attack the Danes, it will be necessary for the Germans first to storm these entrenchments. When these works are captured, the only way of attacking Alsen will be to erect batteries of sufficient power to command the straits, and, under their cover, to throw a pontoon bridge across the channel. Difficult as this enterprise is in itself, its difficulty is increased by the fact that, if the reports prevalent here are correct, the Danish men-of-war will be able to cruise up and down the straits. In fact, barring any sudden panic on the part of the Danes, such as that which led to the abandonment of the Dannewerke, the probability is that the capture of Alsen will be a work accompanied by a heavy loss of life, and even a more serious waste of time.

At the same time, it is not clear whether the Germans can afford to leave Alsen unattacked. If they advance northwards to the frontier of Jutland, they leave a powerful army encamped in their rear. The general impression is that the allies mean to attack the works at Düppel at once, and thus, if possible, finish the war by one decisive action.

I have reason to know that the Austrian Government is most anxious to bring this war to a speedy conclusion. As a purely military measure, I believe the wisest course would be to capture the works at Düppel, and then simply to leave a sufficient force to hinder the Danes from returning from Alsen to the mainland; but, politically, I fancy the German Powers are prepared to make any sacrifice in order to terminate the war by an overwhelming victory, and, therefore, I incline to the belief that, according to the present programme, the last stronghold of the Danes in Schleswig is to be wrested from them, if possible, by force.

All day long the Austro-Prussian Army has been defiling through Flensburg, on its road to Düppel. I was woke up by the sound of drums as the first regiment passed my hotel, marching northwards; and now, long after dark, I can still hear the tramp of troops as they follow on the road to Düppel. The one street of Flensburg has been filled all day with a long straggling procession of baggage waggons, infantry, cavalry, artillery, and provender trains. The hard snow has been beaten into a soft powder by the passage of so many thousand wheels, and the footpaths themselves have been taken up by return carriages, which have been endeavouring hopelessly to make head against the never-ending current. There are soldiers everywhere; every other house has a sentry placed before it; every tavern is crowded with troops.

Passing along the streets you can hear German, Magyar, Italian, Servian, and every language of central Europe, spoken in turns. All the uniforms in the world appear to be gathered into this little town. The music of the grand Austrian bands comes clashing from time to time upon one's ears; then there is the heavy rumble of artillery, as the cannon founder onwards through the broken snowdrift; and then there comes the short, sharp step of the Austrian *jagers*, as they trot briskly forwards. As far as I can see, there is not much fraternisation as yet between the Austrian and Prussian troops. The officers of the two armies sit apart in the public dining-rooms, and in the streets I have rarely seen North and South Germans walking about together

The truth is that there exists considerable jealousy between the two armies. Hitherto, the whole credit of the campaign has fallen to the lot of the Austrians, and, with the exception of the Missunde affair, whose magnitude has been extremely exaggerated, the Prussians as yet have had little opportunity of distinguishing themselves. At the desire of Field-Marshal von Wrangel, the Prussian troops are to take the lead in the march on Düppel. Personally, the Austrians are much more popular here than the Prussians, who act too much as masters to suit the taste of the Schleswig-Holsteiners.

The reception given to the invading army has up to this time been very cool, as far as Flensburg is concerned. It needs very little observation to perceive that the population here is entirely different from that of Rendsburg, or Schleswig, or Kiel. Names with Danish terminations are plentiful. Every second shop appears to be kept by a Hansen, or Petersen, or Jacobsen. For the first time I have seen Danish inscriptions over the shops, and have heard Danish spoken in the streets. The number of flags hung out is comparatively small; and in the back streets, where the poorer part of the population dwells, it is very rare to see a flag at all. Four Danish cannon, which were captured at Idstedt, are drawn up in the market-place; but nobody appears to pay much attention to them. At the hotel where I am stopping the landlady and servants are all addicted to what the Americans would call proDanish proclivities, and hardly make an attempt to conceal their sympathies, though the hotel is crowded with German officers.

As the troops marched through the town I have not yet heard a single cheer given them by the inhabitants. The *Flensburg Zeitung* hardly alludes to the war, and carefully excludes any sentiment which could be construed into an expression of sympathy for either combatant. Moreover, it is obvious enough, even to a casual visitor, that there are two parties in the town. This morning I happened to ask my way of an elderly gentleman I met in the streets. He answered me civilly enough; but, while he was speaking, a working man rushed up and insisted on showing me the way to the hotel I was in search of.

As soon as we were out of hearing of my first informant, my guide told me that the man I had spoken to was a Dane, and that, hearing I spoke German, he had volunteered to assist me himself. The report of the town commission for providing aid for the wounded soldiers expressly declares that its charity will be devoted alike to Germans and Danes; and I have no doubt that public opinion here is pretty equally divided. As a whole, the town is perhaps more German than Danish. The streets have German names; the performances at the theatre are in German; and the great majority of the conversations you overhear are in German. Still you are clearly on the frontiers of Denmark; and there can be little question that whenever Flensburg is passed the Germans will be amongst an alien, if not an unfriendly population. General von Wrangel has given great offence to the German party in the city by declining to remove the officials appointed by the Danish Government.

Up to tonight the headquarters of the allied army are at Flensburg.

Flensburg, February 13.

The march of the army continues northwards. The advance of the Prussian forces is at Gravenstein, some twelve miles from Flensburg, under Prince Charles of Prussia; and the Austrians are stationed at the village of Rinkenis. The headquarters, however, of the allied armies are still at Flensburg. Field-Marshal von Wrangel, lieutenant-General von Gablenz, the Austrian Ambassador, and the Crown Prince of Prussia remain in the town; and though their departure is expected hourly, time passes by, and no forward movement is made. The truth is that the progress of the invading army has been delayed by the state of the roads, and that there is no intention of attacking the heights of Düppel till the Germans can marshal a sufficient force to render any chance of resistance altogether hopeless. The belief in Flensburg is that this will not be possible till some two or three days have elapsed.

However, about war movements decidedly less is known here than is known in Hamburg, and infinitely less than is known in London. The subordinate officers have absolutely no information as to the movements of the campaign, and the superior maintain a silence which possibly only conceals an equal amount of ignorance. Meanwhile, pontoon trains are rapidly passing on to the front, and there is no doubt that the Powers are preparing, if necessary, to storm the island of Alsen itself.

It is impossible to obtain any accurate information. Field-Marshal von Wrangel is bred up in all the traditions of half a century ago, and considers newspaper correspondence on military matters as an evil to be suppressed at all hazards. The correspondents of one or two semi-official German newspapers have, I understand, received permission to accompany the invading army, but no exception has been made in favour of foreign correspondents. In fact, if I am to confess the plain truth, I am afraid these German authorities are not anxious for the criticism of the English press. They know very well that the public opinion of England is unfavourable to the reckless manner in which the war hats been forced upon Denmark, and they have not sense enough to perceive that, the power of English journalism is one worth conciliating.

I spent the whole of yesterday and this morning in an unsuccessful attempt to obtain permission to pass the lines of the German Army. Flensburg is the longest town of its size it was ever my fortune to be in; and, as nobody has any idea where anybody else is quartered, while nine persons out of ten you meet are strangers, and half the other tenth speaks only Danish, it is a singularly hopeless task trying to find the address of any officer you wish to visit. When at last, after wandering about up every lane and alley in Flensburg, I found out my destination, I cannot say that I was much advanced in my object. The letters which had been forwarded me from London were sufficient to insure me a courteous reception, but that was all. I applied first to the Prussian headquarters, and there, after considerable delay and hesitation, I was told that if I confined myself to the truth, and wrote with becoming moderation, I might be allowed to stop at Flensburg.

In reply to this gracious intimation I could only politely express my regret that the Prussian Government did not think fit to allow free reports to be given of the condition of their armies. From the Prussian headquarters I went to the office of the Civil Commissioner, Herr von Zedlitz. There I was informed, with many apologies, that the civil authorities were perfectly powerless, and that, much as they wished for the valued support of British opinion, they could do nothing in contravention to the rules established by the military powers. My last hope was in the Austrian authorities.

At the headquarters of the Imperial Army I was received with a friendliness which contrasted strongly with the scant civility of the Prussian officers. My letters of introduction which had been sent from the Austrian Minister at Hamburg had somehow miscarried, but instead of being passed to and fro from one official to another, I was introduced at once to the General Von Gablenz, commander-in-chief of the Austrian forces; and I should be most ungrateful if I did not express my sense of the kindness with which I was received by him as an unknown stranger.

But, practically, the result of my mission was a failure. All readers of *David Copperfield* must remember how Dora's father, the proctor, was always willing to do everything his clients asked him, if his partner Jorkins had not been so hard a man. Now, Von Wrangel was the Jorkins of the Austro-Prussian firm. Nothing could have delighted the Austrian authorities more than to afford every assistance to the representatives of the English press if the Prussians had only been willing; and I have no doubt that the Prussians themselves, if they had been second instead of first in the firm, would have been equally willing to render me a hypothetical service, if it had not been for the unwillingness of the Austrians.

However, from Prussians, Austrians, and Schleswig-Holsteiners I have practically received the same answer, that I cannot be allowed to pass the lines of the invading army. I may possibly go up to Gravenstein—that is, exactly as far as there is no chance of seeing any fighting—but beyond that I am to go no farther.

Now, it would be absurd to complain because the Germans do not wish to have English special correspondents with their army. A truer understanding of their own interests would probably show them that it was for their own advantage to have the English public made acquainted with the immense force which they have displayed in their present invasion of Schleswig. This, however, is their concern, not mine, and most certainly the tone of my letters will not be influenced by the hope that they may induce the Prussian authorities to acquiesce in my sojourn at Flensburg.

Yesterday I was present at an interesting ceremony. A battalion of Austrian *Jägers* were summoned before the headquarters of General von Gablenz to receive the thanks of the Emperor for the gallantry they had displayed on the field of Over-Soe, which the Germans, by the way, insisted on calling the battle of Idsted, with an utter disregard of locality. The troops were formed up in a square, and the general, standing in the centre, addressed them in the name of the Emperor. Three privates, who had distinguished themselves especially on the scene of action, were called out in front of their comrades, and then and there informed that their names would be recommended for commissions in the service.

Then the troops were told that the emperor and empress took a most lively interest in their hardships and sufferings, and that a special commissioner had been sent from Vienna to report on the state of the hospitals; and, finally, the general announced that during the continuance of the war he should give up the pension he received as a holder of the Maria Theresa Order—amounting to about 50*l. per annum*—for the benefit of the families of those soldiers who died in the campaign. Three cheers were given for the Emperor of Austria, and for the King of Prussia, and for the German Fatherland.

The snow was falling fast, and the scene was picturesque enough. Between each sentence of the general's speech the grand Austrian band clashed in with half a dozen bars of the National Anthem, and the troops waved their hats and shouted "*Hoch!*" at every appropriate pause. About a score of Flensburg people had collected to see the spectacle, and on their part there was absolutely no exhibition of enthusiasm. The longer I stop here, the more I am struck with the coldness of the reception given to the German troops.

If you go into any of the shops where the national colours of Schleswig-Holstein are not exhibited, and where the name over the door has a Danish termination, and if you show that you are an Englishman, you will very soon hear the inhabitants express an unfavourable opinion about the army of the German Powers. As an army, I believe the Austro-Prussian forces have given very little cause of offence. Every exertion has been made to render their sojourn here inoffensive to the inhabitants, and the greatest care has been taken to avoid any step calculated to excite the anger of the Danish population.

The addresses of the Duke of Augustenburg have been torn off the walls, and nothing has been done under the avowed sanction of the allied commanders to proclaim the right of Prince Frederick to the throne of the Duchies. Nothing, however, that the Austrians or Prussians can do will reconcile the Danes to their occupation. The whole question, as I must again and again assert, is one of rival nationalities. Wherever the German element is in the ascendant, the people are for Frederick VIII,; wherever the Danes have the preponderance, the population are in favour of Christian IX. It is not possible to avoid the conviction that Flensburg is the extreme limit of the German portion of the Duchies.

As far as I can gather, the population of this place is entirely a frontier one. Almost everybody speaks German and Danish indifferently. I have happened today to pass my time chiefly amongst persons connected with the Danish Government, and from them I have heard the other side of the story, which I have now had narrated to me so often from German lips. If I were to listen to the Danes alone, I should believe they were the most innocent and unoffending people in the world. According to them, the vast majority of the Schleswig-Holsteiners are perfectly contented with the Danish Government; the sympathisers with the Augustenburg dynasty are only a small number of ill-conditioned Germans, who were unable to get employment under the German Government; and, in fact, the whole Schleswig-Holstein movement is entirely an artificial one.

Now, I am quite prepared to believe, as I have before asserted, that the sins of commission perpetrated by Denmark are extremely few. I am ready, also, to allow that the great bulk of the population would have preferred, subject to certain concessions, to remain united to Denmark. But still I cannot close my eyes to the fact that, up to Flensburg, the Germans are in the preponderance. For the first time in the Duchies, I have come across a strong Danish party; and the further north I go, the less I expect to find of Schleswig-Holsteinism.

February 14.

I am about to execute a retrograde movement, with the view of placing myself in a more commanding position than any I can occupy here at present I am like a Peri at the gates of Paradise—I can see the allied forces marching on to the seat of war. Possibly, if the wind blows in the right direction, I might hear the sound of the distant cannon as they thunder upon the works at Düppel; but practically I should know rather less about the progress of the war than if I were in London. The Flensburghers themselves know nothing, except that great masses of troops are passing constantly through their town, and that a great battle is likely to take place in their immediate neighbourhood. But neither the Prussians nor the Austrians vouchsafe them any further information.

The subaltern officers have very little to tell, and if they had, the mere fact of your being an Englishman, and, above all, a newspaper correspondent, would preclude them from imparting their knowledge to you. If the Germans think fit to close the channels of information conceded in other wars to the representatives of the press, they are perfectly at liberty to do so; but then they have no business to complain if the reports of English correspondents are derived from Danish sources, and therefore tinged invariably by a Danish bias. I leave this morning for Copenhagen, *via* Hamburg, and there, if all accounts be true, I shall meet with the civility which has been denied me in the Austro-Prussian camp.

But, before I leave, I would say something of the strange aspect which this place presents. From early morning to late at night the hotel where I have taken up my abode, like every other place of entertainment in Flensburg, literally swarms with soldiers. The Crown Prince of Prussia is stopping here, and the officers of his staff have more or less appropriated to themselves the smaller of our two public dining-rooms. Princes are as common as blackberries, and nobody seems to be of lower rank than a count. The Prince of Hohenlohe, one of the handsomest military men I have ever seen, is always loitering about the doorsteps, and another prince, who strikingly resembles a Prussian Lord Dundreary, and who rejoices in the longest of noses and the lengthiest of legs, is perpetually standing at the bar.

The white tunics of the Austrian infantry, the blue coats and red cuffs of the Prussian line, the gilt-braided jackets of the *Uhlan* dragoons, and the gorgeous red uniforms of the Brandenburg hussars, are all grouped together in one shifting mass of motley colour. As in most Continental armies, difference of grade makes comparatively little separation in social intercourse. Constantly you will see non-commissioned officers, or private soldiers, enter the coffee-room, make a military salute, and then place themselves by the side of colonels and majors. The cry of "*Kellner!*" never ceases for a minute throughout the day. The waiters are driven to the verge of imbecility; and in their few lucid moments show a marked preference for their civilian customers, who pay more, and bully less. The consumption of liquor and cigars is something appalling.

If headquarters were to remain much longer at Flensburg, I should think the army would be decimated by softening of the brain and delirium tremens. However, to do the German soldiers justice, positive intoxication is very rare. The quantity imbibed is enormous, but the quality is not of a powerful order. The human stomach, after all, can contain a vast amount of Bavarian beer and sugared champagne and diluted claret, without any worse effect than the' production of a state of general haziness. A battle is expected tomorrow; and it is strange to think that, out of the hundreds of officers whose faces I have learnt to know by sight within the last three days, some will, in all human likelihood, have drunk their last glass before the next four-and-twenty hours are passed. However, if soldiers were to speculate on such considerations, I fancy war would be less popular.

At any rate, these German officers are obviously in the highest spirits at the prospect of the coming fight, and the news that the Danes had evacuated the entrenchments at Düppel would, if I am not much mistaken, be received with positive disappointment in the Austro-Prussian camp. As I think I have mentioned before, there is very little appearance of *camaraderie*—to use a French term, for want of an English one—between the soldiers of the two nations. The men of rank of the two countries are of course united by that kind of intimacy which is sure to exist between the upper ten thousand of any nation, but the rank and file of the allied armies have very little in common. "*We are fighting for a common object, but we have no love for one another,*" is a saying attributed to an Austrian officer, which I have little doubt expresses the general feeling entertained towards each other by the soldiers of Northern and Southern Germany.

As time goes on, the real history of the evacuation of the Dannewerke is becoming known. I have learnt some particulars concerning it from a reliable source, which even at this date may be interesting. General de Meza, the Danish commander-in-chief, had always declared that he could hold the Dannewerke with a hundred thousand men, but not otherwise. The Government of Copenhagen, whether relying on the hope of foreign aid, or on whatever ground, had answered that the required number of troops should be forthcoming. When it became obvious that this promise could not be fulfilled, and the Germans, instead of concentrating their forces against Schleswig, were prepared to break the line of the Danish defences at three separate spots, General de Meza and his fellow-officers felt that it was hopeless to attempt holding a line of some fourteen English miles with a force of 25,000 to 30,000 men at the utmost, and therefore withdrew his army only just in time to save it from almost certain destruction.

The Austrian officers who are much fairer in their criticisms than the Prussian, all agree that no other course was open to the Danes, and that their retreat was effected with great skill and courage. Their only accusation against the course pursued by the Danish military authorities is, that, by holding the Dannewerke till the last moment, they sacrificed a vast amount of warlike materials, and, what is worse, subjected their troops to the inevitable demoralisation of a sudden retreat.

The evacuation of the Danish works was, however, totally unexpected by the Austrians. General Waldeck, the present commandant of the town of Schleswig, was the first to receive the news of the retreat of the enemy: commanding the advance of the Austrian position, he was under orders to commence the attack on Saturday. Late on Friday night some of the inhabitants of the city came in to his lines to announce that the Dannewerke was entirely evacuated. The news was hardly credited; but a regiment of cavalry was pushed on in the darkness, expecting to be attacked every moment by the Danes. Their advance was very slow in consequence, and it was not till two in the morning that the general found himself in the castle of Schleswig.

According to his own expression, he kept constantly pinching himself, to be sure that he was not dreaming. A message was forthwith despatched to the Austrian headquarters, enclosing the words:

I am in Schleswig.

It is said that when General von Gablenz received it he turned to his staff, and said, "What a pity! Waldeck has gone mad!"

No time was lost, when once the truth of the story was ascertained, in pushing on in pursuit of the retreating enemy. But the Danes had got too long a start, and their rear-guard were leaving Flensburg on one side as the Germans entered it on the other. The sufferings, I should add, of the Prussians, in their forced march after the Danes, were extremely heavy; and for three nights the troops slept upon the bare snow, without fire, and almost without rations.

Chapter 3

Flensburg to Sonderborg

Lubeck, February 17.

As far as climate goes, it is certain the French proverb—that *the days follow, without resembling*—holds good with regard to the Duchies. It was freezing hard when I went to bed on my last night at Flensburg; and the whole face of the country, far and near, was covered with one unbroken waste of ice and snow. When I woke up in the morning, the sun was shining brightly, a mild south wind was blowing, and on the hills which surround the town you could see on every side great patches of brown bare earth. For the last two days it has been thawing fast, and if this weather goes on there will soon not be a creek along the coast of Schleswig to which the Danish cruisers cannot penetrate.

However, there is a corresponding advantage to the German troops in the fact that they will not suffer so fearfully as they have done hitherto from the severity of the cold. Personally, I could only rejoice at the unexpected change. I was enabled by it to see Schleswig and Holstein under a different aspect from that which, in my eyes, had become their normal and habitual one. Still, though the country looked less cheerless beneath the bright, warm sunlight, it scarcely seemed less desolate. Between Flensburg and Schleswig—that is, for a space of five-and-twenty miles—the country is one flat unbroken "plateau."

The fields are generally of small extent, divided by what are called here "*knicken*," or mounds of earth a couple of feet high, surmounted by meagre hedgerows. These hedges, which, unlike our English ones, have no ditches on either side, would present very little obstacle to a fox-hunter; but they must most terribly delay the advance of cavalry. At the Battle of Over-Soe the Danish riflemen, crouching behind these "*knicken*," fired at the advancing Austrians, and then, as soon as they had delivered their fire, retreated hastily to the cover of the next

71

hedgerow, where they repeated the manoeuvre.

It is said, by the way, that the Danish soldiers used to remark that the Prussians were bad enough, because they fired six times with their needle guns, while they themselves could only fire once without loading; but that the Austrian *Jägers* were worse still, for the moment they had delivered their single round, they charged at once with the bayonet.

Every now and then the fields ceased, and the railroad passed over long swampy morasses, where the only forms of vegetation appeared to be reeds and ' bulrushes. Unlike Holstein, the southern part of Schleswig consists of extremely poor land; and the number of houses visible over the wide flat expanse is so scanty, that the population (except in the towns) must be a very small one. Possibly it is due to this fact, that there was little apparent excitement or enthusiasm to be traced along this portion of our route. At the stations there were none of those crowds which are to be seen at every station south of Schleswig; and at the few roadside houses we caught sight of, no flags were suspended from the windows.

A few miles north of the above-named town, the plateau of which I speak comes to an abrupt end. A low range of hills runs hereabouts from the Baltic to the North Sea, and along this line the works of the Dannewerke were placed. From the railroad you see nothing of the famous wall which has given its name to the whole range of fortresses; but you pass for some miles close to a number of apparently disjointed redoubts, connected by the natural earthworks formed by the low mound-like hills. It is only after the Dannewerke is passed that you seem to come into the genuine, undoubted German country, and at the present moment its aspect is bright and cheerful enough. Immense masses of troops are still constantly passing to the front.

A journey of about eighty miles occupied us very nearly twelve hours, not because our rate of speed when we were moving was a very low one, but because we were always stopping to let heavy trains pass us on their way northwards. The line of rails is a single one, and at every station we stopped, often for hours, till some long, heavily-loaded train came panting up. Trucks laden with immense piles of hay, lengthy trains of artillery, carriages filled with soldiers, and long pontoon boats supported by two or three trucks tied together, formed the material of every one of the many trains that crossed our path during the day. The soldiers going to the war were in the highest spirits, and kept singing and shouting on their way.

At every roadside station there was a crowd collected, partly to learn the latest news from the war, bat still more with the hope of hooting at any Danish passengers who might happen to be in the train. There was not a man to be seen, far or near, who had not the Schleswig-Holstein badge affixed, in some form or other, to his dress. The stations were decked out with flags, and busts and portraits of Frederick VIII., Duke of Schleswig-Holstein, were as plentiful hereabouts as they were scarce in Flensburg.

The conversation, I need not say, was all about the war. To doubt the absolute certainty of the success of the hourly-expected attack on Düppel was obviously considered an unpardonable heresy; and it was only persons of very despondent disposition who considered that the capture of Alsen might not follow immediately on the storming of the heights of Düppel. I am speaking of the talk of the many passengers who dropped in and out at the different stations, not of that of the military men, who filled the greater part of the train. One and all, in speaking to me, acknowledged freely the courage with which the Danes had fought, and looked forward, rightly or not, to a long and embittered struggle.

The dark side of war—the counterpoise of its pomp and glory—was just beginning to make itself visible, and to show to those who would look below the surface that this was not a mere holiday parade. The return freights of the trains to the south were already swollen with the sick and wounded soldiers, who were going home on furlough. The wounds, of course, of soldiers who were able to travel thus early, were naturally of a slight character. Heads bound up with plaster, shattered hands, and great gashes upon the face, half covered over with bloodstained bandages—these were about the worst traces of the battlefield that the sufferers had to show.

The great majority, however, of the returning soldiers were men stricken down with fever and consumptive maladies. In my own carriage there were two non-commissioned officers, who, unless their looks belied them, were returning to their own country only to die. The day was absolutely close, with a damp, reeking heat; but my fellow-travellers burst into a consumptive cough at the slightest breath of fresh air, and seemed to shudder at the mere mention of the sufferings they had undergone. One of them told me that he had been for three days without changing his clothes, on the march from daybreak to dusk, and sleeping at night on the snow without even a camp fire. He told me that he believed he had caught his death on the march from

Missunde, and I am afraid his declaration was true.

As yet, however, the number of returning soldiers has not been sufficient to damp in any way the ardour of popular enthusiasm. The Schleswig-Holsteiners have had no experience hitherto of the miseries that war inflicts on the population in whose midst it is carried on. The Danes cannot, even if they were disposed, ravage districts or destroy towns which they claim for their own. Both parties, so far, have paid for what they have taken; and the increased demand for almost every article of consumption has brought rich gains into the pockets of the Holstein farmers.

There is a common German story, that the Danes seized all the peasants' horses in Schleswig, and paid for them in notes which had passed out of circulation, and were supposed to have no commercial value; but there is so much exaggeration about these stories, I cannot attach much weight to this accusation without fuller evidence of its truth. Just in the same way, there is a report that the Austrian troops plundered a good deal on their march through Schleswig; but in all probability the army has to bear the weight of the sins committed by some stray Croat regiment.

While I am talking of stories, I must mention one which was told me by a German gentleman, about whose sympathy with the Schleswig-Holstein cause there could be no manner of doubt. If my informant was to be believed, the peasants in the neighbourhood of Averselk came out and plundered the wounded German soldiers as they lay upon the field of battle. The story may be true or not; but every candid German I have met, who has gone up to headquarters, agrees about the extent to which the inhabitants of Flensburg and its vicinity sympathise with the Danes. Perhaps it would be more correct to say, that they agree as to absence of sympathy for the Germans.

In 1848 the Flensburgers fired upon the Schleswig-Holstein volunteers as they fled through the town, after their defeat by the Danes. Indeed, the more I learn the more I am convinced that the line between the Danish and German populations begins very little, if at all, north of Flensburg. The Germans, who admit this fact, assert that the Schleswig Danes would much prefer union with Holstein to annexation to Denmark. About this statement I can as yet express no opinion. Let me add, before I quit the subject of the Duchies for a time, that a finer, manlier race of men than its inhabitants it has never been my fortune to see. The typical John Bull of *Punch*—the stout, red-faced, burly grazier, whom we see so seldom in real life in England—appears to me the actual, not the imaginary, type of the Schleswig-Holsteiner. The race is not a very bright or intelligent-looking one; but looks are no evidence if it is wanting in bulldog courage and honesty.

Malmoe, Sweden, February 18.

Every road, the Italians say, leads to Rome; at the present moment the converse of this proposition is applicable to Copenhagen. There is hardly an European capital so difficult of access as the Danish one. All the ordinary channels of communication are cut off; and, in fact, I was advised by some Danish acquaintances in Schleswig to charter a fishing-smack on my own account, and run the blockade, trusting to Providence that I might some day get landed somewhere or other on Danish ground.

However, it seemed to me there were too many probabilities inherent in this cruise of these letters, being brought to a premature and inglorious termination to justify its adoption; so I decided for the less romantic but more secure plan of going round by Sweden. The Germans I spoke to on the matter gave me the comforting assurance that Alsen would be taken and the war be over long before I could get round to the Danish camp by my circuitous route. I had a strong impression that they were counting their chickens before they were hatched, and at any rate I resolved to make the venture.

It was not sufficient to resolve in order to effect my purpose. My first difficulty was to obtain any information whatever as to when or where the boats started for Sweden. At Hamburg nobody knew anything; the papers contained a cheering announcement that a regular line of steamers was to be established from Lubeck to Malmoe, and that the first was to start on that very day. No time was to be lost in seizing this golden opportunity, and I was on the eve of starting for Lubeck when I was informed that the steamer had already sailed. When I had just reconciled myself to my disappointment, I met another traveller, equally well informed, who told me that the departure of the vessel had been delayed for a week; a third assured me that she was positively to sail the next day; and so on till I learnt to look upon the steamer in question as a sort of phantom ship, or Flying Dutchman, destined to haunt me throughout the remainder of my earthly existence.

Whether I should ever have made out anything at all I am much in doubt, had it not been for an institution peculiar to Hamburg. In the free city of the Elbe almost every nation has a post-office of its own; so that if you have correspondents in different parts of Europe you have to go to a dozen places to collect your letters. The Danish Government, amongst others, has a separate postal establishment There, at last, I learnt something positive. The Lubeck steamer had not yet arrived from Malmoe. She might come in every hour, or she might not; and, on the whole, the clerk assured me, if I would take his candid advice, I should go on to Rostock, where there was a considerable probability that I might get a steamer before very long.

With this faint prospect I had to content myself for want of a better, but finding that Lubeck was little out of the way, and that the detour would cause me no loss of time, I made up my mind to give the Lubeck boat one last chance of the honour of carrying me across the Baltic. Nothing could be learnt about her on the spot. A party of English acquaintances, who had been waiting for the boat for days, who had exhausted the novelties of Lubeck, and who regarded me with the interest which squatters in the backwoods of the West feel for a new arrival, were positive in their assurances that the missing vessel must arrive in a few hours, and that I should lose most valuable time by going round to Rostock. In this view I need not say that the landlord of our inn coincided most heartily.

I was happily decided enough to stick to my own resolution, and the next morning found me, shivering and cold, on my way to Rostock. On the road, I heard with a gloomy satisfaction that the Lubeck boat had been seized by a Prussian cruiser, as being a Danish vessel sailing under Swedish colours, and carried off as a prize to Dantzic. Whether the report is true or not I have not yet been able to ascertain. If it is, I hope I shall support the detention of my friends at Lubeck with philosophical resignation. Of my journey through the state of Mecklenburg I shall say nothing, as I only wish to dwell on those incidents in my travels which bear in any way upon the war. Let me, however, mention, as a curious trait of German life, that, if it had not been for a piece of ill-timed economy, I should have been a fellow-traveller with royalty itself.

There was but one first-class compartment in the whole train; and, had I taken a first-class ticket, I should have been its sole occupant in company with a very ordinary-looking little man, who was met by a guard of two soldiers, cheered by four small boys at Schwerin, and who turned , out to be his Serene Highness the reigning Grand Duke of Mecklenburg-Schwerin. Possibly, as I heard an Englishman exclaim, in a moment of elation at having just been presented, at the reception of the Statistical Congress in Potsdam, to the Crown Prince of Prussia, "'Is Royal 'Ighness might 'ave hallowed me to drink 'is very good 'ealth." On such little things do great events depend.

It struck me that the tone of my fellow-passengers, in talking of the war—and they talked of little else—differed very much from that current in Hamburg and the Duchies. They were most of them merchants connected with the Baltic seaports; their great desire seemed to be to see the whole matter brought to a close as soon as possible; and they obviously were keenly alive to the dangers of foreign intervention in case the war should be prolonged. For Schleswig-Holstein itself, they expressed considerable sympathy; but they regarded the cause of the Augustenburgs as hopeless.

By the way, from them I learnt two pieces of information not commonly known, and which I give as specimens of contemporary history. The first is, that England supplied Denmark, by a parliamentary grant, with the funds necessary to carry on the war against the Duchies in 1848-50; the second is, that the English Government has offered Frederick VIII., of Schleswig-Holstein Sonderborg Augustenburg, a million sterling if he will resign his pretensions in favour of Christian IX.; both of which facts I considered should, in the words of Captain Cuttle, mariner, "*When found, be made a note of.*"

I am afraid I bored my fellow-passengers dreadfully by asking them about the Swedish vessel I was hunting after. Nobody could assist me. One gentleman told me I should have to go round by Stockholm; another suggested trying a Russian port, say Cronstadt; a third prophesied that I should have to wait a week at Rostock; while a fourth, who professed to be especially informed, declared that the line I was trying to go by had been suspended as soon as the steamer had started for Lubeck. At Rostock itself I could learn nothing positive; and from thence I set off on what seemed now almost a wild goose chase, for the little fishing port of Warnemünde, whence the packets proposed to sail.

There, at last, to my intense delight, I found the Swedish steamer lying at her moorings; but all the captain could tell me was that he should start some time or other when he got his orders, but when that would be it was impossible to say. Afterwards I discovered the cause of this unsatisfactory communication to be that the captain, a Swedish officer, took me for a German, and to Germans he had a personal antipathy. However, having got to the steamer, I resolved to stop there; and after keeping the steward up beyond his usual time, to his great disgust, in order that I might finish a letter, I betook myself to a berth, and was woke up in the morning by the welcome sound of the screw grating against the pier as we pushed off from the German port. The voyage was cold and miserable.

The only other passenger besides myself was prostrated with sea-sickness; and the stove, which professed to warm the cabin, was always going out whenever the boat rolled, as only screw-boats can roll, and the wind blew as, I think, winds only can blow in mid-winter in the Baltic Sea. However, I shall always feel grateful to the *Dronning Luisen*, as the boat was called. In the first place, she carried me across the sea which divided us from Denmark; in the second, she made a run of 98 miles in little over eight hours; and in the last, her captain, after he had discovered I was an Englishman, made me acquainted with genuine Swedish *schnaps*, a drink not to be despised in this ice-bound country.

Indeed, of the few hours I have spent in Sweden, I am afraid my impressions must be summed up in the one word "cold." Ystad, the little port where the steamer landed me, lies at the extreme end of the Swedish peninsula, but on the eastern side. To reach Copenhagen, therefore, it is necessary to cross the peninsula to Malmoe, a distance of some 40 miles.

My first object on reaching Ystad was to procure some means of conveyance, and I found the speediest method of making the journey was by the "*malle-post*," which left at five the following morning. All the inside places were taken, and so I had to ride outside by the driver. As my luck would have it, the day was so cold, with a bright, hard frost, that even the natives spoke of it as something extraordinary. I am not partial, at any time, to the spectacle of sunrise; and even the most enthusiastic admirer of nature would not desire to witness the "break of dawn" from the top of a lumbering, jolting chaise, with an ice-cold wind blowing straight into his teeth from across the Baltic, and the temperature Heaven knows how many degrees below anywhere.

A sleigh drive in New York always appeared to me one of the most wretched phases of my existence, but it was Paradise compared with this ride. As my sole effort was to bury my face beneath furs, and to keep up some sort of tingling life in my hands and feet, I cannot profess to have seen much of the country through which we passed. What I did see struck me as bare and uninteresting, and preternaturally cold. In the little taverns we stopped at to change horses, I noticed there were frequently pictures of Christian IX. and of the Princess of Wales, as well as of the Swedish Royal family. However, the steamer is nearly ready which is to carry me over the narrow strait of the Kattegat to Copenhagen, so I must say no more of Sweden.

Copenhagen, February 12.

Everybody tells me that in the summer time Copenhagen is one of the brightest of European capitals. A German waiter, who was expatiating this morning on its charms, informed me its sole defect lay in the fact that it offered so many pleasures to the traveller, that he was at a loss which to select It may be so, but in this chill wintry war-time it is not a bright or lively looking city. The streets are narrow; the houses are high and many-windowed, plastered with stone-grey *stucco*, and surmounted by high-peaked slate roofs.

There is little, indeed, to distinguish it from any town of northern Germany, except that it is less picturesque and more uniform than most of the small German capitals. The shops are poor, and of a more miscellaneous character than is common in the great cities of Europe; and the use of signs is still very common. The barber, of course, is known by the brass soup-plate basin suspended before his shop. The tobacconist advertises his trade by hanging up three small gilt rolls of tobacco in his windows. A tin book denotes a bookbinder, and a wooden boot is the trade emblem of a shoemaker. However, civilisation has penetrated to Copenhagen in the shape of Train's street-railroads; cars built exactly upon the American fashion run across the square upon which my windows look; and, as far as I can discover, cause no particular annoyance to the inhabitants. In fact, anything which lessens the noise must be a blessing, for the pavement of Copenhagen is about the worst and noisiest I have ever come across.

Putting aside the Danish inscriptions on the walls and shop-fronts, I think any careful observer would soon perceive he was not in a German city. The people are a smaller, slighter-made race than the Teutonic. The difference between them and the Germans is very much like that between the North Americans and the English. Of any particular Yankee it is impossible to say that he might not possibly be an Englishman; and yet you feel certain that he could never be a type of our English race. And so it is here. Every individual Dane might be a German, but no breed of Germans could ever resemble the one that prevails here. The features are sharper, the hair is straighter, the complexion is more sallow, than is the case with the inhabitants of the Fatherland; a stout person of either sex seems extremely rare, and narrow chests are the rule.

In truth, I am extremely struck with the similarity in external aspects between the Danes and the Northern Americans; they have the same brightness of look, the same sharpness of features, and, let me add, the same frank cordiality of manner. The women one meets in the streets would be pretty enough if they did not remind one so painfully of dried pippins parched by the frost. However, Venus herself would have a red nose in a climate such as this, so that possibly my judgment is based upon insufficient data.

Of soldiers there are few apparently left in Copenhagen. The Royal Guards, with their dark-red cloaks, are as fine a body of soldiers as our own Horse Guards, though scarcely so powerfully built. The ordinary line regiments, of which I have seen several detachments parading through the streets, dressed in greyish-blue uniforms, are not by any means crack troops in appearance. They have not yet acquired the regular military "*tenue*," and look very like the soldiers of an English militia regiment, called out for yearly duty. The men are small-sized and awkward in their gait; but; on the other hand, they have that indescribable look of meaning business which I have seen wanting in armies of much more martial aspect.

The town itself is obviously depressed by the gloom which, for the moment, hangs over the fortunes of Denmark. All trade is paralyzed, and people hear of nothing, read of nothing, speak of nothing, and, I believe, think of nothing, but the war. All the shops are filled with plans of the campaign and with pictures of the battles of 1848-50. The booksellers have obviously removed all German works from their windows, and you see none exhibited for sale except Danish and a few English and French.

All day long the papers bring out handbill supplements, with the latest rumours from the seat of war, which are hawked about the streets by boys and women, and appear to command an enormous sale. Still, as far as I have seen, there is no outward sign of disturbance about the town. The hotel whence I write is the one where the Schleswig-Holstein deputies were mobbed by the populace in 1848; and the square in which it is placed—the "*Kongens Ny Torv*"—is the chosen scene for all popular demonstrations in this capital. As yet, however, I have seen nothing, except a band or two of workingmen marching in procession through the square, and singing patriotic songs. Otherwise, the city is as quiet as London. Indeed, it is impossible to help being struck with the order and air of unguarded security which characterise Copenhagen. There are scarcely more soldiers visible than there are in Manchester, and of any police I have seen no trace as yet. Passports are unknown; and, with the single exception that you are required to sign your name in a book as soon as you arrive at an hotel, you move about as freely and as independently as you would in England.

I have had the opportunity today of seeing several persons—Danes as well as foreigners—well qualified from their position to judge of the position of affairs, and they all agree as to the present determination of the people to continue the struggle as long as their resources will hold out. The arguments which they put forward may, I think, be briefly expressed. I will leave aside all their discussion as to the abstract merits of the question at issue. The Germans may be extremely unreasonable, and the claims of the Augustenburg dynasty may not be based upon any principle of justice; but the question has now passed—and the Danes themselves admit that it has so passed—from the domain of argument into that of force.

Taking, then, "accomplished facts" as the sole basis of discussion, the Danes assert that resistance to the death is their only possible policy. In the first place, they deny the power of Austria and Prussia to make any satisfactory arrangement, even if they were disposed to do so. These Powers, they assert, have been forced into war with Denmark in obedience to a popular passion. When they entered Holstein, they had no idea of invading Schleswig; when they had invaded Schleswig, they had no wish to cross the frontier of Jutland. The necessities, however, of their position have compelled them to follow up one step by another, and the same motive power which has driven them on so far will force them on farther and further, with increased intensity.

But, admitting even that this is not the case, and that the two great German Powers are in a position to offer terms, the Danes still assert it would be inexpedient for them to accept the offer. The utmost that, under the present conjuncture of affairs, could possibly be offered by Germany, would be an independent Schleswig-Holstein, united to Denmark by a purely personal union. Now, an union thus established would only be another name for a separation. German settlers would cross into Jutland; a cry would be raised that the Teutonic nationality was oppressed by the Danish; and the same battle would have to be fought over again with diminished powers on the side of Denmark On the other hand, the course of war can hardly entail any greater injury on the Danes than the loss of Schleswig-Holstein.

Without a fleet the Germans cannot possibly invade the islands which constitute Denmark proper, and, even if there were no moral difficulties, the material obstacles in the way of their permanently retaining Jutland would be almost insuperable. Thus the worst evil that the prosecution of the war is likely to inflict on Denmark is a certain loss of life and treasure, and for this loss the country is prepared. As long as the Danes continue fighting, they can reckon on many contingencies; the "glorious uncertainty" of war may turn in their favour; European complications may give a brighter aspect to their affairs; the unfailing discord between Prussia and Austria, and between these Powers and Germany, may break out anew; and, finally, if they fail in the end, failure will be less disastrous to the nation after a gallant struggle than after an inglorious peace.

Such are, in substance, the views I have heard expressed today, from several quarters of very different character. I am not endorsing them as my own; I am simply repeating what I have had said to me. And it is difficult to believe that my informants were not in earnest in what they said. There was no *braggadocio* or "tall-talk" in their utterances; they appeared to be expressing nothing but a solemn and sober conviction, when they said that resistance was the only path open to them. Personally, I fancy the Danes lay too much stress on the luck which attended them in the last Schleswig-Holstein war, and expect a recurrence of the same good fortune. How far a series of disasters might damp the national spirit, I cannot say; but, in the present temper of the people, I believe that neither the fall of Düppel nor the capture of Alsen itself would render any peace that Germany could propose acceptable to Denmark. For another year, according to the common belief, the Danes can maintain a fleet and an army against any power the Germans can bring against them; and unless the fallacy of this belief should be shown by stem experience, there is, I suspect, little prospect of any compromise being come to.

Nyborg, Island of Fünen, February 20.

Persons who have travelled in America will be familiar with a process entitled "making bad connections." If they wish to enjoy the reality of the operation without troubling themselves about the name, they need not take the pains to cross the Atlantic, but may content themselves with the much shorter, though infinitely more laborious, journey from England to Denmark.

No conveyance in this country ever succeeds in making a good connection. When you arrive at a junction you are always half an hour too late, or a dozen hours too early, for the corresponding means of transport. I myself am at this moment a victim to misplaced confidence in the regularity of Danish postal arrangements. Having left Copenhagen at a preternaturally early hour, I was landed here with extraordinary expedition at one p.m., and now discover that the post-waggon which is to carry me across the island of Fünen, does not leave till one a.m., for some inconceivable reason or other. By seven in the morning I am to be at Assens, and thence, if report be true, I am to find a steamer to convey me to Sonderborg, on the Isle of Alsen. That this may in truth be so is my prayer rather than my hope. For the present, the one thing certain is that I am doomed to spend twelve mortal hours in the dismalest of small Danish towns.

If I were to attempt to give you news of the war from here, I should have to evolve it entirely out of my own consciousness. The French may have invaded the Rhine provinces, the English fleet may be steaming for the Baltic, and what is more, the Austrians may be in the possession of the Isle of Alsen, for anything I, or anybody else in Nyborg, know to the contrary. The more I travel in Denmark the more I am struck with the utter disjointedness of the country. Fünen is as far from Zealand in distance as England is from France, and infinitely further in practical accessibility. Fünen is as far again from Schleswig, and Alsen itself is separated from this island by a strait, as broad in parts as that between Jersey and Granville.

And as these inland seas are very stormy in winter time, and communication is often broken off for days together, the separation is a very real and important one. Each island appears to be a distinct country in itself; and, in fact, unless you adopt the German view, and say that Denmark is Copenhagen, it is as hard to say where Denmark is, as it is to say in what part of the human frame the principle of life resides.

Of direct war news, therefore, I have only this much to tell you, that the Danes attach extreme political importance to the German invasion of Jutland; their idea is that the German powers desire to obtain possession of some purely Danish territory, which they may offer to surrender in exchange for the evacuation of Alsen. It is surmised that the delay in the attack on the works of Düppel is due to a wish to gain a footing in Jutland before any serious onslaught is made on the island of Alsen.

With the view of frustrating this scheme, if possible, troops are being poured as rapidly as may be into Fredericia. However, it is no good to speculate on the progress of events from this out-of-the-way nook of Denmark. Let me tell you rather of what little I have seen and

noted with reference to the war. On my way to the station this morning, I came across a considerable body of troops, on their march to the
railroad. It was cold enough, I should have thought, to damp the most
ardent patriotic enthusiasm; but the troops were in the highest spirits,
shouting and singing as they marched, and escorted by a large crowd
of friends and sweethearts.

I cannot say that their appearance was martial; they looked like
what they probably were, peasants fresh from the fields. They stooped
constantly, seemed hardly to know how to carry their muskets, and
kept very indifferent step in marching. Their uniforms, too, were slov-
enly, and in many cases only half complete; in fact, their resemblance
to the raw levies of the North American armies was very great, and
the contrast they presented to the Austrian and Prussian line regiments equally striking. Moreover, their discipline was obviously very
imperfect. Some allowance must doubtless be made for the excitement of departure; but still the confusion at the railway station was
greater than ought to have existed if regular troops had been awaiting
transport.

The demand for, and the supply of, "*schnaps*" had obviously been
large, and muskets were pulled about in horse-play, in a way rather
alarming to an unexcited spectator. Still, as I said in a former letter,
the men all looked as if they would fight, and with time I have no
doubt they might be turned into excellent troops. But, in estimating
the relative forces of the two combatants, it is only fair to Denmark to
remember that a great portion of her army consists of raw levies, who,
like the troops I saw this morning, have been summoned together in
extreme haste, and sent to fight with but little previous training.

At the station there was the usual spectacle which I fancy attends
the departure of all armies for the war. Mothers and wives were crying; men were cheering; friends were waving their handkerchiefs; and
the troops themselves were singing in response, as our train moved
slowly off. It was curious to notice how much the tone of the air differed from that which would have been poured forth from German
throats. There was very little of the harsh Teutonic accent about the
melody; and, except that the notes were not so rich, I could have fancied, if I closed my eyes, that I was listening to a Garibaldian regiment
singing the "*Va fuori d'Italia*" for the hundred-thousandth time.

During our three hours' journey the troops never ceased singing,
and as they embarked at Korsoer, on the large steamers which were
to carry them to the scene of war, they still continued their chorus

in defiance of the cold. In strange contrast to these troops setting out for the war were a number of disabled soldiers who had just been discharged from the service on account of their wounds, and were returning home to their villages. Those I spoke to complain bitterly of the hardships they had undergone from the cold; but with all the chief regret seemed to be that their military career was ended.

The harbour of Korsoer presented clear evidence of the naval supremacy of Denmark. Half a dozen steamers were leaving for different parts of the kingdom, some with troops, some with stores, others with despatches, all with the Danish flag—the white cross upon the red background—flying at their stern; and not one, as far as I could see, was armed with cannon. It is only in the German harbours that the Prussians can interfere with the vessels of the enemy, and between any two ports of Denmark the Danish ships go as fearlessly and regularly as in time of peace.

The fortifications of the harbour were obviously unprepared for any attack; and, indeed, unless the Great and Little Belts, as the straits are called between Fünen and Zealand on one side and Alsen on the other, were to be frozen over, and the Germans were to repeat the strategy of Charles XII. of Sweden, I do not see that Denmark proper has much cause to be alarmed at the possibility of a Teutonic invasion. As yet, at any rate, it is a contingency not contemplated. About a small town like this from which I write, lying as it does somewhat out of the beaten track, there is little, therefore, to show that the country is involved in a struggle of life or death. There being no apprehension of the scene of war being transferred to this island, the campaign hardly comes home to the daily life of its inhabitants.

The town of Nyborg is rather strongly fortified, but there scarcely seems to be more than a corporal's guard left in the whole place. When you have walked round the ramparts, and up and down the pier, you have exhausted the curiosities of the little market town, which looks very much as if it had been transported bodily from Lincolnshire or the fen country, dropping half its inhabitants on the way. The people themselves, as a rule, seem to me wonderfully grave and quiet. Even amongst themselves, they appear to talk little in public; and in these country towns the *table d'hôte* is got over with a silence and rapidity which a Western American might envy. Let me say, *en passant*, that the living is excellent, and that the breakfasts are something worth travelling to see. Poached eggs, anchovies, sardines, tongue, smoked ham, corned beef, fried herrings, cheese, and oatcake—these are the most elementary materials of an ordinary breakfast that is set before you without any special order. The hotels, too, though very plain, are clean to a degree which you will rarely meet with in Germany.

CHAPTER 4

Sonderborg

Headquarters of the Danish Army,
Sonderborg, Isle of Alsen, Feb. 22.

Just a week has passed since I left Flensburg, and after six days' hard travelling, and after passing through half-a-dozen different States, I have got back to a point about twenty English miles from Flensburg itself. The ill-luck which had hitherto pursued my movements deserted me—I trust finally—at Nyborg. This time I was fortunate enough to find a vacant seat inside the *malle-poste* which conveyed the mails, and, after a long night's journey, rather less cold and comfortless than usual, I found myself in the forenoon set down at the little port of Assens, on the west coast of the Isle of Fünen. Having quite made up my mind to a further detention here, I was delighted to find a steamer actually waiting, with its steam up, to carry on the mails. Then there was a long windy sail down the Little Belt, past the Island of Æro and the Fort of Kaiborg, and then, at last, I found myself in Sonderborg, the headquarters of the Danish Army.

Being there, the next thing was to find a shelter. Considering that the town is a fairly large one, with one main street nearly a mile in length, there seemed but little difficulty in discovering some roof or other under which to hide my head. Experience, however, soon taught me that I was mistaken. At the hotels they laughed at the very idea of giving me a bed, or even of allowing me to use a sofa. Any mechanical contrivance by which a bed could be run up, on any available spot, had been exhausted long ago. At last, after a masterly exertion of eloquence, I got permission to leave my luggage at an hotel, while I went out in search for a room; and then I recommenced my investigations by knocking at the doors of house after house.

My researches were equally unavailing, and I saw no chance of anything except spending my night on the floor of a tavern, with my carpetbag for a pillow, when I recollected that a gentleman in Copenhagen had given me a note of introduction to a friend of his, residing at Sonderborg. As a last chance, I resolved to avail myself of this letter, in the hopes that the gentleman to whom it was addressed might recommend me a lodging. I had no sooner shown my credentials, than I was invited with extraordinary cordiality to take up my quarters at this gentleman's own house, so that probably I am better lodged than any stranger in the whole city.

I cannot speak too highly of the kindness of my hosts, who have literally placed their house at my disposal. I cannot say more than that it is of a piece with the uniform courtesy and civility I have received since I entered Denmark. Nothing can be more striking than the contrast in this respect between the Danish and German Armies. I have not only been granted the fullest permission to pass the lines and go to all parts of the camp, and this without any condition whatever being attached to the favour; but every single officer or civilian I have come across has shown himself not merely willing but anxious, to afford me every information in his power.

Moreover, there is something very gratifying to an Englishman in the absolute freedom of locomotion permitted here in the very midst of war. As far as I can see, there is absolutely nothing to prevent any dozen Germans from coming to Sonderborg, stopping here as long as they please, inspecting all the preparations, and then returning home without let or hindrance, I was never asked a single question during the course of my journey hither; and the very steamboats which carry troops are open as conveyances to any civilian who likes to pay the passage fare.

What renders this liberality the more remarkable on the part of the Danes is that, if they chose, they might really hinder almost all intelligence from penetrating abroad, except what they chose to convey themselves. With the Germans such an attempt is ludicrously hopeless. Every single movement of their army must be known, sooner or later, at Flensburg, and thence diffused through Hamburg over the Continent; but here at Sonderborg we are completely cut off from the rest of the world, and our only means of communicating with the main land is by steamers sailing under the orders of the Danish authorities. In fact, it is difficult to conceive a position more isolated than that of Alsen.

The island—so the inhabitants say—is shaped like a dog sitting upon his haunches; and if you look at its form on the map you will understand the similitude. The dog's head is the promontory of Nordborg; the hind feet are formed by the southernmost one of Sonderborg. Alsen is divided from Schleswig by a narrow strait called the Sund. Its average width I gather to be about three-quarters of a mile; in some parts the strait widens till it must be nearly two miles across. Near Sonderborg, however, it narrows rapidly, and opposite the town itself it is little, if at all, over a hundred yards in breadth. The channel is deep enough for men-of-war to pass up and down; but its narrowness in parts and the extreme rapidity of the current make its navigation very difficult.

At Sonderborg the strait is crossed by two boat bridges almost close to each other. On the Alsen side of the channel, the hills slope down gently to the water, and the one long straggling street of Sonderborg runs up these hills at right angles to the water's edge. On the Schleswig side, however, the hills rise rapidly and steeply, and the main road leads up to the heights of Düppel, or Dybbol, to adopt the Danish spelling. It is on the brow of this hill the works are placed which form the last line of defence of the Danish Army. At this point, exactly opposite Sonderborg, the Schleswig coast juts out into a narrow promontory, across which runs the hill of Dybbol. On the left hand is the bay of Vemming-bund; on the right is the strait of Alsen.

Thus, in order to reach the one point at which the passage of the strait is easy, the Germans must force their way across the hill of Dybbol, whose ridge is surmounted by the line of redoubts on which the Danes place such reliance. If, on the other hand, the Germans attempt to cross the Alsen Sund without storming Dybbol, they will have to throw a pontoon bridge over a much wider distance, while they will be exposed to an attack in their rear by the force which occupies Dybbol.

If this explanation is intelligible it will easily be seen how a comparatively small force can defend the isle of Alsen against an army infinitely larger which has no command of the sea. The real numbers of the Danish Army are carefully concealed; but my impression is that they cannot possibly exceed 18,000 men. When I left Flensburg, an assault on the entrenchments of Dybbol was hourly expected, and Monday last was the day on which the assault was anticipated. What has occurred to delay the progress of the allied armies it is useless to speculate on here. The Danish belief is that the invasion of Jutland was an afterthought of Prussia, and that the attack on Dybbol has been deferred till Jutland is occupied, as a material guarantee. Considerable hopes are based on rumoured disagreements between the Austrians and Prussians; and it is thought that the fearful loss of life which must attend the capture of Alsen may deter the Austrians from sanctioning an attempt whose success is not necessary to their own prestige.

But whatever hopes of this kind may be entertained, they have no influence on the determination of the Danes. Alsen they are resolved to hold, and if they are attacked they will fight for it to the last. Even supposing the heights of Dybbol should be taken by storm, an attempt will still be made to defend the passage of the straits. For my own part, if once the brow of the hill overlooking the town falls into the hands of the enemy, I question the possibility of hindering their further advance. At any rate the town will lie completely at their mercy.

Any hour of the day the Germans may attack the heights, and if their attack should prove successful, the town will have to be evacuated—at any rate by non-combatants. At the house where I am lodging, the children have been sent away days ago in anticipation of such a possibility, and most of the inhabitants, who are not detained here by business or duty, or poverty, have already left the place. The town is completely given up to the army; every house is crowded with troops, and the harbour is filled with war-steamers. Amongst the inhabitants, as far as I can learn, there is a most evident goodwill towards the military. Of course, if there were any German sympathisers or "*Deutsch-gesinnte*," as they are called by the, Danes, they would hardly manifest their existence. But all the names of the people are of Danish origin; you hear nothing but Danish talked in the street; and I find that, in speaking to a common person here in German, it is always better to preface your question by a statement that you are "*ikke tydsk*," or "no German," if you wish to get a cordial answer.

Today we have had almost the first symptoms of the long-expected attack. I had hardly got my pass stamped and signed when the alarm was sounded in the streets by trumpeters riding through the town. In a moment Sonderborg was in a bustle. Orderlies began galloping about recklessly; soldiers poured out of every house and by-lane; and the crowd of horses led up and down before the headquarters of the army showed clearly that the staff was about to move. Confusion there was absolutely none, and everybody seemed to fall into his place with wonderful promptitude and order.

In a little town like this, acquaintances are soon formed, and, in company with some English and Danish gentlemen, I started for the scene of action. We had not gone far up the straight steep road which leads to Dybbol, before we began to meet forage waggons being driven back to the town, filled with wounded soldiers from the front. It was snowing hard, so that we could not hear the fire of the enemy; but every now and then, from the Danish batteries on the crest of the hill, there came that sharp whizzing noise caused by a shell cutting through the air, which, when once heard, it is impossible to forget.

Underneath the brow of the hill, out of sight of the enemy, there were massed a couple of Danish regiments, waiting for the word to advance. The haze caused by the mist and snow was so great, that it was thought possible the Germans might attempt to storm the works under its cover; and everything was ready to have given them a hot reception. Gradually, however, the fire died away, and news came in from the scouts that the enemy's forces were falling back. The mist had cleared up, and three regiments of Danes received orders to advance and reconnoitre the ground.

The men, who had been wearied out by the constant, anxious waiting of the last few days, were delighted at this forward movement, and marched on singing vociferously the song of the "*Tappere land-soldat*," who is ready to die for his Fatherland and his king. Just behind these troops, so full of life and spirits, came the ambulance men carrying the stretchers on which the wounded were to be brought back. We had not to wait long before we saw them return with their stretchers loaded. Two dead men were carried past while I was standing there; one with his arm hanging over the cart on which his body was flung, and dragging lifelessly along the road. Another poor fellow was brought in severely wounded, and his moans, as the stretcher swayed from side to side, could be heard for a long distance off. But all these appeared to have no effect on the spirits of the troops, who still wended gaily forwards, singing still the "*Tappere land-soldat*."

Just then a Prussian non-commissioned officer was brought in prisoner by a guard of four Danes, with whom he was conversing in a most amicable manner. As he passed the troops on their march, they chaiffed him good-humouredly enough, asking him if he was come to order quarters for the Prussians; and the prisoner took the banter with complete apparent unconcern. After I had followed the troops for some distance, I met the staff returning, and as I found that nothing of any importance was likely to occur, I made my way homewards.

As far as the skirmishing went, there is no doubt the Danes had the best of it, and at the close of the day their outposts were further advanced than at its commencement. On the other hand, they could have acquired no substantial advantage, and they must have had some seventy or eighty soldiers put out of service; a loss which is of more importance to them than ten times the amount to their antagonists. Since the morning the attack has not been renewed.

February 23.

I don't know whether other people are constituted in the same way that I am, but to me the moment that occurs between a light being placed to the match and the explosion taking place appears always unaccountably long. If only something would happen—even if the gun itself were to explode—it would be a relief from the state of suspense which the knowledge that all your nerves are about to receive a painful jar causes to a person to whom noise is peculiarly distasteful. Now I fancy that the Danes in Alsen have a very similar feeling about the long-expected attack upon their lines at Dybbol.

If it would only come off everybody would feel relieved. As it is, it is dreary, anxious work waiting and knowing that any moment the attack may come. Another day, however, has passed, and still no symptom is seen of the enemy's advance. Last night it was resolved to push forward a considerable force to reconnoitre the ground supposed to be held by the Prussians; and, in order to avoid exciting suspicion, small detachments of troops were sent out throughout the night and early morning, till a sufficient force was collected at the front. However, the morning was so hazy, that it was impossible to see a hundred yards before you, and the Danes were unwilling to advance far beyond the shelter of their batteries. In consequence, any idea of pushing on to a distance was abandoned, and when I left the outposts towards noon the troops were returning to their quarters. No skirmishing had taken place, and, as yet, the day's list of casualties has been a blank. The gunboats meanwhile sailed up the Sund and fired some stray shots at the woods where the Prussian pontoons are supposed to be concealed, but no response was made, and hitherto the day has been barren of events.

Before, then, the position has become familiar to me by its sameness, let me use this breathing time to try and convey to you some notion of the aspect borne by the scene amidst which I am living. The house where I am quartered stands a little out of the town, on the top of the low bluff which, in this part, runs along the Alsen side of the Sund.

From my windows I look out on an old barrack-like building, in part of which some Danish king—I believe, Christian II., was confined for years by his nobles; to the left the Sund opens out into the Baltic; to the right it narrows into the river-like channel, which barely divides the island from the main land. The snow has been falling again heavily within the last three days, and everything is covered with a white veil, fringed with icicles. Across the channel there ran two bridges of boats, almost parallel to each other, and at but little distance apart; the nearest to the sea is for passengers crossing to the mainland, the further for those returning from it. One of them is quite of late date, and the planks of which it is formed are laid across a number of fishing smacks, moored in the stream, whose masts have been cut down for the purpose, while their hulls are still inhabited by the fishermen's families. Thus, as you pass over the bridge, you can see all sorts of quaint family interiors through the openings underneath your feet.

At the Schleswig end of the bridge there lies the unfinished hull of a vessel of some two hundred tons burden, which was far advanced towards completion when the war broke out The workmen were all summoned off for military services, the builder was left with the vessel on his hands, and she lies there with her bare skeleton timbers as a sort of emblem of the desolation this war is causing. I wonder, by the way, stranded as she is right in the line of fire between the heights of Dybbol and the town of Sonderborg, what would be the rate of premium charged at Lloyd's for her insurance ?

At the bridges are placed the sentries who are supposed to examine the passes of non-combatants, a duty performed on their part with extraordinary laxness. A few steps leads you to the commencement of the works which defend the strait. Bight up the hill stretches the long straight road leading by Dybbol and Gravenstein to Flensburg. On either side you see a large tract of snow-covered field, picked out into squares by the tips of the hedgerows rising above the surface of the snow. The road is hard and slippery on the edges, soft and muddy in the centre, beat down into a squashy pulp by the constant passage of so many thousand wheels and feet. If you choose the side paths, you lose your footing; if you go in the middle, you sink into the mire. However, to those who, like myself, have seen the state of the Schleswig roads during the march of the vast German armies, there is little to complain of in this Dybbol highway.

The snow is not actually falling, but the whole air seems thickened with snowy particles, so that you can see nothing till you come close to it, and, what is worse, can hear nothing distinctly till it comes close to you. The clatter of horses' hoofs almost at your back causes you to jump on to the roadside banks, and the Danish staff come riding by. The tall gaunt-looking officer, with the iron-grey hair and keen eye and wrinkled face, is General Luttichan, the commander-in-chief, in the absence—probably a prolonged one—of General de Meza.

The staff itself consists of some twenty officers, most of them men in the prime of life, the recital of whose names would convey no interest to the English reader. There is no variety of uniform among them—no display of crosses or ribbons; their horses, though strong and serviceable, are not well groomed or caparisoned; and though the officers look eminently like gentlemen, they have not that air of professional preciseness which distinguishes the military men of other European countries. Indeed, about the whole Danish Army there is very little if anything of the "pomp and circumstance of glorious war." There is hardly any distinction of dress in the whole army. Infantry, riflemen, artillery, hussars, and dragoons, all wear the same plain grey-blue coats.

Yesterday, for the first time, we had a band playing in the town; but the men marched without any music except that which they make for themselves by singing. Each company has its own small pennant flag, with the Royal Crown and the number of the regiment placed in the corner of the white cross which runs across the red background; but there are no regimental flags, or if there are they are not brought out on active service. In this dim, dreary light there is something mournful about the aspect of these brave Danish soldiers as they meet you on the roads, and pass from the mist before you into the mist behind you so silently and gravely.

They are fine men enough, of small stature, but strong, wiry build. Their step in marching is free and manly, but they have not the briskness of the French nor the regularity of the Austrians. Except by the numbers upon their shoulders, there is nothing to show you to what regiment or even to which branch of the service they belong. The officers hardly differ in appearance from the men, save that their dress is of better quality, and that they carry a sufficient display of epaulettes and facings to mark their rank. Sometimes they ride in front of their regiment; but more often you see them walking side by side with their men. The soldiers are heavily weighted with their thick woollen cloaks and dun cowskin knapsacks, and the large wooden shoes that most of them carry tied on to their wallets. The uniform of any one company is seldom complete.

The clothing establishment of the Danish Army has not proved equal to the extra demand for uniforms, and amidst the blue coats you see brown and drab garments of anything but military cut; while occasionally hats and cloth caps disfigure the uniformity of the head gear. The troops—many of whom have been but lately pressed into the service—have had a hard life of it of late. From the necessity of the Danish position, the army is obliged to be constantly on its guard against a sudden attack, and the men are harassed by perpetual alarm. Fortunately, they are well clothed and fed, and there is as yet but little sickness amongst the troops, in spite of the hardships they have undergone. Yesterday, at the prospect of a fight, they were in the highest spirits; today the excitement has gone off, and you heard much less shouting and singing as the troops tramped home to their quarters, than when they were marching out, as they supposed, to battle.

The long uphill road to Dybbol reaches the summit by a lonely windmill—whose sails, I should fancy, can never be idle for want of breezes—and then descends, by a less steep but equally straight incline, towards the village of Dybbol. It was expected that the Danes would have reoccupied this hamlet on the withdrawal of the Prussians yesterday, though with what object, except to gratify the troops, it is difficult to see. However, the mist was too dense for the execution of any such idea; and, after I had pushed my way to the outposts, I had to retrace my steps without any chance of seeing the village I had started to visit. If you had looked upon the battle-scene simply as a painter, the mist, I think, would have added to its picturesqueness.

In the fields off the road, and under shelter of the hedges, strong bodies of troops lay waiting for the signal to advance. Straw had been brought up in cart-loads, on which the men lay sleeping, smoking, or eating, with their arms stretched beside them. Every now and then there was a dull sound, which might have been distant cannon, but which probably was merely the noise of some cart rumbling along the road; and then came the sharp note of the bugles, as the signal passed from one company to another. Everything looked an unnatural size against the mist, like the Spectres of the Brocken, and the whole scene had a weird, ghastly air about it.

February 24.

If the German papers are to be believed, by the 26th the Prussian heavy artillery will all be brought up to the front, and then we may expect the long-delayed attack upon the works of Dybbol. However, these things are seldom known beforehand, and all that can be safely stated is that no attempt has as yet been made. For my own part, I fancy that what the Americans would call "wire-pulling" must have stopped the operations of the Allied Powers more than any want of artillery. It is divulging no secret when I say that the Danes, at the outbreak of this war, were found in a very imperfect state of preparation. "Wolf" had been cried so often about the German invasion, that somehow or other the Danes do not seem to have realised that war was actually at hand.

The respite which has occurred between the entry of the Germans into Flensburg on Sunday week and the present date has proved of incalculable advantage to the defenders of Dybbol. The soldiers have had time to recover from the fatigues of their march, and what is of more importance, to regain their spirits after the blow inflicted on the national pride by the evacuation of the Dannewerke.

Moreover, this breathing time has been used to advantage in strengthening the position. Hedges have been levelled, woods cut down, and barracks built; and the Germans will find the storming of Dybbol a much harder task now than if it had been attempted ten days ago. There seems to me a sort of carelessness and habit of taking things easily amongst the Danes, which hinders them even now from doing quite all that might be done in the present emergency; but still a great deal has been done; and, if further time should be granted, a great deal more will be done, to render the line of works which defend the Island of Alsen as strong as possible. That this was likely to be the case must have been obvious to the German commanders.

It is, too, impossible to doubt that they are well informed as to the movements of then enemy. As I have before mentioned, the "surveillance" kept up by the Danes over the movements of non-combatants within the lines is of the laxest character. During the three days I have wandered all over the works it has only once occurred to me to be asked for my permission to pass the lines; and I can entertain no doubt that any peasant acquainted with the country could make his way to and fro with hardly any danger of detection. Now, even the most enthusiastic Dane would not assert that there are no German sympathisers at all in Alsen, or that all the population could be trusted to convey no information to the hostile camp. On these grounds I am forced to suspect that political or diplomatic rather than strategical motives have induced the Germans to defer the assault on Dybbol.

However, the immediate effect of the delay has been greatly to raise the spirits of what I suppose may be called the besieged army. When the Danes first retreated here, I gather that the defence of Dybbol was regarded as a sort of forlorn hope, and that the resolve of resistance was due rather to a sense of honour than to any prospect of success. Gradually I see that public opinion is growing somewhat more confident. Encouraged by the obvious hesitation of their enemies, the Danes believe that the contest will not be so unequal as they at first supposed, and serious hopes are entertained that if the Germans should venture on an attack they will meet with a severe, if not an overwhelming, repulse. There can be no question about the temper of the army.

As I walk about with my opera-glass—which I am proud to say is the best I have yet met with in the camp—hung over my shoulder, I am constantly stopped by the common soldiers to ask for a peep. Their invariable desire is to see if they can catch a glimpse of the enemy's patrols, and their equally invariable mode of returning thanks is the expression of a wish that the Germans would lose no time in coming to be shot. Whenever there is a rumour of an advance and the troops are marched forwards, they begin their unfailing song, whose burden is that "they are going to fight the Germans, and drive them home again." Amongst the officers, though the tone of conversation is naturally more moderate, it is not less decided. A lieutenant, whom I was talking to today at the works, said to me very solemnly:

"My one prayer is that I may never live to see the day when this position is abandoned; and that if we are to be driven out of it by the Germans, I may be left here amongst the dead."

And this is the general tone of quiet middle-aged men, who have long outlived the hot enthusiasm of youth. Indeed, it is curious to observe how completely the inhabitants of Sonderborg have got acclimatised, as it were, to the idea of danger. To foreign lookers-on, like myself, the worst evils that the entry of the German Army is likely to bring would be the loss of my luggage, and possibly the passing of what Rabelais called un *mauvais quart d'heure*.

But to the Danes amongst whom I live, the occupation of the town by victorious Prussian troops—to take the most favourable view of the matter—would mean not only national humiliation, but the ruin of their fortunes and exile from their homes. Yet, somehow or other, the prospect appears to have lost its terror by familiarity. The daily life goes on much as usual. After all, as I once remember reading in a book whose name I have forgotten, "*if the end of the world was known to be coming the day after tomorrow, people would still want to dine tomorrow,"* and even though Sonderborg may be occupied any hour by the invading army, that is no reason why its inhabitants should not live comfortably while the town remains untaken. I must not be misunderstood as if I meant to say that at this moment there was anything of reckless gaiety about the Danish population. On the contrary, everything is quiet and still to a degree that is almost depressing; but yet the ordinary social life is by no means devoid of comfort, and we sleep and smoke, and eat, and listen to music in the evening, as if there were no possibility that any moment the sound of cannon and the sharp notes of the alarm-trumpet might tell us that the enemy were at hand.

There appears, indeed, to be a settled conviction that the attack, whenever it does take place, will occur in the morning. The calculation in itself is not unreasonable. Even assuming that the German armies carried all before them with uninterrupted success, the storming of the Dybbol heights would be a work requiring all the daylight of these short winter days; and in the present state of the country, covered as it is knee-deep in snow, a night attack is out of the question. I have no reason to assert, or even to suppose, that there is a want of vigilance in the outlook kept up by the Danes during any hour of the four-and-twenty; but still there is something almost comical in the fixed idea which appears to prevail that no attack can possibly be made after eleven o'clock, or noon at the very latest.

Today I was talking to an officer in one of the outworks, and asked him if anything was likely to happen. He pulled out his watch, consulted it, and said, "No, it's past eleven;" and seemed to consider this reason as conclusive as if he had said that it was too late to present a cheque in London because it was past four. Thus, hitherto, our life here has gone on with monotonous uniformity. Every morning there springs up a rumour that something is going to happen at the front. With that the corresponding public, whose number at present, native and foreign, consists of five, hurries out to the front; and then, after two or three hours' rambling about the works, the troops begin to return home, and we return with them.

This morning there was more than the usual excitement; a report had reached the town that the Germans were likely to commence their attack, and a very large body of troops was sent out to reconnoitre. The day—for the first time since I have been here—was literally clear, so that the Danes were able to advance with safety for some distance beyond their batteries. A long undulating valley lies between the heights of Dybbol and the hills which run parallel to them towards the creek of Nybol.

The land between these two parallel ranges of hills is a sort of debateable ground, which hitherto has been alternately occupied by Danes and Germans. The whole country is intersected by stunted hedgerows and copses of wood, or what in Leicestershire would be called "spinnies," behind which troops may with extreme care be concealed. Moreover, when fields are all covered with snow, the distant hedgerows look so much like lines of troops that it is very difficult to distinguish one from the other.

Today, too, three regiments of Danish troops advanced cautiously to a considerable distance beyond Dybbol. Before each successive hedgerow was passed, skirmishers were thrown out in twos and twos, but no trace of the enemy could be discovered; and after advancing perhaps a couple of miles beyond the batteries, the Danish troops were very wisely recalled. On the slopes of the hills on the western side of the valley I could see a considerable force of German troops encamped in the snow; but nothing could be seen at a nearer distance, though the enemy are believed to be very close at hand.

Probably, last Monday's skirmish has taught the Danes the necessity of caution. It seems that after the enemy had retired, two Danish regiments, the 11th, I understand, and the 22nd, pushed on in advance, and occupied two small works which lie about a mile beyond their outposts. Here they were fallen upon by the Germans when out of reach of their supports, and had a hundred and fifty men taken prisoners before they could make good their retreat. The mishap was kept very quiet, and now that it has become known, the excuse put forward is that the troops engaged were raw levies of peasants, which I have no doubt is true. But still, a small army like the Danish cannot afford such mishaps, and the lesson was not uncalled for.

February 25.

Letters from this place resemble, in one respect, the bread spoken of in Scripture, namely, that they must be cast upon the waters, in the hope that they may be found somewhere after many days. The general want of preparation and organization, which characterises all the arrangements of the Danes, is especially manifest in their postal system from the seat of war. When, or how, or where letters go, after they are dropped into the box of the military "*feld-post*," is a mystery that nobody—the post-office officials themselves included—appears to have been able to solve. Theoretically, there is a steamer every morning for Copenhagen; but the practice is not equal to the theory. This morning, for some unaccountable reason, the steamer did not sail for Körsör; and in all probability the letter which I wrote you yesterday will reach you at the same time as this.

Fortunately, however, or unfortunately, the delay will be of comparatively little importance, as today has been as blank of events as yesterday.

This morning about six o'clock the town was woke up by an alarm that the enemy was advancing in force. Nothing, however, came of it, and we are still waiting for the attack to come. Strange to say, the Danes appear to be most imperfectly informed of the movements of the German Army. The population of these parts are a quiet, unenterprising race, amongst whom it is very difficult to extemporise spies; and, though the peasantry of the mainland are probably more friendly to the Danes than to the Germans, they do not appear ready to make any great exertions on behalf of their defenders.

However, the approach of daylight showed that the Prussians have again advanced very close to our works. At this moment the Danish lines do not extend much beyond a mile or so from the summit of the Dybbol-hill. A few houses which lie along the main road from Dybbol to Grasteen have been set on fire, and all the hedges on the hill-side have now been cut down, so that the whole face of the hill is clear. On the hillside of the ridge, which runs parallel to that of Dybbol, you can see the Prussian encampments; and their patrols were visible today on the shores of the Wemming-Bund, within range, I should think, of a Minié rifle.

The woods which were the scene of Monday's skirmish, and which lie between the two ranges of hills, are probably in the possession of the enemy; at any rate they serve to conceal his movements. It is a misfortune for the Danes that their attempt to burn down these woods proved unsuccessful, owing to the dampness of the timber. Since last evening the frost has broken, and, if the present thaw holds on, in another day the ground will be clear of snow. If the attack on Dybbol is to be made at all, it is not likely to be delayed much longer. This, at least, is the opinion of Sonderborg.

Meanwhile the one incident of the day has been the burial of the soldiers who fell on Monday last. The churchyard of Sonderborg must be a pretty place enough in the pleasant summer time. It lies a little off the town, on the brow of the low hills which run above the quay.

From the narrow lime-avenue which divides the churchyard from the burying-ground itself, you can see the snow-covered heights of Dybbol, surmounted by their crest of batteries; the broad deep Als Sund flowing like a river between the island and the mainland; and the great fiord-lake of the Wemming-Bund, stretching calm and motionless beneath the low-wooded hills of the mainland shore.

If it were not that everything looked so chill, and cold, and grey, I know of few prettier burying-grounds than this of Sonderborg. The graves are decked out with chaplets, and wreaths, and crosses, and the hum of the little town scarcely reaches to that quiet *"field of God."* It was here they buried these dead soldiers. But, except for the presence of death, the scene was not, I thought, impressive. The soldiers who were to escort the dead to their last home looked what I have no doubt they were—cold, tired, and out of humour. The majority of the officers in attendance stood chatting with the chaplain, smoking, and making unsuccessful efforts to keep their feet warm by stamping on the ground.

The whole affair was ill-arranged as a spectacle. The bodies lay within the dead-house, a couple of hundred yards from their grave, each cased in a black deal coffin of the most cumbrous make. It was with difficulty that the six soldiers who acted as bearers could toil up the slippery avenue with their gloomy burden. Nearly an hour elapsed before all the twenty-two coffins could be placed in the broad trench, where they were laid side by side together; and then the chaplain, who wore a white starched frilled ruff, about the size of a cheese-plate, round his neck, such as you see in Vandyke's pictures, and who had been laughing before, assumed the professional look of deep depression, and commenced a funeral address about the holy character of the war for King and Fatherland, in which the dead had died.

Amongst the bodies was one of a German soldier, whom the Danes had buried with their own people. At the time I could not help thinking of the possibility that the poor fellow had been present a week ago, at the military burial in Flensburg, when a chaplain of his own nation descanted to his hearers on the fact that his countrymen had perished in a holy war. Happily, the dead, whether Danes or Germans, are not likely to be perplexed with the difficulty of how it is that God's blessing is always announced with equal confidence, as appertaining to the combatants on either side of every war.

Then the dust was thrown upon the coffins, and the solemn words commending the dead to God's keeping were pronounced, and a discharge of musketry was fired across the grave, and just at that moment the guns boomed forth in the distance from the heights of Dybbol. All was over, and the soldiers were left to sleep in their last resting-place, close to the grave of the men who, as an inscription on a stone pillar tells the stranger, died for their Fatherland in the last Schleswig-Holstein war. Half-a-dozen small boys and one or two peasants were all the spectators that had collected to see the sight from the town of Sonderborg. Whether this was due to want of curiosity or absence of enthusiasm I cannot say, but the fact is worth recording.

February 26.

Every day which passes contracts the narrow area of our mainland domain. The island of Als of course is open to us. In this strange war, though we are only divided from the continent by a strait whose width varies between that of the Thames at Richmond and at Graves-end, yet we are as safe from any water attack as if the Channel lay between us and Schleswig. If the German Powers had anything approaching to a fleet, they could land their forces in an hour or so on any part of the island, and have the whole Danish Army at their mercy.

As, however, they have nothing of the kind, this island fastness is perfectly secure, unless the enemy can throw a bridge across the straits; and this attempt is believed to be impracticable, unless the position of Dybbol is first captured. Thus, we can ride or walk about the island as much as we think good, and leave the war entirely out of sight and mind.

A Danish gentleman, residing at Sonderborg, told me that the other day he had occasion to go to the little peninsula of Kainaesk, which runs out into the sea at the southernmost part of the island, and found peasants there who had never heard that there was a war going on at all. But the disadvantage of these inland excursions for a correspondent is, that they throw him entirely out of the way in case anything were to happen; and, therefore, I find myself daily crossing the bridge to stroll about the little strip of land which Denmark still holds on the continent of Schleswig.

Having ridden or walked now over pretty well every part, I think I can give the reader a very fair idea of it in a few words. The Danish possessions west of the Als Sund consist, in truth, of nothing but a low, round-shouldered hill, very much resembling in shape an old-fashioned plum-pudding. This hill is, in fact, a promontory, jutting out into the Baltic. The sea surrounds three-fourths of the area of its base. The waters of the Als Sund and the Wemming Bund approach very close to each other at the exact points where the hill ends on the western side. It is probable that at some remote period, Dybbol itself was an island separated from Schleswig by a strait, like that of Als.

This hill, which is called Dybbol, from a neighbouring hamlet, is exactly bisected by the high road from Flensburg to Sonderborg, and on the crest of the hill, stretching from the Wemming Bund on the south, to the Sund on the north, are the Danish fortifications. Today, according to the German papers, was the date fixed for the commencement of the bombardment; and if any serious attempt is to be made, it cannot, I think, be long delayed. As soon as the enemy opens fire, all parts of the hill beyond the ridge will become unsafe for spectators; and therefore my strolls on the mainland are likely every day to become confined to the eastern slopes of the Dybbol hill.

Today I took what very likely may be my last walk beyond the brow of the hill. The works have made good progress ever since I have been here, and every object which could protect the enemy in his advance up the hill-side has been diligently removed. The few cottages along the road have been burnt down; the hamlet of Dybbol is utterly deserted; soldiers are quartered in the empty houses; and broken chairs, tables, and bedsteads lie scattered about the fields.

The Prussian encampments can be seen in front of the church of Nybol, a village about two miles from Dybbol, and the outposts of the two armies are within sight of each other. This morning the Danish iron-clad, the *Rolf Krake*, sailed into the Wemming Bund with the object of shelling-out some batteries, which the Prussians are supposed to have constructed on the further side of the bay. If the *Rolf Krake* had started at daylight for her cruise of a couple of miles, she might have raked the whole shore with ease. As it was, she did not start till near eleven; and by the time she had taken up her ground, a heavy snowstorm came on, which rendered it impossible for any object to be distinguished at a hundred yards distance. So she returned without doing anything. However, since her return, the Danes assert that no batteries have as yet been erected by the Prussians within range of the shore—a fact about the truth of which neither I nor, I expect, the authorities themselves have much means of judging.

Living, as I happen to do, amongst Danish officials, I hear a good deal about the Schleswig and Holstein question; and it may perhaps be worth while to put before you shortly their view of the case as between Denmark and the Duchies. Their defence, then, amounts to this: that Denmark governed the Duchies justly and fairly, according to the best of her knowledge; that she made no attempt to oppress the German nationality, except in as far as revolutionary agitation caused her to act in self-defence; that she solved the problem of dealing with a mixed population as equitably as it is possible to solve it; and that the great bulk of her subjects were perfectly contented with her rule, and were only led by professional grievance-mongers to imagine that they were oppressed.

Or, in fact, to put the case more tersely, no adequate reason can, in their opinion, be alleged why Denmark deserves to be deprived of possessions which are her own by right and law. Now, I have no doubt of the sincerity with which these assertions are made. I am not given to take an unduly favourable view of the average truthfulness of mankind; but I can truly say that I have seldom met in any class so many men who impressed me with a strong conviction of their kindness, honesty, and uprightness, as amongst the Danish officers and gentlemen with whom my lot is thrown at present; and in a great measure I believe that their statement is true in fact as well as in intention.

My own observation in the Duchies led me to the conviction that the Schleswig-Holsteiners had not been subject to any acts of grievous oppression. The country is too prosperous to have been tyrannised over for any length of time. Moreover, if you sift the German accusations against Denmark to the bottom, you can find little evidence of anything worse than—to say the utmost—a vexatious assertion of supremacy on the part of the Danes. I picked up the other day a German historical novel about the wrongs of the Duchies, and the instances of actual cruelty which the writer could bring forward were, that the deputation from the Duchies to Copenhagen in 1848 were hooted at and pelted by a Danish mob, and that a certain German doctor was cruelly ill-used during the war by some peasants in Jutland. It is clear, too, from hearing both sides of the question, that the quarrel between Denmark and the Duchies is a good deal one of two antagonistic political systems. The Duchies are governed by a land-owning aristocracy; Denmark is ruled by a democracy.

But yet, allowing all this, as I am perfectly willing to do, I am not able to follow my friends in the inference they draw from their assertions, namely, that the restoration of Danish authority over the Duchies is the one thing to be desired. I leave the constitutional and dynastic questions entirely out of the case, as not being of primary importance. If the November constitution were repealed, and the Duke of Augustenburg himself were made King of Denmark and Duke of Schleswig-Holstein, I believe the arrangement would only secure a temporary cessation of hostility. The cause of quarrel does not lie in any question of dynasties or abstract political rights, but in the antagonism between two opposite races.

The Danes seem to me at this moment to entertain a not very dissimilar feeling towards the Germans from that which the Northern Americans have towards the English. They resent bitterly the extent to which their culture and civilisation are imported from Germany, and are anxious to cut themselves off from all connection with Fatherland. It is with reluctance they will ever speak in German, and I constantly find that Danes, who know German as well as they know their mother-tongue, will torture themselves to stutter out a few words of broken English, sooner than hurt their ears by the accents of the German language.

It is quite natural they should dislike the Germans; but then this dislike is a bad qualification for ruling a country in which the German element preponderates. Nobody can see the gallant effort made by the Danes to repel an overwhelming force without honouring their courage; nobody can live any time, I think, amongst them without liking and esteeming them. As far as the present struggle is concerned, I wish them success most heartily against their immediate enemies; but I cannot see my way to claiming the reinstatement of Danish rule over the German part of Schleswig.

February 27.

Sonderborg, in its normal condition, must be one of the dullest of towns. It is not lively now, but to the inhabitants its present state must seem an approach to delirious excitement. Nobody, as far as I can learn, ever heard of any public amusement at Sonderborg, and the utmost dissipation that the natives ever dreamed of was an excursion once or twice in their lives to Copenhagen. In truth, here, as in almost all parts of the peninsula—a fact, by the way, worth bearing in mind—Hamburg was much more the commercial capital of the country than the metropolis of Denmark.

You could drive from here to Flensburg in three hours easily, and from thence the railway took you to Hamburg in five hours; whereas, in ordinary times, the journey to Copenhagen involved two sea passages, a wearisome drive across the island of Fünen, and an expenditure of the better part of two days. Alsen lay out of the line of travel between Zealand and Hamburg, and the traffic—on this side of the island, at any rate—went towards the mainland, not towards the insular possessions of the monarchy.

However, the value of this disquisition as to why the communications of Alsen should have tended westwards rather than eastwards is somewhat impaired by the fact that Sonderborg does not seem to me to have ever been much in communication with anywhere. A sleepy, quiet little island town, it minded its own business, and had very little to do with any other part of the world. The population scarcely numbered two thousand souls, and it was only a strange freak of nature which converted the place into a fortified stronghold.

One long, straggling street, which appears to have grown piecemeal—each piece being at a different angle to its preceding and succeeding joints—constitutes the greater part of the town; of private residences there are hardly any; every house almost is a shop or a tavern; the dwellings are mostly of one story high, with lofty roofs of tiles and gable ends, and wattled with plasters of every hue that is cold and dingy. Danish is obviously the language of the locality. One tavern only in the whole place—the *"Holsteinisches Haus"*—has a German name.

About twenty families, I am told, speak German amongst themselves, but I have never heard it spoken in the streets, and when I use the language in speaking to the common people, I find that their knowledge seems limited to those common phrases which are certain to be picked up by a population living so close to the frontiers of a German-speaking nation. A town-hall or *"rad-huus"* of the humblest dimensions, a church, and a post-office are the only public buildings of the town; and the one sign of modern progress is the existence of gas. However, lest this should be considered a reckless innovation, I am glad to say that the lamps are never lit on nights when the calendar declares that the moon ought to be visible. If anybody, in truth, desired to select a spot where he could pass his life, *"the world forgetting, by the world forgot,"* I should recommend him to choose Sonderborg, supposing he could guard against the risk of war.

But at the present day lovers of repose should avoid Sonderborg with the utmost diligence. The town is literally turned upside down and inside out. Everything is changed. The climate, indeed, must be regarded as normal. It is true that everybody assures me such a winter was never known in Alsen. But then I have always observed, in all parts of the world, that whenever the weather is particularly bad, the inhabitants assure you that, they never knew such weather before, I have no doubt if I could get within the Arctic circle—which heaven forbid!—I should be informed by the dwellers in those parts that they had never been a whole day before without seeing the sun; and whether normal or not, the weather here is simply to be described by epithets which begin with the fourth letter of the alphabet.

A thick undercoating of snow covered with successive layers of slush is the nearest description I can give of the surface of the ground. Every six hours a thaw comes on, sufficient to melt the snow in the streets and to render the footpaths impassable, in consequence of the showers of rain-drops which pour down from the overhanging eaves of the houses; then we have a sharp frost, which renders the roads as slippery as ice; then we have a fresh fall of snow, then another thaw, and so on *da capo*.

Our one street is steep and naturally slippery, and nature has been improved by a pavement of small round stones, scattered about the road hap-hazard, and supposed by a popular fiction to represent a "*chaussée*." All this, as I said before, is more or less normal. But the confusion of our present condition is due to the presence of the Danish Army. The barracks which were to hold the troops engaged in the defence of the works of Dybbol were, like most of the Danish arrangements, incomplete when the need arose for them, so that till quite recently the whole of the defending army has been encamped in the town.

Quarters which were meant to hold four thousand people have been forced to hold six times that number, in addition to their original inmates. In one house, where the family consisted of six persons, I have known forty privates quartered, not to mention the officers, who lived with the family. The uniforms far outnumber the unmilitary dresses in the streets, including the peasants and waggoners. At every door you see soldiers standing about; they are looking out of every window; they are crowding into every shop. All day long troops are marching through the town, going to the front, or returning from it.

Even at the quietest time of the day—that is, about noon—it is hard work passing through our one main thoroughfare. Orderlies keep galloping up and down with no apparent object; long trains of forage-waggons straggle across the road, and get blocked up upon the footpaths in apparently inextricable confusion. Before the headquarters, which are over an apothecary's shop, there is always a *mêlée* of horses and sentries and officers. Still, the confusion is nothing like what it was at Flensburg, or what I remember it at Mola di Gaeta, when the Sardinian army occupied the town during the siege of the fortress.

All the supplies, with the exception of forage, come by water, and, being landed close to the bridge, do not need to pass through the town. Moreover, somehow or other, there is, considering the circumstances, a strange absence of life or noise. As I have before mentioned, nothing can be conceived more sombre or colourless than the aspect of the Danish Army. The dull, faded blue is but seldom relieved by the red cloaks which, as a matter of theory, the soldiers ought to wear. A quieter or better-behaved set of men I have never seen. They march along with a dull, loitering gait, very different from the spirited step of French or Austrian troops.

Whenever there is a prospect of battle their step quickens, and they begin to sing lustily; but, as a rule, they exhibit singularly little animation of any kind. During the whole of the week I have stopped here I have never yet seen a drunken soldier; and in the taverns and inns very little drinking of any kind seems to go on. The men look strong and healthy, and since they have been housed in Sonderborg have had no cause to complain of their treatment. The inhabitants—though they appear to exhibit no particular enthusiasm about the war—are on the friendliest terms with the soldiery, and are perfectly willing to supply them with everything that is at their own disposal.

To do these people justice, the idea of taking advantage of the sudden demand made upon their resources, in order to fill their own pockets, appears never to have entered into their heads. Prices have not been raised in consequence of the war; and even the few persons who let lodgings have not altered their tariff. An English gentleman, who could not speak a word of Danish, managed as a great favour to secure a bed in one of the most decent houses in the street, without making any bargain beforehand, and on his departure was charged a shilling a day for his bed, and ninepence for his breakfast and supper. I quite admit that both board and lodging were indifferent; but then they were as good as he could have got elsewhere.

I believe this moderation is due in main part to the honesty of the people; but it is due also in no small measure to a certain want of energy which appears to characterise them. No adventurous trader has come to cater for the score of wants which the presence of an army is sure to create. One Hamburg Jew-pedlar, indeed, opened a store for cigars, which ought, one would have thought, to prove a good speculation; but nobody, as he informed me, ever bought a cigar worth selling; and this morning I find he has decamped for some place where enterprise is more appreciated.

We have three events here in the course of each day. In the morning, about ten o'clock, the steamer leaves for Korsoer, to catch the train for Copenhagen. Every day a batch of sick and wounded soldiers are sent off home. Those who are able to walk are helped down to the wharf, their friends carrying their knapsacks as they hobble up the ship's side; those who can bear jolting over the stones are brought down in the ambulance vans; and those who can neither walk nor ride are carried to the vessel on stretchers, and laid upon the deck wrapped up in rugs and blankets. God help them on their cold, weary voyage! Then, at four, one of the worst military bands I have ever heard plays for an hour in the main street to some hundred soldiers and a score of boys and servant girls. And then, after dark, the steamer arrives from Copenhagen, and the town is filled with soldiers wandering helplessly about in search of unknown quarters. Unless there is a rumour of an attack, these are all the diversions a day at Sonderborg has to offer. By nine the streets are empty, and by ten everybody is abed and asleep.

February 29.

Three weeks have elapsed since the Danes evacuated the Dannewerke, and a full fortnight has passed since the Austro-Prussian army marched as conquerors through Flensburg. When I left that town the attack on Dybbol was believed to be imminent. I heard myself the Austrian commander-in-chief use words in addressing his troops which had no signification unless they pointed to an immediate attack on the Danish defences; and I know that officers of high rank in both armies believed that this day fortnight was the time fixed for the assault. Nothing whatever has been done, and the position of the Danes is decidedly stronger than it could have been at the period alluded to. With the exception of one or two insignificant skirmishes, the Danes have been left utterly unmolested; and far from the Germans being nearer to the attainment of their avowed end—the expulsion of the Danes from the territory of Schleswig—they are apparently further from it than at any previous period of the campaign.

Nobody is more astonished at this inaction on the part of their enemies than the Danes themselves. The explanations offered of it in the camp are manifold. Amongst persons likely to be well informed, the delay is attributed to the interference of diplomacy, and there is an uneasy suspicion that some compromise may be on foot by which the solution of the Dano–German question may be removed from the arbitrament of war.

Any prospect, however, of such an occurrence is so bitterly unwelcome to popular feeling that it is rather hinted at than foretold. With the older officers of the army the cause of this unaccountable delay is sought for in the difficulty the Germans have experienced in bringing up their artillery, owing to the state of the roads and the inclemency of the weather. Now there is no doubt that the climate is detestable, and the roads infamous. Still these obstacles are not insurmountable.

The Austro-German Army marched to Flensburg in infinitely worse weather than the present; and as to the roads, they are not to be compared in badness with those through which I saw the Sardinians drag their siege train to Gaeta, or those over which I have ridden to the encampments of the Federal army in Virginia. The siege train which passed through the streets of Flensburg two weeks ago was considered sufficient for an attack on the Dannewerke—a work which assuredly was far better supplied with artillery than the fortifications of Dybbol.

Even if heavier guns had been needed, the Germans can bring them by railroad as far as Flensburg with perfect ease, and the distance from that town to the Danish outposts can be barely fourteen miles. Moreover, though the information obtained by the Danish generals appears to me strangely inadequate, considering the importance of obtaining it, yet, such intelligence as is received does not show any vigorous preparation for the assault on the part of the invading army.

Amongst the younger officers and the common soldiers, the explanation given is a much more simple one. They assert, and I have no doubt believe, that the Germans—and especially the Prussians—are afraid to attack them on anything like equal terms, and that it is want of courage which keeps the Germans hanging back. For my own part, I incline to the first of the three hypotheses I have stated and can give no credence to the last, as no candid person can suspect either Austrian or Prussian troops of lacking personal courage. But the prevalence of this belief is likely to produce no small influence on the political as well as military upshot of the war.

With the delay in the attack the Danes have acquired fresh confidence. They are convinced that they can hold the Dybbol heights against the overwhelming numbers of the enemy, and nothing but the test of experience is likely to shake their conviction. Whenever there is a rumour of a battle, the troops raise the song that "we are going to beat the Prussians," and even educated men have seriously told me that they would back one Danish soldier against three Germans, and would gladly leave the issue of the war to be decided by one battle in which the odds against the Danes should not be more than two to one. The universal feeling amongst the army is that no terms of peace can be entertained till their country has had an opportunity of showing that her soldiers are not cowards, and until the stain inflicted on the national honour by the evacuation of the Dannewerke has been washed out in blood.

The other night, two regiments stationed here received orders to march for the outposts at dawn, and the belief was that they would be called upon to attack the enemy. An officer in command assured me that the men could not sleep all night for excitement, and passed their whole time singing patriotic songs in anticipation of the coming battle. According to the assertion of my Holstein informants, the ardour of the Danes is of a spasmodic character, and dies away as suddenly as it springs up. I have not been long enough in the country to convince myself how far this is true; but, judging from outward appearances, I should be inclined to doubt its truth.

There is little trace of excitability about the Danes I meet with. On the contrary, they seem to be impassive and sober on ordinary subjects to a strange degree; but, if once you touch upon the question of the war, you find in every quarter a determination to hold out to the very last. Up to this time, it should be remembered, the Danish Army has met with no crushing defeat On the contrary, in the few skirmishes which have taken place, the Danes—bearing in mind the inequality of numbers—have more than held their own. And in an attack on Dybbol they will fight at an absolute advantage.

At any rate, the delay of the last fortnight has raised the spirits of the nation. Every day that passes is thought to increase the chance of some foreign complication, which can scarcely fail to turn to the advantage of Denmark. Moreover, the position of affairs can hardly be more desperate now than it was in 1849; and yet, owing to the division of her enemies, the Danish kingdom came out of her dangers with little loss. In the words of a German writer:

One million and a half of Danes, strong in union, conquered forty millions of Germans, weak by disunion.

It is hoped that the same causes will produce the same effect, and the calculation is not unreasonable. It is idle for me to speculate here on the motives which have induced the Allied Powers to prosecute the war with so little vigour. This much, however, I can confidently assure you, that their delay has been most prejudicial to the prospects of any compromise which involves the surrender of Alsen. The idea of a purely dynastic union between the Duchies and Denmark cannot be entertained while Danish forces hold a position from which—in the absence of a German army of occupation—they could invade and reconquer Schleswig at any moment; yet nothing but absolute defeat will reconcile the Danes to the abandonment of Dybbol and Alsen. The saying, "*What thou doest do quickly,*" applies with force to all acts of violence and aggression, and the Germans have not done wisely in neglecting its teaching.

Since Monday last not a shot has been fired in earnest, and the respite has restored the spirits of the Danish Army. Moreover, a sort of petty retaliation is exercised by the Germans in Schleswig, which can hardly fail to exasperate a high-spirited nation. The statue of the Lion at Flensburg, raised to commemorate the battle of Idsted, has been taken down by order of the Prussian Commissioner; the Schleswig papers are ordered to give all intelligence from Copenhagen under the heading of "foreign" intelligence; and the Battle of Oversee, where the Austrians overtook the Danish rearguard, is called in the German papers the victory of Idsted, though this place lies twelve miles away from the scene of action; the obvious motive of this erroneous designation being to remove the disgrace which the real victory of Idsted, in 1850, inflicted on the German troops.

Nothing, too, could create a greater impression of weakness than the "*Bombastes Furioso*" address issued by Prince Charles of Prussia to his troops after the unsuccessful assault on Missunde. When to all this energy in words there is added an inexplicable want of vigour in action, it is not surprising that the Danes should begin to underrate the powers of their adversaries.

This morning intelligence was received from Copenhagen that General Gerlach has been appointed commander-in-chief of the Danish Army. The officer in question is a Holsteiner by birth, and is said to speak Danish with a very marked German accent. Not the slightest suspicion rests, however, on his loyalty towards the cause of Denmark. He took an active part in the former Schleswig-Holstein war, and was in command the other day at Missunde, where the Danes consider that he acquitted himself with great ability. His appointment, however, I believe, is due to negative rather than positive merits.

He happened, unlike General Luttichau, not to be present at the council of war which decided on the evacuation of the Dannewerke. He is free, therefore, from the responsibility of that most unpopular step, while the fact of his not having voted against it renders his appointment less of a slur on General de Meza than the nomination of an officer such as General Luttichau, who opposed the opinion of the late commander-in-chief. General Gerlach till yesterday commanded the first division of the army stationed at Sonderborg.

CHAPTER 5

Camp Life

Sonderborg, March 1.

Last night, on returning home from my usual evening's excursion in search of news, I was informed that a letter had arrived from England. Letters are so rare in this most inaccessible of places that the intelligence was most welcome. Judge of my disappointment when I discovered it was a communication from Elizabeth Cottle. That mysterious lady has been sowing her missives broadcast over the Danish camp. My friends—whose knowledge of English is limited—were lost in astonishment over the announcement that "*the wicked Duke Ernest of Saxe Gotha shall go into everlasting fire,*" and that the Lord (Clanricarde) shall give help unto the needy (Danes). I myself was still more startled by the news that the "beloved John" (Scott), "after eating his Christmas (Cottle) Turkey," had testified to the truth of every word written in Mrs. Cottle's *Book of Life.*

I remembered with regret that when I was in Rome, some years ago, I received an autograph missive from the same quarter, directing me to seek an interview with his Holiness the Pope, and present him with an extract enclosed from the *Book of Life*, which could not fail to convert him from the error of his ways, and induce him to avow himself a convert to Protestantism. If I had but obeyed the injunction, I, too, might have eaten my Christmas Cottle Turkey in company with "John the Beloved," instead of ruining my digestion—as I am doing now—on the liquorice soup and fat pork which constitute the usual diet at the hotel where I dine daily.

However, it is no good fretting over the opportunities one has thrown away in life; so I was obliged to console myself with the reflection that the opinion of Mrs. Cottle was in favour of the Danes, and could, therefore, be shown confidently to my friends, who watch with an almost painful eagerness for any symptom of English sympathy. There is no good in concealing the fact that, as a nation, England is not popular at this moment in Denmark. Personally there seems to be the kindest feeling towards individual Englishmen. Indeed, there is so much in common in character and tastes and habits between us and the Danes that this could hardly fail to be the case. The misfortune is that people here believe, whether rightly or wrongly, that hopes have been held out to them of English support which have not been realised.

Men fighting, as they deem, for national honour and existence cannot be expected to be altogether reasonable; and, if you point out to them that they have not been entirely in the right in their conduct towards the Duchies, they set you down at once for "*Deutsch-Gesinnt*," and conclude that you have been talked over by German sympathisers. I have had serious complaints made to me that I speak, sometimes, of "Schleswig-Holstein." This heading, I am told, assumes the whole question: there is no such state in existence as Schleswig-Holstein; and I ought to describe the Duchies invariably as Schleswig *and* Holstein.

If, again, I try to explain that England has a score of Imperial interests she must consider before she espouses the cause of Denmark—even if it were desirable for her to do so at all—it seems incredible to my hearers that any consideration can be more important to Great Britain than the maintenance of the integrity of the Danish kingdom. At the same time, I own that the Danes have some show of reason in feeling more irritation at the neutrality observed by England than at that observed by other Powers who apparently are more closely connected with the matter than ourselves.

As far as I can learn, the aid of Sweden alone is not much desired in Denmark. It is believed that the utmost Sweden could do would be to send some 20,000 troops to the assistance of her sister kingdom—an assistance which, however gratifying, would not materially affect the relative strength of the combatants, while the interference of a foreign Power would deprive Denmark of the moral advantages conferred upon her by the fact that she is fighting single-handed in her own quarrel. The aid of Russia is felt to be so dangerous that it is feared rather than wished for; and France, it is thought, can take no active step without the concurrence of England. The Danes fancy that we have only to make a show of action in order to paralyse the power of their enemies.

They commit, I fancy, the mistake—which many persons committed at home—of underrating the determination of the Germans in this Schleswig-Holstein matter. They believe that the mere presence of an English fleet in the Baltic would have arrested the march of the Austro-Prussian armies; and, therefore, they are angry with us for not making a demonstration in their favour, which they imagine would have cost us nothing, while it would have proved of incalculable advantage to themselves.

As I am touching here on political questions, I would also say that I can see no indication of any popular wish for annexation with Sweden. Supposing the Duchies to be virtually separated from Denmark, the remaining Danish possessions would only become at last a dependency of the Scandinavian kingdom. The Swedish language differs sufficiently from the Danish to make the rule of Sweden that of a foreign power; and the memory of the long and bloody wars between the two countries has left behind it a legacy of mutual jealousy and distrust between Swedes and Danes, which tells heavily against the possibility of a cordial union. The whole constitution of the twin powers is different; Denmark is democratic; Sweden aristocratic, both in government and in popular feeling.

Moreover, the Danes have been an independent Power and a sovereign State for too many centuries, to reconcile themselves willingly to the idea of merging their national identity in that of Sweden. The union of Calmar, it should be remembered, consisted in the annexation of Sweden to Denmark. At the present day the process would have to be reversed by the annexation of Denmark to Sweden. If the worst should come to the worst, the Danes may possibly accept the idea of a Scandinavian kingdom in order to save themselves from extinction, but in their present frame of mind they will not do so until the hope of preserving their individual existence has to be abandoned as hopeless.

In truth, if I were a Dane, I should be loath to exchange my present condition for any problematic advantage. If people do not dislike a six months' winter of ice and snow, they could hardly find a pleasanter land than this of Denmark. Poverty, in our English sense of the word, seems to be unknown in the country districts. A beggar is a sight you never meet with; and the clothing even of the lowest classes is warm and comfortable. If you ride about, as I have done within the last two days, over the interior of the island, you can fancy yourself back in the most prosperous parts of England. When the hills are green, and the leaves are out, and the sky is blue, it must be pleasant wandering amongst these wooded lanes and through these cosy hamlets.

Unlike the mainland of Schleswig, the country must be densely populated. Small well-to-do cottages, with high thatched roofs and clean white-washed walls, are dotted all over the fields. It is true that the hedgerows have got no trees, as with us; but then on the brow of every hill you have large beech-woods, which now stand grey and gaunt and bare, but which in summer time must be pleasant spots to wander about at your will; and the glimpses of the sound which you catch from the brow of every hillside in the island must give the same charm to the scenery that the view of the sea does to our lanes in Devonshire.

Today I have had the pleasure of dining on board the Danish iron-clad the *Rolf Krake*, and can hardly speak in too high terms of the hospitality with which I was received as a stranger. From the captain to the cabin boy, everybody on board spoke English, and the mere fact that you were an Englishman seemed to be a sufficient passport to the goodwill of these Danish seamen.

Of the vessel itself my report cannot be altogether as satisfactory. During the engagement at Eggernsunde she suffered far more severely than the Danish papers admitted. The Prussian batteries fired with extreme accuracy, and even after ten days' refitting and repairs her hull bore marks of serious damage. The contrivance by which her cupolas are lowered struck me as being too elaborate, and it was proved in action that a well-aimed shot, which struck the cupola in the centre, twisted it so much that it was impossible to turn it afterwards. The grating, too, that covers the top of the cupolas is so wide, that the particles of the shells which struck it rained down into the hold; while the bolts which connect the plates of iron together gave way beneath the concussion of the blows inflicted upon them by the impact of the cannon balls.

The *Rolf Krake*, according to all accounts, steers badly, and is not a vessel that any sailor would like to trust himself in in a heavy sea. On the other hand, the noise occasioned by a ball striking her was not found to be painful by any of her crew; and the broad fact remains, that some 150 shot struck her in different parts without a single casualty occurring, and without any injury being inflicted which could not be repaired in a few days' time.

March 3.

One day here is very like another; but still the days have a strange character of their own, and those who, like myself, have lived at

Sonderborg while the assault of this island stronghold was daily and almost hourly expected, will not soon forget a curious phase in their existence. Let me try and describe some of its minor incidents while they are still fresh in my memory, passing, as it were, before my eyes. I myself—thanks to the hospitality of new-found friends—am quartered luxuriously.

In the first place, I have a bed—a possession in itself most difficult of attainment. In the second place, I have a bed to myself—a comfort which is to be hoped for rather than expected; and, lastly, I have not only a bed but a room of my own—a luxury for which I am an object of general envy. One of my friends has a doubtful tenure of half a loft, another sleeps at night on board any steamer which happens to be at anchor in the port, and a third is supposed to sleep somewhere, but where he has never consented to reveal.

The one objection to my domicile is, that I am woke up at a preternaturally early hour. My room is a passage into another, occupied by a Danish engineer officer, employed upon the works of Dybbol. As soon as it is daylight some messenger is sure to come in from the lines, and I am startled out of my sleep by the trampling of heavy boots and the jangling of swords and spurs. From my windows I can look across the Wemming Bund to the heights of Dybbol; and so, when I have assured myself that there is no smoke to be seen, and no cannon to be heard, I get to bed again; and by the time I am just falling off to sleep, I find the hour for breakfast has arrived.

We are early on foot here, and our morning meal is of the simplest. Some half-dozen officers are quartered in the house (where, I am ashamed to inquire), and we all meet at breakfast and repeat the monotonous intelligence that there is nothing going on at the front, and no symptom of an attack from the enemy. Our meals are never very long. Indeed, to anyone accustomed to the tediousness of German repasts, it is a comfort to live with people who can get through dinner in half-an-hour; and after we have eaten an enormous quantity of bread and butter we separate about our several businesses. I should, however, say that we are always shaking hands.

I never met a people who performed this ceremony with such punctuality. We shake hands all round before every meal; we shake hands after every meal, saying invariably, "*Wel-bekomme*," or welcome to each other; and whenever we meet, at any period of the day, no matter how often, we shake hands again.

Then I wander up the High Street of Sonderborg in pursuit of intelligence. Somehow or other I always come across a dragoon regiment riding to the front, and have to shelter myself on the steps of some house to avoid being trodden under foot Here they come, two and two together, trampling down the steep, narrow, winding street Somehow—I say it with no disrespect—they remind me always of Don Quixote, when he rode forth on Rosinante with the barber's basin on his head.

Their great heavy helmets, surmounted with the brazen crest, are for all the world like the head-gear which Roman charioteers used to wear, if the pictures in Smith's *Dictionary of Antiquities* are to be believed. Their long blue serge cloaks hang down almost to their feet; their stirrups are all cased in wisps of straw, and their necks are wrapped up in woollen comforters of every variety of colour. The short muskets are hung by the right side of their heavy, swaddled-up saddles, with the muzzles pointed towards the ground, and the scabbards of their swords peep out at every kind of angle from beneath the folds of their cloaks. The horses are rough, dirt-stained, and shaggy, and the long, unkempt, bushy hair of the riders bristles out beneath their helmets. Slowly and gravely they tramp along, smoking solemnly, with the heavy, porcelain-bowl pipes hanging from between their teeth. Still, I should not like to be in their way if the order came to charge, and I should not be surprised if the Danes are right in believing that these heavy, stalwart dragoons could ride down the light, brilliant *Uhlan* cavalry of Austria if they once got the chance.

But, with the exception of my friends the dragoons, there is not much stirring in the forenoon in the streets of Sonderborg; the troops—whose chief occupation, like that of the King of France, appears to consist in marching up a hill and then marching down again—have gone to the heights of Dybbol in the early morning, and have not yet returned. So I make my way over the miserable pavement, hopping, sparrow-like, from stone to stone, wherever I can get a footing, to the great hotel of Sonderborg, where a large room, occupied by two brother writers, is a sort of headquarters of the press. Anything dirtier than this gathering room cannot well be conceived. It has not been swept for ages, and the floor is littered with a nondescript medley of empty bottles, torn-up newspapers, dirty shirts, slops and fragments of defunct repasts.

Of course, there is no news to be heard—there never is any news here at present—and the only thing to be done is to stroll about the works, and make vain endeavours to catch sight of some German outposts with the help of telescopes and field-glasses. If it were not so cold it would be pleasant enough wandering about the Danish camp, to anyone who has a taste for quaint, picturesque, living pictures, after the style of Teniers or Rembrandt. There are scenes enough to be imprinted on the memory. Here, a group of soldiers, with their arms stacked beside them, are labouring sturdily at raising earthworks.

These rough Danish peasants seem more at home, I fancy, with a spade in their hand than with a musket on their shoulders, and the work goes forward merrily enough. In a field hard by a relief party are sitting in the slosh and snow round a camp-fire, munching great hunches of coarse black bread, and smoking between every mouthful. Then, again, a suttler, seated on a truck drawn by dogs, is dispensing beer from squad barrels to a knot of thirsty labourers; and further on a company, quartered in a roadside cottage, are tinkering up a scarecrow intended to represent a German soldier.

Scenes of this nature are to be witnessed by the score. But of any real warlike movement there has of late been scarce an indication. Moreover, compared with other military spectacles I have witnessed, it is very still life indeed. The Danish soldiers are wonderfully quiet and sober—almost impassive in their demeanour. Except when they are marching to battle, they rarely sing; and I have never yet seen a quarrel or dispute amongst them. A stranger may walk or ride right through a crowd of soldiers without seeming to excite their attention, and their good-nature appears to know no bounds.

Then comes the great event of our day—dinner. At the hotel I have spoken of there is a *table d'hôte*, frequented by the officers stationed in the town. But even here there is singularly little conversation. The officers come in, bow to each other, and get through their meal without wasting much time on superfluous remarks. Moreover, the "menu" is not exactly calculated to promote a genial state of temperament.

We have, first of all, sweet soup of a gluey consistency, and savouring of treacle; and then we have fat pork, a slice of which contains about one inch of lean to three inches of greasy fat As soon as we have gorged ourselves sufficiently with this viand, which goes here under the name of "*speck*," the dinner is at an end: the cigars are lit, and the company breaks up. It must not be supposed that this repast is more satisfactory to the Danes than to strangers. On the contrary, they complain of it bitterly. But somehow or other it appears that the resources of our hotel can never rise beyond "*speck*" and treacle broth.

By the time dinner is over, and we have heard the band play in the street, it is growing dusk, and the steamboats have come in. There is one consolation this hour affords to us who are now entitled to consider ourselves old inhabitants of Sonderborg. We can watch the new arrivals wandering disconsolately about the town, and knocking ineffectually at door after door to try and find a lodging. Then the faint flickering gas-lamps are lit, few and far between; and the streets are again crowded with troops splashing their way home to quarters from the front, and we have at least the satisfaction of knowing that we have got through another day "*tant bien que mal.*"

March 4.

This morning, General Gerlach, on assuming the command-in-chief, has issued the following address to the army:—

Soldiers,—His Majesty the King has most graciously confided to me the command of the army in the field. Mighty foes are opposed to you; but I, who have lived amongst you for fifty years, know what you can do, know that you will follow your officers. In the war of 1848-50, every man under my command followed his colours and his duty. I, your old general, will engage my word for you that, like true and brave Danish men, you will show yourselves worthy of the confidence which the king and the nation repose in you. It shall be my task to provide for your welfare to the best of my ability. As a recompense, I demand your implicit trust. Fearless we will march against danger, with the aid of God, for our king and our country.

A quieter or more sober address could hardly be issued at such a crisis as the present. To do the Danes justice, all their war bulletins and orders of the day have been singularly simple and unboastful. The "tall talk" in which the Germans so much delight is obviously distasteful to the national instincts of Denmark. But still this manifesto of the new general-in-chief is thought to lie on the side of tameness. If there was any intention of attacking the enemy, or indeed if there was any expectation of an immediate assault, it seems incredible that bolder and more defiant language should not have been used. In truth, the impression—of which I have written to you frequently before—that no serious movement is intended for the moment on either side, gains ground rapidly.

Amongst the common soldiers and the younger officers there is a strong idea that General Gerlach is not a man to let the grass grow under his feet, and that his assumption of the command is sure to be followed by some decisive action. But amongst the superior officers there is, I think, very little hope of any immediate change in the position of affairs. The apprehension is that the war will be allowed to languish on till the energies, and resources, and spirit of the Danish people are exhausted by the immense efforts they are making daily; and that then some disastrous compromise will be extorted from the government, to which the people will reluctantly consent.

Any day may falsify these expectations, and the officers are too deeply interested in the issue of the question to be fair critics of its prospects. I quote their opinions, therefore, rather to show the temper of the army than for their intrinsic value. Yesterday I spent the day in company with a number of Danish officers at one of their outposts. Of their courteousness and kindness I cannot say more than that it was such as I have ever found it. But, I own, what struck me most forcibly was their bitter discontent with the conduct of affairs, and their fierce exasperation against the Germans.

There is a story circulated here which might easily account for their irritation. At Flensburg there was a bronze lion erected in the burying-ground to the memory of the Danish soldiers who fell in the Schleswig-Holstein war of 1848-50. It was a work of considerable artistic merit, designed by Herr Bissen, a Schleswig sculptor of reputation, and the ablest of Thorwaldsen's living, (1864), pupils. According to the popular report, the Prussian soldiers have cut off the head and tail of this lion, and sent the mutilated trunk to be exhibited for money as a trophy at Hamburg. In all probability the story is exaggerated; if it is true, it is a singular instance of brutal barbarism; but, whether true or false, it is believed here, and has created intense indignation.

I had a proposal made that a new lion should be prepared, to be carried in triumph through the streets of Flensburg by the first Danish troops that re-enter the town. The news, too, that the South-Schleswigers have, more or less, fraternised with the Germans, or, at any rate, showed no animosity towards their invaders, has not tended to conciliate the Danes. The reluctance to use the German language seems to me increasing: one officer assured me with an oath that, except to an Englishman, he would never speak a word of German again while he lived. Another gravely asserted that nothing good had ever come out of Germany; and, even amongst sober men, the openly avowed assertion is, that everything which savours of Germanism must be rooted out of Danish ground. Now, these sentiments are natural enough; and, while you are talking with Danes, it is difficult not to sympathise with their authors.

But yet the painful consideration must force itself on any candid mind, how, if the Duchies should be restored, are men with such feelings, however just, to hold and govern permanently a German population? As an old man who had passed his life in Alsen said to me the other day:

> The sad thing is, that neither success in war nor diplomatic arrangements can permanently help us. Every year I have lived, I have seen the Germans pushing further and further northwards, and no effort can keep them back.

And of the truth of this saying I am more and more convinced, from what I have seen of both sides in the contest. The present difficulty may be arranged; but the real cause of quarrel is not the November Constitution, nor the death of King Frederick VII., nor the German Confederation, nor the Augustenburg dynasty, but the gradual invasion of the Jutland peninsula by German settlers. All other causes of dispute might be removed; but, as long as this remains, the old quarrel between the Scandinavian and Teutonic nationalities will keep on festering.

Meanwhile there has been somewhat more activity on the part of the Danes within the last two days. Yesterday a force was sent out to occupy the wood of Ragebol, a little hamlet half way between the villages of Dybbol and Sattrup. The wood was occupied without opposition, and the Danes cleared away as much of it as they could, and then withdrew their forces. If this war lasts a week or two longer, there will not be a hedge left standing anywhere within a couple of miles of the Dybbol batteries.

I rode today along the outposts, which stretch all round the base of the hill. The day was the mildest we have yet had here, and there was about it a certain vague flavour of the coming spring. Not a leaf, indeed, or a bud could be seen; but the larks were singing, and the ground was soft, and almost clear of snow, except upon the hillside or underneath the tall hedgerows. The troops at the outposts seemed in better spirits than I have seen them of late, and the lookout for the enemy was kept up with unusual vigilance. The brow of every piece of rising ground was dotted over with sentries; the lanes were blocked up every hundred yards or so with rough barricades made up of broken carts and logs and bushes. The villages were all deserted; the doors stood open; the paper was torn from off the walls; the floors were littered over with straw; the household furniture lay scattered about the gardens; a few peasants stood loitering wistfully about their empty homes; and an air of desolation reigned over the whole country.

March 5.

Today, if the Germans had had any regard for dramatic propriety, they would have advanced to the attack of Dybbol. The one ostensible pretext that Austria and Prussia have ever condescended to put forward in defence of their invasion of Denmark was, that the extension of the Rigsraad to Schleswig constituted a violation of the rights of Schleswig-Holstein. In order to save the sister Duchy of Holstein from the humiliation of sending deputies to a Parliament assembled at Copenhagen, the armies of the allied Powers have advanced into Jutland. So imperative was the urgency in their opinion, that they refused to allow time for the withdrawal of the Constitution, and declared their intention of abrogating this obnoxious enactment by fire and sword.

Yet today this monstrous iniquity, to prevent the occurrence of which Europe has been plunged into war, was allowed to be perpetrated quietly almost within sight and hearing of the German armies! The island of Alsen has not yet been wrested from the clutches of Denmark; and, though the whole place is beleaguered, the elections to the Rigsraad have been permitted to take place without the slightest attempt on the part of the saviours of Schleswig to disturb their course. Not a cannon was fired to protest against the enormity; not a shell was thrown into the town as a harbinger of the deliverance which the Germans are about to bestow on enslaved and persecuted Schleswig.

Everything—I am ashamed to say, for the honour of the Fatherland—went off as tranquilly as possible. No excitement, indeed, of any kind was visible; not a placard of any kind was to be seen about the town; and it was only through private information a stranger could have guessed that the question which has agitated all Europe was about to be brought today to a practical issue. The island of Alsen is divided into two electoral districts, of which Sonderborg forms the first, and Augustenburg, with the other villages, the second.

For the elections to the "*Folk-ting,*" or Lower House, every man can vote who is upwards of thirty, and has not been convicted of any offence against the laws. For electors to the Upper House, a property qualification is requisite of 1200 *rigdalers* income, or about 140*l.. per annum.* Today the elections for the Lower House were held; those for the Upper House do not take place till the 29th of March. In the district of Sonderborg there are about five hundred men over thirty on the list of electors; but a great number are away from home, in consequence of the war. Two candidates offered themselves to the constituency—the *burgomaster*, Herr Finsen, and a lawyer. The proceedings were of the most orderly and unexciting character.

The election was held in a long, bare, whitewashed room in the town hall. Two deal tables and a low platform constituted the whole furniture of the room. About eleven the electors began to assemble, and by twelve we had—when we were at the fullest—some hundred people collected. They formed an assemblage worth studying. The majority were peasants or fishermen—rough, sturdy-looking customers, with great brawny arms and shoulders; and ragged hairy faces.

If you were to go into any one of the smaller seaports of our eastern coast, and pick up a hundred men at hazard loitering along the jetties or hanging about the taverns, you would compose an audience very like that which I beheld today. The only difference would be that our countrymen, I think, would look fresher and less weather-beaten than these Danes, and also that our men would not wear the small gold earrings which here are almost universal.

The proceedings began by the town clerk reading out the writ, and then the candidates were proposed in two short speeches: one by a farmer, the other by a butcher of the town. As far as looks went, there could be no doubt as to the eligibility of the rival candidates. The *burgomaster* was a handsome portly man, with a bright eye and an open face, and a frank, pleasant smile. With the cross of the Dannebrog sparkling on his great broad chest, and wearing the dark-blue frock-coat faced with gilt buttons which constitutes the uniform of Danish officials, he looked like the *beau-idéal* of a gallant English sea captain. His rival was tall, gaunt, and thin, and whatever pretensions he may have had at any time to good looks were marred by the fact that he had lost the use of one of his eyes.

Moreover, not even the Apollo Belvidere would appear to advantage if attired at midday in a suit of seedy black, his neck, encased in a huge soiled white neckcloth, and his hands imprisoned in kid gloves which once were white. It was evident that on the present occasion—though there were no women in the crowds—the popular verdict was in favour of the best-looking of the two candidates.

They both made speeches, which I confess my knowledge of Danish was not sufficient to enable me to follow. The *burgomaster's* address was short, and unaffected in manner. Whatever his oratorical merits may have been, the advocate had a fatal fluency of language, and succeeded, at any rate, in wearying his audience; for stragglers began to drop out of the room as he poured forth period after period, in which every other word appeared to be "Fatherland "or "men of Denmark."

At last, however, he came to an end; then the town clerk called for a show of hands, which was overwhelmingly in favour of the *burgomaster*. His antagonist was allowed a quarter of an hour to demand a poll; but the result was so certain that he gave way, and Heir Finsen was declared unanimously elected. Loud, hearty, English-sounding hurrahs followed the announcement; then another cheer was given for "*Kongen og Faedreland*"—a cheer so powerful that it shook the walls of the old "*Raadshuus*," and then the meeting broke up.

I have seen a good many elections in foreign countries, but I can truly say that this was the only one I ever saw out of England where the electors appeared to take any interest in what they were doing, or to care the least about the result But the real interest of the event to me lies in the peculiar aspect to which I have before alluded. This morning, as usual, there was a skirmish at the outposts when the soldiers changed guard at daybreak. One Dane was killed, and a Prussian soldier was seen to fall and not to rise again.

Why, I could not help asking myself as I gazed upon the election, had these two poor peasants died in the full prime of life? Why, in all likelihood, are thousands more to fall—before many days are passed—both in front and behind the works of Dybbol? Simply and solely, in order that two deputies from this out-of-the way little island should not be allowed to represent Alsen in the Copenhagen Chambers; simply in order that the delicate honour of Prussia may be saved from any stain, by the sacrifice of God knows how many sons and husbands and fathers. The Danes at Alsen are fighting for their own country; the Germans are bent on slaughter in order to annul the election of Herr Burgomaster Finsen. Surely a wickeder war, or one for a more paltry object, was never waged.

March 6.

Yesterday it was believed—or, at any rate, asserted—at headquarters, that today was fixed for the attack on Dybbol. I had heard the statement too often to place much confidence in its truth; and, though an acquaintance of mine who had only just arrived was extremely anxious to let him call me at four, in order that we might be in time to see the opening of the battle, I steadily refused to accede to any proposal of the kind, or to leave my bed on any pretence whatever, until I was woke up by the sound of the cannon.

My scepticism was justified. The day has passed over without a symptom of an assault, and the only difference between today and any other of its fifteen predecessors is that it has rained, instead of snowed. The sole apparent justification of the rumour lay in the fact that two regiments of Austrians are reported to have been moved from Aabenras to the village of Sand Bierg, a little hamlet on the banks of the Sund, and about two miles north of Dybbol.

Why the conclusion that an attack was imminent should have been drawn from so small as indication, may appear strange to the reader. Under our present circumstances, however, we exist upon rumours; and, moreover, the above explanation of this reported Austrian movement was in accordance with a foregone conclusion, which is now generally adopted by the Danish army. The popular belief is that the Prussians are afraid to attack the works of Dybbol, and that the delay in the assault is simply due to the fact that the Prussian troops cannot be induced to advance under fire. I am now told constantly that at Missunde, the attack had to be abandoned because the Prussians could not be brought to charge after they had seen their comrades fall around them beneath the fire of the Danish batteries; and that in the skirmish of the 22nd the officers could be seen striking their men with their swords, in a vain endeavour to urge them forwards.

Now, without imputing want of courage to the Prussian troops, it is possible these stories may be true. There is scarcely a man in the whole of General von Wrangel's army, with the exception of the commander-in-chief himself, who has ever seen a shot fired in earnest, or heard the ghastly whizzing of a rifle-ball as it comes flying over your head. The bravest troops in the world need the baptism. of fire; and that sacrament has never been seriously imparted to the Prussian Army since the campaign of the Hundred Days. On the other hand, I must own that such reports of lack of courage on the part of the detested Prussians have gained marvellously in consistency within the last few days. When I first heard them, they were given as mere hearsay reports; now they are stated as acknowledged facts. The Prussians are infinitely more unpopular with the Danes than their allies; and I believe firmly that a battle which ended in the capture of Dybbol by the Austrians, but which was accompanied by a signal repulse of the Prussians, would be welcomed almost as a triumph throughout Denmark.

The wish in the present instance is, I suspect, further to the thought.

The Prussians are supposed to have found themselves unequal to an assault on Dybbol; Austrian troops must therefore be summoned to lead on the Northern Germans against the Danes; and, by this chain of argument, the conclusion was arrived at that the rumoured presence of a couple of Austrian regiments within the Prussian lines was a certain signal that the assault was about to commence.

As far as the army is concerned, I can see no indication whatever of its ardour being diminished by the prospect of an impending engagement. Both men and officers are eager for a combat, in which they are confident they should win the day, or, at any rate, inflict such damage on the enemy as would avenge the wrongs suffered by their country. The townsfolk of Sonderborg are naturally less anxious for a battle. However well conducted an army may be—and the Danish troops are wonderfully well-behaved—it must always be a terrible nuisance to any town where it is quartered The prolonged occupation is beginning to wear out the patience of the less enthusiastic inhabitants.

Some of the wealthiest tradespeople have as many as three or four hundred soldiers collected upon their premises, and the remuneration given by the government—about a penny a day, I believe, per private—is utterly inadequate to the expense and trouble entailed.

Svenborg, March 8.

Where is Svenborg? is a question which, even in these days of competitive examinations, would be asked in vain, I suspect, in most schools of England. Yet in every part of the world—in the Pacific, the Mediterranean, and the China seas—there are vessels sailing under the Danish flag which hail from Svenborg, and whose owners dwell in the streets of this little seaport town. If you look at the map of Denmark, you will see that the island of Fünen lies between the Great and the Little Belts, and that between the southern extremity of Fünen and the island of Taasinge there runs a narrow channel, called the Thorsenge, or Straits of Thor. On the northern banks, then, of this channel lies the town of Svenborg.

The cause of my writing from the town of Sven—who, if I am not mistaken, was the son of Thor, who was the son of Odin—was after this fashion: I had observed that our periodical rumours of an approaching assault on Dybbol occur at regular intervals, in obedience to some unknown law of nature. Whenever a day has been positively fixed for the long-deferred attack, and has passed over without fulfilling its promise, we have a period of three days' rest, during which all idea of any assault at all seems to be abandoned. Sunday last was to have witnessed the commencement of the bombardment.

As the event did not come off, I was confident that for a couple of days at least we should be left undisturbed by false rumours, and I felt at liberty to desert my post of observation for some thirty hours. It so happened that there was at Sonderborg an English friend of mine, who is making his annual business tour through the towns of Denmark He promised me that if I would accompany him to Svenborg I should see an old-fashioned Danish town, and, through his introduction, something also of the household life of the inhabitants. The offer was too tempting to be refused, and so, at the risk of the Germans being inconsiderate enough to attack the heights the moment that my back was turned, I started this morning for Fünen.

Fighting has ceased so completely of late, that the boats from Sonderborg are no longer filled with the return freights of sick and wounded soldiers, with which they were crowded during the first weeks that followed the retreat from Schleswig. We had but few passengers on board. What soldiers there were were chiefly Schleswigers who had received their discharge. Some days ago, at the outposts, a score of Schleswig soldiers deserted in a body, and ran over to the lines of the enemy.

This circumstance is only one of many indications which have created a belief that the German-speaking Schleswig troops are not much to be relied upon; and, in consequence, with the usual good-nature of the Danes, a discharge from service has been granted without much difficulty to many Schleswigers serving in the Danish Army. With the exception of these soldiers, the company was chiefly composed of landowners from the neighbouring islands, who had come over to see the army. They complained bitterly of the difficulty of getting labour for their fields.

A great many of the island peasants are half mariners and half landsmen; and, in consequence of the merchant seamen having been taken from their ships to man the Danish Navy, the peasants have been tempted by high wages to go to sea. Thus, in addition to the regular drain of the conscription, the supply of labour is diminished by the demands of the merchant service. Had it been a bright summer day, instead of a cheerless wintry one, our sail would have been beautiful enough. We kept ever winding in and out amongst the thousand islands which stud this Baltic archipelago. Bare and bleak as they looked now, they must wear a very different aspect when the fields into which they are mapped out are green, and the great birch woods, which grow down their banks to the edge of the sea, are covered with leaves.

Near Svenborg the channel winds and narrows till all glimpses of the open sea are lost, and the great ships which come sailing past have hard work to tack up and down the landlocked passage. Nestling in the centre of the Thorsenge is the port of Svenborg. On either side of it stretch the tideless waters of the strait which leads from the "Store" to the "Lille Belt;" behind it rises the low sloping forest-crowned upland, and in front is the shoal-like wooded shore of Taasinge. But, beautiful as the position is, there is nothing in the look of the town, seen from the water, to add to its picturesqueness. A confused mass of low red-tile roofs, the high whitewashed tower of the parish church, and a few lofty warehouses—these are all the features that catch your eye as you sail up towards the port.

When you enter within the town, there is not much to please a painter's eye. The streets are narrow, winding, and irregular, but there is little beauty even about their want of symmetry. With the exception of a few new *stucco*-covered dwellings of modern dimensions, the houses are very small, and very low. Even in the main streets there are many houses not more than one story high; most of them are plastered over with a sort of gritty compost, such as you see used in English village cottages, painted pink or slate colour; windows are very plentiful, and the panes very small; each house has stone steps before its door; gable-ends and high-peaked roofs are common; foot-walks there are next to none, and the pavements are constructed of round sharp stones, dreadful to walk upon, and worse to ride over.

The shops are about of the same stamp as you would find in a small English market town; taverns are not plentiful, and any place of public amusement appears to be unknown. The one charm about the place, to my mind, consists in the exceeding cleanness and tightness of the dwellings. Not a brick is out of its place, not a tile is loose upon the roofs, not a pane of glass is stuffed up with paper, even in the poorest houses. In the whole of Svenborg I have not seen a dwelling where a rich man in England would be likely to live, or where, as far as warmth, and shelter, and outward cleanness are concerned, any reasonable man would complain of being forced to live.

The same absence of marked contrast between wealth and poverty is visible in the look of the townsfolk. Everybody is decently dressed—nobody handsomely. Every woman, belonging in any way to the well-to-do classes, is in mourning—as is the case over all Denmark—for the late king; common women wear white caps, and warm woollen dresses of sombre colours. Crinoline has hardly made its way here, and hats are but seldom seen. Men and boys wear cloth or fur caps, and long brown coats, reaching down to their heels. Wooden shoes are very common, and everybody has a superabundance of woollen comforters and worsted mittens.

Of private carriages I have not met one about the streets; but then I have also not seen a single beggar. I have spent most of my time here in going round with my friend to visit the different merchants and shippers with whom he has business connections. Everybody is friendly, everybody is hospitable, and everybody takes it unkindly if you and your friend, and your friend's friend, will not smoke and drink at his expense, and shake hands a score of times, with or without the slightest provocation. To those accustomed to English merchant life it seems incredible that these homely, shabby-looking traders, with the air and dress of elderly clerks not over well-to-do, can be men of capital, or that business of any large amount can be transacted in these poky little dens of offices. You go into a small room, the whole furniture of which consists of a deal desk, a safe, and a couple of rickety chairs, and are told to your surprise that all the vessels whose pictures you see hanging upon the walls belong to the firm, and are sailing in the Indian Ocean, plying between China and Amsterdam, or Liverpool and Rio.

Altogether, I felt as if I had got transported back to the days of the old-fashioned English traders whom you read about in Defoe's works. The offices of these Svenborg merchants form part of their dwelling-houses. The sons are the fathers' clerks, and everything is done by the principals themselves, from copying letters to accepting bills. Business appears never to be at an end. From daylight till late in the evening the traders are hanging about their offices, and, though the streets are empty by nine, the shops are kept open till near eleven.

It was my fortune to see the interior of a Svenborg household, belonging to one of the wealthiest merchants in the city. We were invited to take supper there at seven; but, on our arrival. we found our host still at his desk, and it was nearly eight before he could get away from the throng of sea-captains who kept calling in to ask him one question after the other.

At last the office was empty, and he led us up a narrow carpetless wooden staircase to the upper part of his house, where the family resided. Everything was wonderfully neat and wonderfully simple. The supper-table was covered with all the varieties of sandwiches, hard eggs, and anchovies, in which the Danes delight, and we had the never-failing *schnaps* and beer and tea, the three liquids which are always apparently drunk in succession at a Danish supper.

The lady of the house acted not only as hostess, but as attendant, and no servant was visible; and then, when in obedience to the kindest pressure we had eaten much more than nature could possibly approve of, and much less than our hosts desired, we went into the drawing-room, where we, as guests, were placed upon the sofa, while the mistress of the establishment sat in the corner of the room knitting stockings. There was a piano of very excellent quality, but this was about the only article of luxury in the house. On the walls were the portraits of Napoleon I. and Frederick VII., which you see in every Danish household, and over the doorway was a picture of a favourite ship belonging to our host.

The sons of the family talked English, and every member of it was a person of education. But of display, or luxury or wealth, there was no trace to be witnessed. It was only from the conversation about business matters and relations, on which our talk chiefly ran, that I could have supposed our entertainers were men of fortune. We smoked cigars and drank punch, and listened to music, and then smoked again, till at last we took our departure in trepidation at the proposal of more punch.

And from there—to finish the night—I was taken to the Svenborg Club. Its resemblance to a London club-house was, I own, closer in name than in character. It consisted of two rooms at the back of an ion, a card room and a conversation-room. The former part of the establishment seemed to be in little request, and the members then present sat solemnly round a green baize table, smoking and drinking beer out of large glass mugs.

However, I have passed duller and certainly less profitable evenings in many more brilliant clubs. There was not one of the Svenborg merchants to whom I was here introduced who had not travelled and seen a great deal of the world. Indeed, there was one of them who, to my astonishment, knew so much more about the mechanism of Hoe's printing machines than I did myself, that I was reduced to indorsing every one of his statements about the London press without venturing to question them. Altogether, I passed a very pleasant evening; and the only fault I can possibly find with the institution, of which I was elected an honorary member, is that they put too much sugar into their punch.

The Danes are beginning, literally as well as metaphorically, to get their house in order. At last, the barracks are finished, and occupied by the troops. The sight presented by this camp is a curious one. The hill of Dybbol does not rise straight from the Sund, but consists of a series of layers, rising, terrace-like, one above the other. On the broadest of these slopes are placed the temporary barracks of the army. They have been a long time building, for labour is not plentiful here; and, besides, the Danes do not possess the Yankee talent for running up something or other to suit the purpose of an hour.

They have this quality in common with ourselves, that whatever they make or build is substantial in character—a quality whose value I should be loath to depreciate, but which may at times be carried too far. This, I think, has been the case in the present instance. Whenever—if ever—the bombardment begins, the first shell which strikes these wooden sheds will probably set them all in a blaze; and the moment the war is over there is no conceivable purpose to which they can be turned. Sheds knocked up in a couple of days would have lasted out the time during which they are likely to be wanted; and any sort of shelter would, for the last few weeks, have been of great service to the Danish army.

Hitherto the troops have had to march daily backwards and forwards between the town of Sonderborg and the works; and, though the distance is short, the unnecessary fatigue to which they have been thus exposed in this inclement weather has been very great. Now that the Dybbol barracks have been completed, their labour will be much lessened. Each regiment passes six days in country quarters towards the back of the island, and the next six at the front. Of this latter period, two days are spent in the town of Sonderborg, two in the camp at Dybbol, and two at the outposts.

This Dybbol camp consists of a dozen rows of wooden sheds of considerable lengthy looking like elongated hencoops. They are built of stout deal planks fitted together tightly and neatly, and are supported by a framework of strong poles. Even the storms of wind and rain and snow with which we are afflicted in this dreary climate would beat in vain against such substantial dwellings. When you enter one of the common soldiers' huts in the daytime, you fancy you have got by mistake into an empty stable.

At either end of the hencoop-shaped shed there is an entrance tall enough for a man of average height to pass under without stooping;

and along either side there runs a broad wooden trough filled with hay. The soldiers sleep in the hay side by side in pairs, and about sixty men are accommodated in this way in every shed. There is no fire, but it is said that the breath of so large a number of men warms the shed—a fact which seems probable enough, as, though the winds are bitterly chilly, the actual temperature of late has been rarely below freezing. The sheds are kept wonderfully clean, and the flooring is very dry, owing probably to the deep trenches that have been cut round each of them.

The officers' quarters are made after the same manner as the common soldiers' except that the planks are covered over with thatch, and that the roof, instead of being fixed in the ground, is placed upon low walls of clay, some couple of feet in height; the huts are also famished with brick-built chimneys. If it were summer weather, the troops could hardly desire better quarters. In the rare glimpses of sunlight the long clean rows of sheds look bright and cosy, and the whole camp bears a close resemblance to a new settlement in the Western prairies.

Unfortunately, our intervals of sunlight are few and far between; and, as a rule, the camp is buried in a Slough of Despond. The heavy day loam of this Danish soil has a tenacity of wet not given to ordinary clay, and no attempt has been made to drain the ground—I suppose, because it was felt that any such attempt was utterly hopeless. So the spaces between the huts—which by courtesy are called roads—are quagmires of more or less depth, through which luckless wayfarers have to wade to their destination. The different quarters of the camp are designated by signboards; and the roads are marked out, not without need, by a series of high poles stuck into the ground at frequent intervals, with a wisp of straw tied across them near the tip, with the view, I suppose, of guiding the traveller in case the pole itself is half buried in snow.

Above the camp is the long line of batteries and earthworks, which crown the hill. Some hundred feet or so below it stretches the Als Sund; and if a painter were to throw in a little warmth and colour into his picture, he might make a pretty sketch enough of this Danish encampment, and poetise even the slosh itself. The time to witness the scene at its best is towards noon, when the men are off duty, and come trooping home for dinner. Whether rightly or not, all danger of an attack is considered to be over for the day; and the soldiers not engaged in the trenches or at the outposts are at liberty to make themselves as comfortable as they can under the circumstances.

I cannot say that the endeavour is attended with much success. There is no animation visible about their gait or expression; they have not the air of being dejected or dispirited, but they look dull and uncomfortable. Most of them loiter about, with their hands buried in their trousers pockets, and their long pipes hanging lazily from their mouths; and though I have the most cordial sympathy for these two weaknesses of the Danish soldier, I cannot say that they add to his martial appearance.

The ground is too wet to lie down upon, so that there is very little for anybody to do except to slouch, and this is the chief occupation of the day when no work has to be done. Wherever a dry spot can be found, the men make up a fire of brambles and broken hedge-rails and stray ends of planks, over which they boil great cauldrons of greasy soup and porridge. Huge hunches of black, or rather brown bread, are the chief food provided for the soldiers; and once a day they have a slice of fat pork and about half a pint of *schnaps*, which is ladled out of a wooden pail in a tin pot, and distributed solemnly to each man as his name is called in turn.

What would happen if anybody missed his turn I cannot say; but nobody apparently ever does. Those who can afford it, smear their bread over with goose fat, or season it with slices of sausage. Itinerant sutlers frequent the camp about the dinner hour, and sell hard-boiled eggs and plumless buns, and lumps of "*speck*," for which luxuries they charge accordingly: and their trade must be a good one, as all payments are cash, and no credit is allowed.

A number of old women, too, of preternatural ugliness, hang about the camp at meal times, and, I suppose, supply some article—possibly *schnaps*—which the soldiers are in need of, though apparently the only mission of these "mothers of the regiments" is to give an extra tinge of gloominess to the aspect of the scene. The private sale of liquors of any kind within the camp is strictly forbidden; but I observe that every man carries a leather-covered bottle, which must hold a quart at the least, and I can hardly fancy he dilutes half a pint of *schnaps* with water to that amount.

The Danes, unfortunately for themselves at the present moment, have not that power of long stolid enjoyment of their meals vouchsafed by Providence to their German kinsmen, and as much time is not taken up by dinner as might reasonably be the case. When this is over, the men have nothing to do except to slouch and sleep till bedtime. It is too cold to read out of doors, even if the soldiers were so disposed. Indeed, amongst the common troops, newspapers or books appear almost unknown. I was told by a Danish gentleman, as a proof of the education of his countrymen, that ten thousand letters are received daily at the post-office here for the army; and even if the statement is exaggerated, I have no doubt that the knowledge of reading is almost universal; but, for all that, I do not think the Danish soldier is given to reading to anything like the same extent as the ordinary American private. The only amusement I could see in the camp was the performance of a *charivari* with tongs and kettles in front of a scarecrow placarded "General Wrangel," which performance seemed to afford intense delight to the troops, and is to be repeated daily till further notice.

I went over the camp with a French gentleman very well disposed towards the Danish cause, but who, after the fashion of his countrymen, judging everything by a French standard, could not fancy there was much military excellence in troops so utterly unlike *Zouaves* or *Chasseurs de Vincennes*. When he has seen them, as I have, marching out to action, his opinion will doubtless be modified. It is wonderful how the approach of danger brightens up these dull, listless countenances. Dash or *élan* can hardly be expected; but when the hour of danger comes they will hold their own, unless I err, with a dogged courage which French troops might envy.

If this war should continue, its results will throw light on a question which cannot fail to be of great interest for a pacific Power like England. I mean the question, what length of time is required to manufacture an efficient soldiery. The army of Denmark is raised by conscription; and with the gradual increase of wealth and growth of popular power the period of service has been shortened, till, practically, the common soldiers only serve for one year consecutively; in the second year they are called out for a month or so, and then, with very few exceptions, they leave the service.

In the cavalry, I believe, and in the artillery, the obligatory time of service is somewhat longer, and even then it is extremely short. The consequence of this state of things is that nothing resembling a military caste exists in Denmark. The soldiers return to their employment as labourers or mechanics as soon as their time is out, and very soon forget the military training they have received. Thus, in reality, there is no standing army; and, undoubtedly, this fact is one of the chief causes of the internal prosperity of Denmark. Whether its effects are as beneficial in time of war is not equally certain. The Danes are naturally brave; they are fighting in a cause which has given courage to very inferior nations; the soldiers have stood fire excellently, and have held their own against veteran troops like the Austrians.

Indeed, the Prussian Liberal party, who have long been agitating for a reduction in the time of service, assert in their organs that the excellence of the Danish Army is a proof that a very short period is sufficient to make good soldiers. How far this view is correct, experience alone can show. My fear is that individual bravery will not supply the want of training and discipline. The officers themselves complain that, though the men are excellent material for soldiers, there is not time enough to turn them into good non-commissioned officers.

On the few occasions that I have seen any large bodies of troops here in marching order, I have been struck by the want of precision and regularity in their movements. In fact, the army looks like what it is—a levy of peasants. According to all reports, the men who were formerly in the service, and have been called out again under arms from the "*Arrière-Bah*," are not equal to the new recruits who have just commenced their training. That the Danish Army knows how to die, it has shown already; but it is not yet clear whether it knows how to carry out a war.

March 11.

To give the Danes their due, they have not shown any excessive precipitancy in claiming honours for the events of this campaign. The national sentiment appears to have been hitherto that in a war like the one now waging every man, when he had done his best, had done no more than his duty towards his country; and that to single out individual soldiers for distinction was in some sense to confer a kind of slur on those who were not so distinguished. The spirit, too, of the people in this hour of Denmark's trial is not inclined to exultation; the time for that may come, but not yet. However, some annoyance was felt in the army at the absence of any official recognition of their services, and today the first decorations were distributed in commemoration of the Battle of Missunde. Four weeks ago, day for day, I witnessed the distribution of crosses to the Austrian soldiers at Flensburg, who had taken part in the skirmish of Oversee.

There was not much of pomp about that; but still it was a dramatic spectacle compared with its counterpart this morning in the Danish camp. At Flensburg we had a brilliant staff, a formal and lengthy harangue, a body of well-drilled troops, who moved and cheered and waved their caps with mechanical precision; and last, though not least, a splendid Austrian band, which seemed to warm the blood of the bystanders, even beneath the cold, pitiless snow which covered us as we gazed upon the scene. Here everything was almost painfully simple. At twelve o'clock, a couple of regiments were drawn up beneath the batteries of Dybbol; a perfect tempest of rain and wind raged at the time, and the chill damp of the air was worse even than the clear biting cold of a month ago.

Something delayed the arrival of General Gerlach, who was to distribute the medals, for nearly half-an-hour; and the spectators, who consisted of myself, three other Englishmen, and one Dane, began to grow extremely impatient of the delay. At last the one band of the Danish army in Sonderborg came trudging wearily up the hill, playing the most dolorous of tunes; and then a small troop of horsemen, some twenty in all, could be seen galloping along the heavy stone-paved road. In front rode General Gerlach.

The new commander-in-chief is a stout, somewhat squat personage, with keen sharp eyes, buried beneath black bushy eyebrows, and a good-humoured smile playing about his mouth. Considering that he was an officer fifty years ago, he is wonderfully hale and well preserved; and it is only when you get close to him that you see the signs of age in the deep wrinkles and puckers which furrow his face. Many a young rider, however, might have envied the pace at which he dashed up the steep slope that leads from the high road to the batteries; and his staff, well-mounted as they were, had hard work to follow him. Immediately on his arrival the troops presented arms, and then were formed into an open square.

Into this open space there advanced without their muskets about a hundred soldiers, forming the company, or rather the remains of the company, which had most distinguished itself in the field of Missunde. The general was welcomed with a loud hurrah, and then three cheers were given for the king and the country. After that, one officer and three privates were called out from amidst the company which occupied the post of honour, and were presented with a large official-looking envelope containing their nomination to the order of the Dannebrog. I suppose General Gerlach made a speech on the occasion; but the wind was so high, it was impossible for anyone not standing next him to hear a word; and, if he did speak, he can only have said half-a-dozen words. The band struck up the tune of "*Den tappre Landsoldat;*" the troops defiled past the general and his staff on the way back to their quarters; and the whole ceremony was over in a quarter of an hour.

Amongst the spectators of the presentation there were to have been two Japanese officers, who, to the astonishment of the natives, have arrived here upon their travels. I had the honour of being introduced to them this morning, in the very dirty tap-room of a small pot-house, where they have been driven for shelter through want of accommodation. They are two very young and rather pleasing-looking men, with Asiatic features, not unlike Frenchmen in figure. If imperturbability is the chief characteristic of high breeding, they ought to be gentlemen of the most exalted rank in their own country; for, being themselves objects of general observation, and placed in a medium where everything must be strange to them, they seemed as indifferent and as much at their ease as if they had been bred in Sonderborg.

Communication with them is not easy, as. their interpreters speak nothing but Japanese and Dutch, with neither of which languages is there much acquaintance here. Everybody, however, agrees that they are well-bred and intelligent young men, and they certainly distribute photographic likenesses of themselves with extreme amiability. One of them is writing a narrative of his travels, and he constantly takes out his note-book, and, beginning at the bottom of the page, makes a series of hieroglyphics in a straight line rising vertically upwards. Unfortunately, the narrative of the distribution of the Dannebrog orders will not appear in the *Jeddo Gazette*, as something hindered the Japanese from being present. At any rate, I hope, for the credit of Japanese "*littérateurs*," that this may prove to be the case.

Before visiting Denmark these foreign travellers went to the Prussian camp, where they were also treated with great courtesy, but were refused permission to pass the lines by General von Wrangel, under the impression, I suppose, that the Danes might derive news of the Prussian position *via* Yokohama or Nangasaki which might prove injurious to the prospects of the besieging army. At the rate at which the siege is being pushed forwards, these apprehensions are not altogether groundless. If the last month is to be a specimen of the progress the Prussians are likely to make, there is no reason why the siege of Dybbol should not last as long as that of Troy.

139

CHAPTER 6

Fredericia

Strib (opposite Fredericia), Isle of Fünen,
March 13.

Just as there are names of personages which, you never meet with out of a novel, so there are names of towns which seem to belong naturally to the domain of farce. Strib, I think, is one of them. How any place ever came to be called Strib is a mystery. However, there is a sort of appropriateness in its having a name which no association can render dignified. Strib is to Fredericia—or Friederitz, as the Danes call it—what Birkenhead is to Liverpool, or Jersey City to New York, or Gosport to Portsmouth. It exists solely by virtue of its position as an adjunct to the great Danish fortress. It is here that the ferry crosses from Fünen to Jutland, and to this circumstance is due the fact that, probably for the first time in the history of Denmark, a letter is sent to England dated from Strib.

The war makes sad havoc with the course of Danish travelling. If you look at the map, the journey from Sonderborg to Fredericia will seem short and simple enough. By land, an excellent high road goes directly through Apenrade and Kolding, a distance of some thirty miles. Unfortunately, a couple of miles out of Sonderborg, you come upon the German outposts, where you would be arrested as a spy if you were not first shot as an enemy. By sea, too, the voyage through the Als Sund, and then through the Little Belt, is short and expeditious. But both these straits, in parts narrow to the size of the Thames near London Bridge, and are—or at any rate may be—commanded by the masked batteries which the Prussians and Austrians are believed to have erected on their western banks.

So the only practicable, or at least the shortest, means of passage between the two Danish strongholds, is to cross over to Assens, and thence to traverse the island of Fünen till you come again upon the Little Belt at Strib, directly opposite Fredericia. It is by this road that I have come this far upon my journey. Few seas have a prettier name than the "Lille Belt," and few look, upon the map, more land-locked on every side and more secure from storms. The Little Belt, however, can be very creditably rough within its inland waters, and our cockle-shell of a steamboat rocked and pitched and rolled in a manner which a Calais packet could hardly have excelled.

The result was that, instead of reaching Fredericia, as I had hoped, on the same evening, I was obliged to sleep at Assens. Weary as I was with the noise and bustle and dirt of Sonderborg, it was pleasant to step all at once, as it were, out of the range of the war. At Assens I seemed to be a hundred miles away from the scene of conflict. Till you have lived in Denmark it is difficult to realise how completely the insular character of the country separates one part from another. Though Assens lies upon the sea shore, without fortifications of any kind to defend it, it is practically as safe against any attack from the Germans as if it was situate in the heart of England.

The only way in which the war has come home to the little sea-port town is through the detachments of sick and wounded Danes, who are carried daily through its streets on their way to the hospitals of Odensee. While I was there a boat full of invalided soldiers came in from Sonderborg. It was a melancholy sight to see numbers of young men, lads almost, in the full prime of strength and life, conveyed along on stretchers, pale, maimed, and haggard, shivering beneath the icy-cold wind which tossed the coverings from off their limbs, and laid bare their bandages and swathings.

The sight, however, had grown too common to attract much notice, and the Danes, as a nation, are not demonstrative. Otherwise, tokens of the war there were none. In the town itself people seemed to know very little about the campaign. The latest papers at our hotel were Copenhagen ones, some two or three days old, containing meagre paragraphs about the progress of the war, stale, according to our English notions, even at the time when they were printed. Still there was a charm about the peacefulness of the place; it was so neat, so quiet, and so sleepy.

Moreover, there was an exquisite Dutch neatness visible in its streets, peculiar to Denmark proper, and which is not, as far as I have seen, to be found in the Duchies. The pavement was excellent, and the tidy houses seemed all to have been built at the same time, and all kept in excellent repair from the day they were first built.

It is an odd fact about Denmark that, though it is one of the oldest of European countries, I have hardly ever seen in it a building of any kind which appeared to be more than a hundred or a hundred and fifty years old. Everything seems to date from about a century ago, and the interior of the dwellings is, I suspect, very like that of our English homes in the days when George III. first came to the throne. As Danish towns go, Assens is a place of considerable importance, and the inn where I stopped is reckoned the best in the town.

Carpets, however, were unknown there, and private sitting-rooms equally so. The deal floors were strewed with sand; the bed-rooms had no furniture, save unpainted wooden washing-stands, straight-backed chairs, and a squat, four-legged table. In truth, with the exception of an iron stove, the equipment of the room closely resembled that of the prophet's chamber in the Bible. Coarse coloured prints of Napoleon crossing the Alps, and of Frederick VII. in his soldier's uniform, are hung on the walls of every public room—an honour, by the way, to which Christian IX. has not yet attained. Easy chairs, sofas, or curtains, are luxuries only to be found in the hotels of Copenhagen; and the place of mirrors is supplied by one small square of looking-glass stuck in a frame of painted tinwork. However, out of Sonderborg everything is clean, and the prices are as primitive as the accommodation.

An extra post took me today from Assens to Strib. As the extra post, with two horses, travels at the rate of five miles an hour, it is difficult to imagine what can be the speed of ordinary posting. The roads are far superior to those in the Duchies, and are as good as they can be on this thick, heavy soil. According to the Danish story, the superiority of Denmark proper in this respect is owing to the circumstance that the Duchies were allowed to manage their own affairs, and mismanaged them accordingly. The version, on the other hand, current in Holstein, is that the money, which ought to have been used in making roads for the Duchies, was expended exclusively in Denmark .

Possibly there may be a certain amount of truth in either explanation; but about the fact there can be no manner of question. The whole of the island of Fünen, on its western coasts consists of a long series of low round lulls, sloping down to the sea; the highest, I should fancy, being scarcely a hundred feet above the water level. You are always going up and down hill, and as your driver invariably walks his horses wherever there is an incline of any kind, your progress is inevitably slow.

But yet my drive today was a very pleasant one. For the first time since I have been north of the Elbe, we had an hour or two of feeble sunlight, and a sky whose uniform grey tint was interspersed with streaks of pallid blue. The snow had almost vanished, except in drifts beneath the hedgerows and in patches on the open hillsides. The Little Belt lay close upon the left of our road, and whenever we reached the summit of one of the endless hillocks we could see its waters between the bays and headlands and fiords of the indented coast, while the great bare expanse of the broken country stretched far away inland.

Anything more brown and colourless than the fields of Fünen at this season of the year cannot, I think, be found. Not a bud or blade of green grass, or even a roadside violet, was to be seen. Fields, roads, and trees were bare alike. Indeed, the one bright feature in the view consisted in the churches. Their number, compared to the apparent amount of the population, is enormous, and one and all have a quaint family resemblance to the toy churches of our childhood. There were two sorts of imitation churches with which I was familiar as a child. The most elementary formed part of a village, and consisted of a square block of white wood, surmounted by a red roof, with an erection in the centre, which began as a tower and ended as a dumpy steeple; the second, made of porcelain, with a roof and tower cut out into steps, stood habitually upon the chimney-piece, and was lighted up on grand occasions with a piece of taper inside—a ceremony, by the way, which generally ended in its destruction.

Now the idea of all these children's churches must have been taken from Denmark. The ordinary church is a long whitewashed barn, with a red tile roof, and a squat white tower, capped with a pointed triangular roof, also of red tiles. The exceptional churches—the *provst-kirchen*, or dean churches, as I believe they are called—differ from the others in the fact that their fronts and towers are cut out into steps, so that if you had legs long enough you might walk up one side and down the other.

All these stand invariably, on the top of a hill, and their whitewashed walls and towers can be seen far away on every side, sparkling in the sunlight. If the multitude of places of worship is sufficient token, Denmark ought to be one of the most religious of Protestant countries. We met a good sprinkling of country people going to and from the different religious edifices, and there was no work going on in the fields.

But the roads—probably in consequence of the war—were crowded with carts carrying heavy loads of hay and straw. Every now and then we passed through great beech woods, and then through little country villages, where the low thatch-covered cottages seemed to cluster round the great farmhouses, or "*gaards*," built in the shape of a square, with the house in front, and the farm-buildings forming the square behind. Of modern agricultural implements or high-class farming I could see nothing; but the buildings, down to the poorest, were wonderfully substantial, and cosy in look; the fields were well hedged and tilled; and every part of the country, down to the sea shore, was brought into cultivation.

Even a speed of five miles an hour, excluding stoppages, gets one over the ground at last But by the time I had reached Strib the weather had changed. Snow had come on—there is always any quantity of snow on hand in the air of this country—and the wind had lashed the waters of the Little Belt into such a storm that it was not therefore advisable to cross the straits in an open boat, the only means of transit available. So here I have taken up my quarters for the night. From time to time the sky has cleared up, and then the town of Fredericia lies clear before us.

On Tuesday last, when the Germans took Erritsö, they fired a dozen shells or so at the little jetty which runs out in front of our hotel. The shells did no damage, but the inhabitants of the village fled away in terror, and have only returned since the enemy evacuated Erritsö with as little apparent reason as they entered it. The strait varies in width from half a mile to a mile, the widest portion being here, where the Belt opens into the sea by Fredericia; and the narrowest, about three miles hence, just below Middelfart.

It is from that town, in ordinary times, that travellers cross the straits; but the whole Jutland coast is so overrun by German troops, that it is not safe landing short of the fortress itself. From here to Middelfart there runs a series of low sandy cliffs, which might be easily enough defended by batteries, and were, indeed, so protected in the Schleswig-Holstein war of 1848-50. The current, however, is so strong and rapid, that it would be a very difficult enterprise to throw a bridge across the channel, even if the attempt were unopposed; and it is not probable that the Germans would venture on the risk of sending any large force into the island as long as Fredericia remains untaken, and as long, therefore, as they would be liable to have their retreat cut off at any moment. Little fear, apparently, is entertained of any German inversion.

All through the night the wind howled and whistled, and our ill-closed windows kept blowing .open, startling us from our sleep at the most unseasonable hours. When the morning came, the outlook was anything but cheering. A perfect tempest of wind was blowing from the north, and the "Lille Belt" was crowned with white-crested waves galloping wildly out to sea. Fredericia lies full in sight, about three-quarters of a mile distant as the crow flies, but for any practical purpose it might as well, or better, be thirty miles away. The inn is crowded with travellers, waiting, like myself, to make the passage; a drove of oxen are fastened in front of the hotel, destined to terminate their existence as soon as they can be transported to Fredericia, where, in the dearth of fresh meat, their arrival is anxiously expected; the post-cart, laden with letter-bags, has been drawn up by the pier for hours.

But still there is as yet no prospect of either men, oxen, or letters getting across the channel Early this morning the officer in command of Strib telegraphed to Fredericia for a steamer to convey the mails; but, though we can see three steamboats lying in the harbour opposite with their steam up, no response has yet been made. When this hope failed, the owner of a small open fishing smack offered to transport any passengers who were willing to risk the passage. I volunteered at once, in company with six other gentlemen, who, like myself, are weather-bound at Strib.

We all got ready, prepared to be drenched to the skin; but when it came to the point the courage of our ferryman gave way. He first asked for a quarter of an hour's delay to get some breakfast, then for an hour, till the wind had abated, and finally he adjourned the prosecution of his enterprise for an indefinite period. So here we are kept for the present, waiting till a steamer shall venture out of Fredericia, or till the ferryman can make up his mind that there is any chance of working his way across the channel against the wind and tide.

The resources of Strib are not manifold. The whole village consists of the post-house inn and of four cottages. The wind is so strong that it is impossible to walk out, and inside the house, there is nothing to be done. A local Fünen newspaper and an odd number of the Copenhagen *Folksblad* constitute the literary resources of the establishment; and its culinary efforts do not rise beyond sandwiches of brown bread and cheese (called "*smörbrod*") and *schnaps*. The guestrooms are crowded with peasants and soldiers, loafing about drearily, and flattening their noses against the window panes, in the vain hope of seeing some change in the aspect of the sky; while the commercial travellers, who constitute the *élite* of the society, are noisy, after the wont of bagmen in all quarters of the globe.

Moreover, though it may seem ungrateful in me to say so, their affability is rather burdensome as a permanent institution. They kindly insist upon my drinking bad beer, and worse *schnaps*, at all unseasonable hours; and also, knowing that I am an Englishman, they refuse to address me in anything but a few words of broken English, only partially intelligible to themselves, and utterly unintelligible to me, which we have subsequently to translate into German for our mutual comprehension.

So, upon the whole, I prefer the quiet of my own room to the charms of Strib society. There, too, I have the great advantage that I look straight out upon the channel and across to Fredericia. The aspect of the Belt in this part is very like the Mersey below Liverpool. The straits are about the same width as the English river near its mouthy and the low sandbanks which mark the Fünen and Jutland shores might well be taken for those of New Brighton and Egremont.

A long line of red tile roofs stretching from the water's edge to the crest of the low cliffs—a line broken only by windmills, rows of poplars, and factory chimneys—this is all I can see of Fredericia from my windows. Towards the Belt the Jutland shore sinks away till it becomes almost level with the water; while towards the north it stretches out in a succession of bold headlands, jutting one beyond the other into the far distance. Fredericia itself stands at the extremity of a semicircular-shaped promontory, bounded by the Belt on one side, and the Ost-See on the other.

At the nose of the promontory is the citadel, whose batteries can be seen clearly enough from Strib. At the back of the town, along the brow of the hill, there runs, if charts are to be believed, a range of works reaching from sea to sea; and almost close to these works upon the western side there is a fiord—the Over Sommelsee—extending a mile or so inland from the Little Belt

Whether I shall be able to give you a more detailed account of the Jutland fortress than this cursory one is doubtful. In the first place, the wind is rising every hour, and the time that I can afford to wait here for its subsidence is limited. In the second place, it is very possible that, even if I succeed in reaching Fredericia, my area of observation may be confined to the town itself. The commandant-general has the reputation of not erring on the side of amenity. Every officer to whom I have mentioned my intention of visiting Fredericia has thought it necessary to warn me that the general has a very abrupt manner, and is not fond of amateurs of any kind.

In the last war he sent back the chaplains, who were forwarded from Copenhagen to the army in Jutland, with the curt message that his soldiers had got something else to do besides saying their prayers; and numerous stories are told of his peremptory, offhand way of dealing with the officers under his command. However, I have letters and papers enough to secure me against any worse fate than being ordered to leave the town; and, weather permitting, I mean to try whether the general's bark is not worse than his bite.

The obvious inferiority of Fredericia to Dybbol consists in the fact that, instead of lying higher than the neighbouring country, it is surrounded by heights of at least equal altitude. On the other hand, it would seem as if, from its position, the Danish gunboats could co-operate in its defence far more effectually than they can at Alsen. It appears to me, however, that the Danes are far less confident of their power of defending it than they are about the Dybbol works. And if weather like this were to last for many days, it is difficult to see how the town could be provisioned, now that the enemy occupy all the surrounding country, and the supplies have to be brought by water.

Fredericia, Jutland, March 15.

In these inland seas storms sink as rapidly as they rise. I had scarcely posted my letter yesterday from Strib, when the landlord rushed up to tell me to get ready at once, as the wind had fallen, and a boat was going to cross with the mails. It was getting dusk, and Fredericia could hardly be seen over the dull waste of angry seething waters which lay between Fünen and Jutland. Personally, I entertained a wish that the wind, as it had thought fit to storm all day, would have kept up a character for consistency till daybreak. However, the opportunity was one not to be lost, and I took my seat in a large, open, flat-bottomed boat, filled to the edge with letter-bags and chests and boxes, and rolling to and fro in a manner which suggested uncomfortable doubts as to the nature of our passage.

The result proved better than I expected; our sails filled out as they caught the dying puffs of the falling breeze, and we shot merrily enough across the straits; we could almost see the water of the Belt levelling itself as the wind dropt; and before we had got half over the channel there was not a breaker to be seen far or near, and we glided as gently into the harbour of Fredericia as if we had been cruising on the Medway or the Orwell. Before night was over, another storm sprang up, and the communication was interrupted again.

It is strange that, though the sea is open to the Danes, there is no regular mode of transit between Fredericia and the capital except by the lengthy and wearisome passage across the island of Fünen, and that no means have been taken even to secure uninterrupted access to Fünen itself. The railroad between Strib and Odensee is very nearly finished; but, not being quite finished, it is of course useless. In all military matters, *a miss is as good as a mile*—a proverb whose importance the Danes hardly seem to me to appreciate sufficiently.

My first thought on reaching the fortress was to find shelter for the night. Of course there was nobody at our landing to act either as guide or porter.

Denmark resembles America in this respect, that it is devoid of that class, to be found in all other European countries, which is always on the look-out to earn a sixpence. The people are wonderfully civil and obliging, but it never enters into their heads to do anything which lies out of their ordinary routing. There is not traffic enough here to support professional porters, and an amateur was not to be thought of. The same want of vigilance prevailed which I have already had occasion to comment on in Sonderborg. Though Fredericia is a fortified place, invested at this moment by a hostile army, whose outposts are within gunshot of the town, and though it is commanded by an officer whom the Danes consider a martinet of martinets, I was allowed to land without showing my permission, or being asked any question by anybody, and to walk off into the town at my pleasure.

There was hardly a person out of uniform visible in the streets of Fredericia when I arrived; and as the lamps were not lit, and nobody could tell me the way, it was mortal hard work toiling about the ill-paved slippery streets in search of an hotel, loaded as I was with the heavy furs and wraps which it is necessary to carry with you in this miserable climate. At last fortune, rather than my own efforts, guided me to the one inn of the place, the Hotel Victoria. In ordinary times it must be a comfortable house, but everything now is at sixes and sevens. In the last war a shell fell through the roof of the hotel, and nearly knocked it down. The owners, therefore, are naturally alarmed for the safety of their property, and have been dismantling the rooms of their furniture as expeditiously as they were able.

Forty officers are quartered on the premises; the landlord is ill in bed; and new guests are positively unwelcome. I soon found that any idea of a room, or even of a bed, was as futile as a child's wish for the moon; and I was thankful when I obtained a qualified reversionary interest in one of the staffed benches which lined the guestroom.

As soon as this favour was secured I started for the headquarters, with the view of facing the redoubtable General Lundig, who is reported to entertain a peculiar dislike to amateur observers in general, and to newspaper correspondents in particular. The other day the editor of an unhappy little local paper, the *Fredericia Avis*, received a first *avertissement* for publishing a list of the killed and wounded in one of the petty skirmishes which have taken place at the outposts, and was warned that the consequences of a second offence would be of the gravest character.

Happily, I was furnished with letters to an officer of the staff, who acted as intermediary between myself and the supreme power. First of all there was some talk of telegraphing to Copenhagen for instructions; but on showing my permission from the commander-in-chief to pass freely over all positions occupied by the Danish Army, as well as other letters of recommendation with which I was furnished, any further difficulty was waived, a special order was granted me to pass through the lines, and I was introduced forthwith to an artillery officer, who is to accompany me over the works tomorrow.

In fact, as far as I am concerned, I have every cause to speak well of General Lundig, and am truly glad that my reception at Fredericia has afforded no exception to the uniform civility I have received from all Danish military men. My one solitary complaint is, that they sit up unnecessarily late. When you have been tramping about all day, and are tired out, it is trying to mortal patience to see a row of officers sitting on the sofa where your couch is to be laid, and lighting cigar after cigar, and ordering *schnaps* after *schnaps*, till close upon midnight. Their conversation, I admit, was courteous and instructive; but on this occasion their room would have been infinitely preferable to their company.

This morning I have spent in rambling over Fredericia. The town has that uncomfortable look which always pervades places built to suit a preconceived plan. The works were not made for the town, but the town for the works. In shape it is exceedingly like a quadrant, the two sides of the triangle being formed by the Lille Belt and the Ost-See, and the semicircular base by the ramparts, the *Kastel* being at the apex of the triangle. Roughly speaking, the length from the *Kastel* to the termination of the ramparts on either shore is half a mile, and that of the ramparts themselves about a mile.

In the triangle included within the sea and the ramparts the town is built. All the streets are at right angles to each other, those feeing the sea rising up the slope of the low sandy shore. The result of this system of building is, that every street is cut short abruptly, either by the sea or the ramparts; and as the town has not prospered except as a garrison, the original plan has never been carried out, and the place has an unfinished untidy look, which is not prepossessing.

Moreover, at this moment it is almost deserted by its normal inhabitants. The dread of a second bombardment has driven away the greater part of the citizens. All the houses are crammed with troops; on every door there is chalked up the number of men who are to be quartered beneath its roof; most of the shops are shut up; those few which are open have empty shelves, and are selling off their stocks as rapidly as they can; while on the sea shore you see stacks of household furniture, chairs and tables, and chests of drawers, piled up, waiting for the means of transport. The one sight of the place is the statue of the "*Tappre Landsoldat*," a bronze figure of colossal size, cast from the guns taken by the Danes at the Battle of Istedt in 1849. The inhabitants believe—not without good ground—that the Prussians, if they enter the town, will either mutilate or carry off the chief monument of their city, and they have petitioned for its removal to some safer place; but as yet their wishes have not been complied with.

Middelfart (Fünen), March 16.

The strength of Fredericia is not, I think, sufficiently appreciated even in Denmark. Thanks to the kindness of the military authorities in that fortress, I have had unusual facilities allowed me for visiting the works; and I own, for the good of Denmark, I should be glad if Dybbol and Fredericia could be made to change places. A stronger position than the latter against a land attack cannot well be imagined. The bastions of the ramparts which surround the town are splendid specimens of earthwork. Strange to say, they were constructed at a period when stone fortifications were the fashion of the day, so that their constructor was absolutely in advance of his age in preferring earth to stone. The guns of the town sweep the whole of the low bare plain which slopes slowly down from the cliffs of the Ost-See towards the Little Belt; and if the Germans have to advance to the attack across this plain, they will find themselves in what in Yankee phrase is called a "tight place."

The reason, I fancy, why Fredericia is comparatively less thought of by the Danes than Dybbol, is because the former fortress was very nearly being taken by the Schleswig-Holstein army in the last war. There is some force in this consideration, but fortunately Fredericia is not at all the same place now, (1864), as it was in 1849. In that year the Germans had not only got batteries below the fortress, by which they commanded the passage of the Lille Belt, but they had erected works on the cliffs which face the open sea, north of Fredericia; and if these had been completed, it would have been impossible for any vessel to leave the harbour of the fortress, no matter in what direction it sailed.

Thus, if the Danes had not made their famous sortie from the garrison, all communication with the island of Fünen would have been cut off; and, unless the siege had been raised, the fall of Fredericia must have been a mere matter of time. A similar danger exists no longer. On the very hill where the German batteries were erected in 1849, the Danes have made an entrenched camp. The work has been pushed forward with extraordinary energy; so that, at the present moment, this Danish outpost would be more difficult, I think, to capture than Fredericia itself.

As long as the entrenched camp is held by the Danes, the communication by sea is kept open, and even if the camp was taken by a sudden attack, the guns on the bastions of the town must be silenced before it can be permanently occupied by the enemy. The officer who was commissioned to show me round the works assured me that with twenty thousand more men Fredericia could now be defended for any length of time. My only fear is that the great chain of works recently erected by the Danes labours under the same defect as the Dannewerk, namely, that it requires a force to man it, which the Danes cannot reckon on possessing. I satisfied myself, however, that, contrary to a statement I had heard at Sonderborg, there is no eminence in the immediate vicinity of the fortress from which it can be commanded by the enemy. Though not much, still Fredericia is decidedly above the surrounding ground, and a bombardment from a distance would effect little damage on a town whose streets are so broad, and whose area is so little covered over with buildings of any kind.

The Prussians are supposed to be in considerable force both north and south of Fredericia. The Danish outposts are now not more than a mile beyond the walls; and the whole face of the country is scoured over by the enemy. It is odd that amidst a hostile population no attempt has been made to inaugurate a guerilla warfare against the Germans. There can be no question about the dislike the Jutland peasantry entertain towards their invaders; but yet the invasion is acquiesced in with a strange outward apathy. Thus far the enemy has contented itself with investing the fortress on the land side, but there is no indication of active operations being about to commence.

Under these circumstances I saw no object in prolonging my stay after I had seen the position and the defences of the great Jutland stronghold, and have come to Middelfart, on my way back to Sonderborg. A little below this town, between Kongebro on the Fünen side, and Snoghoi on the Jutland side, the Lille Belt is at its narrowest, and is only 2000 feet across. To guard against the risk of an invasion of Fünen, two or three small batteries have been thrown up on the bluffs near Middelfart; but I think the Danes place their chief reliance on the rapidity of the current, and on the fact that the Germans cannot venture to cross into the island in any force while the fortress of Fredericia remains untaken in their rear.

Everything is so quiet here, that an hour ago I myself saw a troop of German dragoons riding slowly along the opposite bank of the river, and return dragging away a cannon that had been left in the waterside village of Snoghoi, without a single shot being fired at them from the Danish shores.

CHAPTER 7

The Beginning of the End

Sonderborg, March 18.

I was sitting at my dinner in the little hotel of Middelfart, rejoicing in the prospect of a good bed—after sleeping for two nights on chairs without change of clothes—when an officer entered the room and informed me that the bombardment of Dybbol had commenced in earnest The news appeared to be authentic, though, up to two hours before, it had not been heard of in Fredericia; but even the mere possibility of its being true determined me to hasten my return to Sonderborg.

All thoughts of bed had to be abandoned; a carriage was ordered forthwith; and in half-an-hour's time, in company with an English fellow-traveller, I was on my way back to Alsen. Through the long dreary night we posted over rough roads, with worn-out horses, in the hardest and clumsiest of carriages. So much time had to be lost in waking up ostlers at unseasonable hours, and waiting at each stage till fresh horses could be got, that it was eight o'clock before we reached the little seaport town of Faaborg, though the distance we had traversed was under forty miles.

From this place the regular ferry crosses to the island of Alsen. But everything is out of order at the present time; and we were told that our only chance of crossing lay in going on to Svenborg, and waiting there for a steamboat. As, however, I found that the bombardment of Dybbol had certainly commenced, and that the sound of cannon had been heard again during the morning, I resolved on a final effort. By dint of persuasion, combined with pecuniary enticements, I induced a fisherman to take us across the straits in his smack.

Such a boat I never sailed in before, and fervently hope never to sail in again. Her builder would have been puzzled to say which was

153

her stem and which were her bows. It would have taken a dozen stout rowers to force her through the water, and we had only one sailor, who paddled lazily with a single oar. There was hardly any wind, but what there was, like the wind of the Irishman's mill, was uncommonly strong, and was moreover almost dead against us.

Our only means of making any way at all was by a system of constant tacking; and whenever we tacked, our old barrel-shaped boat swung round the opposite way to that which was intended. Hour after hour passed, and still we kept tacking to and fro between two little islands about a mile from each other, without ever succeeding in passing either. In a cold winter's day it is not pleasant to lie becalmed on the Baltic in an open boat, without food or shelter.

And what added to my annoyance was the fact that we could hear distinctly the sound of heavy firing across the water. Happily, at the moment when we had begun to despair, and were thinking of turning back and trying our luck by some other channel, the wind freshened, and veered round a point or two in our favour. Thanks to this good fortune, we got clear at last of the narrows, and somehow or other made our way to the east coast of Alsen, having sailed over ten miles in about eight hours.

Our troubles were not yet ended. Some twelve miles of impassable cross-country roads lay between us and Sonderborg. The spot where we were landed was a mere hamlet, and our sole chance of getting a conveyance was at a ferry-side tavern. When I first asked for horses I was told by the landlord that he had none. When I asked again what, if so, was the reason of his having stables, he changed his ground, and said that a terrible battle was going on at Sonderborg, that it was impossible to reach the place, and that nobody was allowed to enter; and further, he wished to know why I should want to go there when everybody else was leaving.

The question was one difficult to answer to his comprehension, so I assumed as stern a look as I could, pulled out my permission to pass the lines, stamped with the seal of the commander-in-chief, and declared that I must proceed at once on "military business"—a statement which I trust was true in the spirit, if not in the letter. The sight of the official seal was sufficient. The landlord engaged to drive us as far as the entrance to Sonderborg, and as the sun was setting we set off once again on our journey.

A prettier and yet a sadder drive than that evening one of ours across the length of Alsen I never remember to have taken. . The waters of the Baltic were blue with the reflection of a sky that for once was cloudless. The wind had sunk, and the air was still, and almost warm. For the first time the tokens of spring were clearly visible. The hedge-rows were laden with kit-cat blossoms, and every now and then in sheltered nooks you saw tender buds of green peeping out from amidst the bushes. Birds were chirping everywhere; while the few faint patches of snow left standing on the bare hillsides only served to recall the winter that seemed well nigh past.

In the west, beyond the low heights of Dybbol, the sun was setting amidst red-streaked golden-edged clouds, and in the east the moon was rising slowly from out the Baltic. Our road lay through long winding country lanes, quiet cosy homesteads, and past old-fashioned Danish churchyards, decked out with flowers and crosses.

And yet every step we took brought the presence of war closer and closer to us. As the evening darkened, we could see the sharp lightning flash of the guns as they were fired from the Dybbol batteries; then, after a few seconds, which seemed at first like hours, there came the dull heavy boom of the cannon; ever and *anon* a thick pillar of smoke, gilded with the rays of the setting sun, rose slowly up into the sky; and we could tell that some shell had burst with deadly effect.

Across the liquid waters of the Als Sund—lying like a silver lake at the foot of the white wood-surrounded castle the Augustenborgs claimed, before they sold it, as the birthplace of their race—you could see dark clouds of fire and smoke rising from the villages, which Germans and Danes were alike burning down, lest they should prove a shelter for each other's troops. But it was not only in the distance that the misery and sorrow which war is causing here, as everywhere, were brought before our eyes. By the roadside we passed soldier after soldier, lying on the damp chill ground—stragglers who had broken down in the march, and were trying in vain to recover a little breath and strength to struggle on after their comrades who had gone before.

Ambulance vans were driving hastily between the hospitals at Augustenborg and the scene of action. Carts came by us with wounded soldiers, pale and haggard, lying in the straw which barely covered the rough planks that form the bottom of these Danish waggons. Saddest of all to me of the sights we saw was the long string of carriages and carts of every kind, in which the poorer inhabitants of Sonderborg were flying from their houses. Tables, chairs, bedsteads, pictures, looking-glasses, were piled up in these conveyances in a strange medley of confusion. The articles themselves seemed so worthless, that it was clear those to whom such sticks of furniture were of value must be ill able to afford their loss.

In the midst of these piles of household goods there sat whole families of exiles from their homes. Old men, too feeble to walk, little children, young mothers with babies at their breasts, crouched and shivered amidst the wrecks of their belongings. There seemed no end to this dismal exodus. It had been going on, I was told, all day; the coming of night had not stopped it. As fast as conveyances could be found, these poor creatures were making their escape from the town where they had been born and bred. Where they were to find shelter for the night, or how they were to get food for the morrow, Heaven could alone know. And as they flitted past us in the dim gloom, the sound of the distant guns grew constantly nearer and louder.

But, with all these stoppages, it was dark before we reached Sonderborg, and the battle of the day was over, because there was not light enough to carry on the work of killing. I found a welcome again beneath the same hospitable roof where I have been sheltered so long; and then my first care was to make out what I could of the history of the attack. On Monday last the Danes opened fire on the batteries which the Prussians were believed to be constructing between the village of Broager and the shores of the Wemming Bund. No reply was made, and apparently no damage was done.

On Tuesday, either because the Prussians had completed their works, or because the weather suddenly became so clear that guns could be aimed with effect, or from whatever cause, the enemy commenced firing from the Broager batteries, and have continued doing so till this evening. On the first day 350 shots were fired; on the second 560. The number fired today is not yet known, but probably it was much greater than the foregoing, as 240 shots were thrown into one single battery. On the first day a dozen shells or so were fired at Sonderborg, but without doing any injury; and since then the town has been left unmolested, though it is clear the enemy has got the right range.

If the bombardment should be continued, it will be a most wanton piece of useless barbarity, as the bridges which connect the town with the mainland lie out of reach of any shell aimed from Broager, and thus the only result of firing at Sonderborg would be the destruction of much life and property. Hitherto the whole force of the enemy's fire has been directed against the left flank of the Dybbol lines of defence; that is, against the batteries 1 and 2 on the northern shore of the Wemming Bund. The distance between these batteries and those of Broager, according to the government map, is close on 10,000 feet; and, though the practice of the besiegers is excellent, little effect has been produced by their three days' bombardment Whatever injury has been done to the Danish works by day has been easily repaired by night, and, unless the enemy can bring his approaches nearer, the heights of Dybbol seem in little immediate danger.

Meanwhile, the Prussians are not relying on their Broager batteries alone. They have seized the low heights of Avn-Bierg to the north of Ragebol, and are erecting batteries there, from which they can to some extent command the right flank of the Dybbol line. This morning a Danish force was sent out to drive the enemy from Ragebol; they were met, however, by overwhelming numbers, and compelled to retire. The Prussians then attacked the Danish entrenchments in the churchyard of Dybbol village, and after three unsuccessful charges drove the Danes from their position. By these movements the enemy has established himself at the very outskirts of the Danish defences. This morning, however, an attempt is to be made to drive the Prussians a second time out of the village of Dybbol.

The loss on the Danish side has, of course, been heavy. Though the numbers are not known, it is said that as many as seventy have been killed in three days' fighting. One shell which burst into a bombproof shed in one of the batteries, killed ten men who were under cover there, and wounded seven-and-twenty more. An infantry colonel is amongst the dead. No estimate can, of course, be formed of the German loss; but, from the number of shells which were seen to burst amongst their columns, it is supposed to be much heavier than the Danish.

On the whole, I should say that the result of these three days' fighting has been favourable to the Danes, as far as the strength of their position and the efficiency of their artillery are concerned. Their failures, if I can call them so, arise solely from that fatal inferiority in numbers to the enemy, for which no courage or skill can compensate. Tonight everything is quiet, except that about once an hour a shot is fired from the batteries, with what purpose it is difficult to say. With daylight, unless the Danes lose heart, the battle will again begin in earnest.

March 19.

Writing as I did last night, amidst a host of conflicting rumours, I was obliged to take several of the statements as they came to me coloured by the natural bias of my informants. On fuller information I find, to my regret, that I somewhat underrated the importance of the German successes—for such, I fear, they must fairly be called—during the three first days of the siege. Nothing would please me better than to give rose-coloured pictures of the position of affairs; but, in so doing, I should be rendering a very doubtful service to the Danish cause, and should not be following the example of the Danes themselves, who confess their own weaknesses and failures with an almost touching frankness. Let me try therefore and cast up fairly the balance of loss and gain to the Danish side, which the progress of the attack has shown thus far. And first for the debit side of the account

The Danes have already lost the use of the harbour of Sonderborg for any practical purpose. As soon as the guns of the Broager batteries commenced their fire, it was found they could sweep everything off the face of the Wemming Bund. The only possible justification for the bombardment of Sonderborg lies in the hypothesis that the Prussians wished to drive away the Danish shipping from the quays of the town. If so, the attempt was perfectly successful All the vessels cleared out at once, and the harbour is utterly deserted by everything, except a few fishing smacks.

The mail steamers now sail from the little port of Horuphav, four miles east of Sonderborg, and no reinforcements or supplies can be safely landed at the mouth of the Als Sund. Thus our means of communication with Denmark proper are sadly curtailed. Moreover, the insecurity of the town itself has been fully demonstrated; only a dozen shells or so were fired, and no casualties occurred; but it is clear that, if the Germans choose to do so, they may render Sonderborg untenable as a residence, even without capturing the heights of Dybbol. According to the admission of the Danes themselves, the practice of the Prussian artillery is excellent The enemy seems to have directed his fire on Tuesday against the little red-tiled steeple of the Sonderborg Raads Huus, and every one of his shots fell within a short distance of it.

Perhaps it may seem strange to you that these results should not have been anticipated beforehand. The only explanation is, that till the batteries on the shore of the Wemming Bund actually opened fire, the Danes had no positive information as to their existence, or, at any rate, as to their strength, while it was imagined that no serious damage could be done by shells fired at a distance of nearly three miles. People who are wise after the event say that the Danes committed a great blunder in ever allowing the Prussians to obtain possession of the Wemming Bund shores.

If you look at the map you will see that just below Dybbol the Schleswig coast runs out into an irregular peninsula, called Broagerland, surrounded east, south, and west, by the waters of the Wemming Bund, the Flensborg Bucht, and the Nybol Nör respectively, and connected on the north with the mainland by a narrow isthmus. No doubt this peninsula might have been defended without much difficulty, and, had it been so, the position of Dybbol would have been infinitely stronger.

Unfortunately, the one fatal objection was that the Danes had not men enough to spare for any object except the defence of the Dybbol heights, and could not have safely detached any large force for the occupation of Broagerland. Courage will do a great deal in war, but it will not enable one man to occupy two positions at once. Hitherto the gun-boats have proved of uncommonly little service in defending the coasts. The *Rolf Krake* failed to destroy the bridge which connects Broagerland with the Schleswig coast at Eggernsund; and, after one abortive attempt to shell the Prussians along the shores of the Wemming Bund, she has assumed a position of inaction, which may be masterly, but is certainly ineffective.

The excuse made for this inaction is, that the Danes cannot afford to run the risk of losing their one iron-clad; but my own suspicion is that the result of the action at Eggernsund was to show that the *Rolf Krake* is not a match for land batteries manned with guns of heavy calibre. Very little reliance, too, seems to be placed upon the ordinary gunboats. In spite of the presence of three of these vessels, the Prussians contrived the other day to make their way across the Femeren Sound, and occupy the island of Femeren, off the Holstein coast; and yet the width of the above sound, if my map is to be trusted, is twice that of the Als Sund in its broadest part

A more serious blow, however, to the Danes than either the loss of the Sonderborg harbour or the demonstrated insecurity of the town, is the successful advance of the Prussian troops yesterday towards Dybbol. In a description I gave you of the Danish position in a former letter, you may possibly remember that I stated Dybbol was, in fact, a low, plum-pudding shaped hill, surrounded by the sea on three-fourths of its circumference, and connected with the mainland on the fourth; the valley, which forms the base of the hill on the land side, being also the narrowest part of the isthmus, washed by the Als Sund on the north, and the Wemming Bund on the south.

On the western slope of this valley there runs an irregular range of hills, or rather hillocks, lower, but not much lower, than Dybbol-hill itself. This range, roughly speaking, starts at a little hill called Avn Bierg, on the shore of the Wemming Bund, passes through Dybbol churchyard, skirts the village of Ragebol, and ends at Sand Bierg, on the Als Sund. Till yesterday the Danish outposts occupied this ranges more or less completely. They have now all been driven in, and the Germans have got possession of the heights which front Dybbol. In using these terms—ranges, and heights, and hills—I must caution you that they are only used relatively, as there is hardly an eminence in the whole neighbourhood which, even in England, we should call a hill.

Thus the Germans have secured a line of attack very little more than three-quarters of a mile from Dybbol heights, on which they can erect batteries whose slight inferiority of position may be atoned for by the great superiority of their artillery. The importance of the position was keenly felt by the Danes, but the enemy advanced in such overwhelming numbers that resistance was almost impossible. There is no object in concealing the fact that, after one or two unsuccessful efforts, two of the Danish infantry regiments could not be brought to attack again.

It would be almost incredible if, in an army of raw and untrained troops, such events did not occur; and it is no slight on Danish courage that these peasant soldiers should for once have been daunted by a murderous fire of artillery, to which they had no power of replying. Many of the regiments fought excellently, but nothing could resist the vast numerical strength of the enemy. In an ordinary war such an incident would be of very slight importance; as a Danish officer said to me today, while telling me these facts:

But the misfortune of this war is that the little army which defends Dybbol cannot afford even a slight diminution of its strength or effectiveness.

It was believed that an attempt would be undertaken today to retake Avn Bierg and Dybbol, but no movement has been made on our side, and therefore I fear that the enterprise has been abandoned as too perilous.

On the other hand, the result of these three days' fighting has in some respects been very encouraging to the Danes. The batteries have received but little damage, and what damage has been done by day has been easily repaired by night. With the exception of the fearful casualty in the block-house, very few lives have been lost in the works; and the men are becoming daily more and more hardened under fire. The weakness of the Danes is the great superiority of the German artillery over their own.

The Danish shells, which explode with fuses, constantly burst in the air before they reach their destination, a defect to which the Prussian percussion shells are not liable. Still, as a net result, the Dybbol position remains as strong as ever. Only one gun has been dismounted, and nothing as yet has occurred to demonstrate the possibility of the works being taken without either a protracted siege or a desperate attack.

Today has been comparatively blank of incident. The Broager batteries have been firing at intervals, but their fire has been slack, and has appeared designed to keep the Danes constantly on the alert rather than to effect any practical purpose. The number of guns in these Prussian batteries has obviously been diminished, and it is supposed that some of them are being removed to the ridge of Avn Bierg. My suspicion is, that we shall have an interval of a day or two of comparative quiet, till the enemy has completed his new batteries, and then a terrible fire will be opened against the whole line of the Dybbol entrenchments.

The Danes have scarcely replied today to the straggling fire of the Prussians, and though large bodies of troops have been drawn up all day under cover of the hillside, waiting the signal to advance, nothing has been done up to the hour at which I write.

I went this afternoon through the camps. The weather was almost warm, and the sky was as dear as an Italian one. Tonight it is freezing again slightly, so that we are promised a continuance of these bright days—pleasant enough to a spectator, but too favourable, I am afraid, to the invading army. The troops were cheered up by the warmth and sunlight, and by the comfort of having dry ground to stand upon, and appeared to be in excellent spirits.

Meanwhile the exodus from the town is going on rapidly. Shops and dwellings are closing one after the other, and vans are standing in front of every other house loaded with furniture, which is to be carried away inland. In the house where I am dwelling the ladies have gone away, the walls are being stripped of their pictures, the floors of their carpets, and everything has a dreary "flitting" look.

Now that the war is coming home to us in earnest, it is impossible not to feel painfully the fearful odds against which the Danes are struggling gallantly rather than hopefully. David is doing combat with Goliath, and the age of miracles is past.

March 20.

It is curious what a difference there is in real life between the passive and active aspects of every question. It is true that schoolmasters, while wielding the birch, inform their victims that the infliction of the punishment is as painful to them as its reception by the sufferer; but, practically, I have found that the flogger and the flogged, the debtor and the creditor, the man who shoots and the man who is shot at, regard one and the same transaction from an entirely different point of view.

My lot in life has enabled me to experience, as an amateur, the sentiments both of the bombarder and the bombarded. Three years ago I was present as a spectator at the bombardment of Gaeta, as I am now at that of Dybbol. There is much of outward similarity between the two scenes. In Italy, as in Denmark, the shots were fired across a narrow bay; and here, as there, the artillery of the besiegers is superior to that of the besieged. For the last few days, the sky and the sea have been as blue as if Sonderborg stood on the shores of the Mediterranean, instead of on those of the Baltic; and when I get sheltered from the cruel east wind, and can bask in the warm sunlight, I might almost fancy that this tardy northern spring was the short Italian winter, when the *Tra-Montana* wind is blowing from across the snow-tipped Apennines.

The atmosphere, too, is so dear, that every sandhill and tree upon the shores of the Wemming Bund can be seen with the naked eye. The occupation of my time is not unlike what it was on the occasion I have spoken of. Then I used to lie for hours amidst the olive groves which rise above the Borgo di Gaeta, and look down on the Villa di Cicerone, where the great Cavalli guns were planted, and watch the shells as they flew across the bay to the doomed fortress which the unhappy Francis II. held as the last stronghold of the kingdom of the Two Sicilies.

Here I sit upon the sea-shore, under shelter of the low sand cliffs, and watch the shells flying from the Broager batteries towards those Dybbol heights which guard the last patch of mainland ground that still owns the sway of Christian IX as sovereign of the two Duchies. The sight has the same strange ceaseless attraction for me as it had in 1861. First there comes the small white puff of smoke, standing out against the clear blue sky like the cloud not bigger than a man's hand, which the prophet's servant saw in the old Bible story.

Then this puff rolls itself slowly out in long spiral coils, like some great serpent unfolding its length ready for a spring. Then, if your eyes are quick, you can see the shell describing its parabolic curve through the air; and then comes the dull solemn boom of the cannon as the smoke dies away.

But to make the parallel complete I ought to be sitting on the southern shores of the Wemming Bund, not on those of the Als Sund. At Gaeta, where my lot was thrown with the bombarders, it was impossible to avoid a feeling of satisfaction whenever a shot told, and I could see by the smoke rising from the fortress that some damage had been done. This feeling was not due to sympathy with one side in the conflict, but to a sort of abstract sentiment of fitness in a shot performing the object of its mission.

Here my instinct is of an entirely opposite character. Every time a shell misses or explodes in the air I experience a feeling of relief; and this, I am afraid, is due not so much to my good wishes for the Danes as to the instinct of self-preservation. Though I am only a lodger, yet the destruction of the house I am dwelling in cannot be a matter of personal indifference. After all, I am one of the people who are being fired at, and the mere reflection that the billet which every ball is said to have may, by some remote possibility, be destined to be found in a portion of my own person, is quite sufficient to give me a prejudice in favour of the failure of the shells whose course I sit and watch.

I have no wish to exaggerate the dangers of my position, and I admit candidly that the risk I am exposed to is probably not greater than any one of my readers is subject to any time he enters a railway carriage. But yet I perceive that the simple ingredient of danger gives a kind of bias to my mind which it is impossible to overcome. I mention this only because I suppose my own state of feeling is a fair sample of the average sentiments entertained by those in the same position as myself. As a rule, I should say that everybody here has grown wonderfully soon acclimatised to the presence of danger.

Those whose ordinary temperament is merry and lively are most depressed and agitated by the bombardment; but the great bulk of the population take the matter with supreme philosophy. Even at its briskest, the fire of the enemy has never been frequent or loud enough to affect ordinary nerves, and our daily life goes on with very little alteration. In spite of the swarms of families who have left the place, the town is still full of children—the Danes have a *spécialité* for large families—and for the little urchins of Sonderborg I suspect this bombardment era is a good time.

There are no lessons, I have no doubt, and everything" must be new and strange for them, So they play about the streets, and run between the soldiers' legs, and never even turn their heads at the sound of the cannon. At night there is very little firing, and the sound is one that you very soon get accustomed to. I know an officer here whose comrades declare that the other night, at the outposts, he was not woke up by two shells which passed through the roof of the room where he was sleeping; and though the officer himself disputes the fact, he admits that he did not think it worth while to get up and see what the noise was about.

The fishermen's wives may be seen in their cottages, in the back parts of the town, knitting and spinning as if the war was hundreds of miles away. The panic which half emptied the town on the commencement of the bombardment has hitherto been confined chiefly to the tradesmen. These shopkeepers have fled first partly because they had more to lose, partly because they had the means of making good their escape.

For my own part, I think that, considering Sonderborg is nominally in a state of siege, the military authorities would have done more wisely to forbid the removals of household furniture, which are going on all day and every day, and which can hardly fail to have a disheartening effect upon the troops.

However, it is contrary to the genius of the Danish people to interfere in any way with personal liberty, even in a time of war, and, moreover, there is an utter disregard here of any sentimental considerations. The great open space before the castle, which the troops have to pass every morning on their way to the front, is filled with carpenters making coffins; and, though the Danes attach extreme importance to a decent and orderly burial, it is scarcely conceivable that the reflection of there being stout deal coffins ready to receive their corpses should reconcile the troops to the prospect of being killed.

Meanwhile the siege itself has not been pushed on with much vigour for the last three days. Every morning between nine and ten the Prussians commence firing from the Broager batteries, continue for an hour or so, and then recommence firing for about the same time towards four or five. The object of this desultory fire is obviously to harass the enemy; but no other end can be served by it. From the

Wemming Bund the Prussians can, if they like, destroy the town of Sonderborg, but they can scarcely silence the Dybbol batteries. Except as a matter of military necessity, it is not likely that they would recklessly destroy the town itself, and at any rate the necessity has not yet arisen.

Meanwhile, it seems certain that the attack is being suspended until the Germans have got their batteries finished on the range of Dybbol village and Avn-Bierg. Their works are being completed rapidly; and today for the first time they have opened fire from a small battery near Avn-Bierg against redoubt No 2 of the Dybbol line. The immediate issue of the contest will depend upon the question how far these new batteries, at a range of some three-quarters of a mile, can silence the Danish guns.

At this distance the Prussian artillery, though far superior to the Danish, will be placed on comparatively equal terms. The Danes hitherto have found it impossible to reply with any effect to the fire of the Prussian batteries, because they were placed out of reach. Now, at close quarters even old smooth-bore cannon may prove as efficacious as modern rifled ones. We shall have, in fact, an artillery duel, and experience alone can decide which is the strongest of the two combatants in this hand-to-hand war fare.

Up to this time the whole force of the enemy's fire has been directed against the left of the Danish line, and especially against battery No. 2, The night has sufficed to repair the day's injury, but it is not certain that this may be the case when the Prussians can fire their guns from about one-third of the distance which lies between Dybbol heights and the Broager batteries. It is also right to remember that the proximity of the Prussian lines renders a sudden attack by storming parties less impossible than it was formerly. It is probable, however, that the enemy will, at any rate, attempt to silence the Danish batteries before they incur the risk of an assault.

The prevailing impression is, that the grand attack will be made on Tuesday next; but I cannot discover that this impression rests on any evidence except the fact that it happens to be the birthday of the King of Prussia. As I have frequently spoken to you of the low estimate which the Danes placed upon the Prussian troops, it is only justice to mention that since the engagement of Thursday last the Danes themselves admit that the Prussian soldiers fought with great courage. The war is a cowardly one, no doubt, on the part of the German Governments, and there is little glory to be won in a campaign where the odds are twenty to one in favour of the invaders. But when it actually comes to fighting regiment against regiment, it is little consolation to the troops engaged to know that if they fall there are plenty to fill their places; and wherever men fight bravely, be their cause what it may, I think credit should be given them.

Meanwhile this slackness in the Prussian fire since the affair of Thursday has raised the spirits of the army, which, perhaps, were unreasonably depressed by the discoveries that the Germans could fight after all, and that the artillery of the enemy was superior to their own. Today a regiment of the Copenhagen Guards has arrived at Sonderborg. A finer body of men, I think, I never saw than these Danish grenadiers. I am not short myself, and should be accounted a tall man in Denmark; but there were scores of these men, not much above their fellows in height, who seemed to tower above me as I passed by them, by a head at least

Our own household brigade, or the Imperial Guard at Paris, are not more splendid specimens of muscular humanity than these Danish foot guards. With their tall bearskin caps they look a race of giants, and have, indeed, that professional military air which is not possessed by the rank and file of the Danish Army. In the death-struggle which is believed to be at hand, the material aid of a few hundred men, more or less, cannot be decisive. It is thousands that are wanted here, not hundreds; but the moral importance of this new reinforcement far exceeds its material value.

The arrival of the guards, whose absence hitherto has been severely commented on, is taken to indicate a resolution on the part of the Danish Government to risk everything on the defence of Alsen; and the army is cheered by the impression that their cause is not despaired of at Copenhagen. For many days I have not seen the troops in such spirits as they were in today. The march of the regiments to the front, in order to relieve those on duty, which usually takes place without notice, was almost a triumphal progress, and the soldiers themselves pressed forward with a briskness and precision of step I have not often observed amongst them. The very scent of battle seems to stir up the somewhat sluggish blood of these Northern nations.

March 22.

Not having a classical dictionary at hand, I cannot say whether the Ides of March are really past; but I know that, metaphorically, they may safely be said to "*have come and gone.*" The sixty-seventh anniversary of the birth of His Majesty Frederick William Louis, King of Prussia, has passed over without becoming memorable in history as the anniversary also of a great German victory. The disgrace of the campaign of 1848-50 has not yet been wiped out in Danish blood; and the island of Alsen still remains disunited from Schleswig. In fact, the long-promised attack on Dybbol is adjourned till further notice; and when the time is to come, if at all, is a problem that we in Sonderborg shall be the last persons in the world to solve. If the firing had ceased altogether, I should be disposed to attach additional faith to the various rumours of diplomatic negotiations for an armistice which are floating about the town.

Unfortunately, it is difficult to reconcile this belief with the fact that the Prussian fire has been more brisk today than it has been since Thursday last, though the real result of the bombardment has been no greater than usual. From day to day it is most difficult to judge of the march of events, or of the progress of the siege. It is only by looking back over an interval of time that you can form any fair impression of the advance that has been made. Since the retreat of the Danes from the Dannewerke, there have been four distinct stages in the invasion of the Duchies.

The four events which mark the intervals between these stages are—the entry into Flensburg, the occupation of Broagerland, the inroad into Jutland, and the capture of Avn-Bierg and Dybbol. The periods between each of these events have been unaccountably long, and, according to the same law, a long interval ought to elapse between the capture of Avn-Bierg and the next decisive step against Dybbol. Each one of these steps appears to have been taken reluctantly, as if it had been delayed as long as possible,; and it is hard to avoid the conclusion that the allied Powers—for causes which I do not profess to divine—are not anxious to push on the war at all costs and sacrifices.

After all, the Germans have done next to nothing hitherto except drive the Danes before them by sheer weight of men and metal. They have overrun the peninsula as far north as Hobroe, if not further still; they have engaged in a few skirmishes of doubtful issue, of which one alone, that of Oversee, can by any pretence be called a battle; and they have fired a few shells without result. This is all that has been yet done. The two strongholds of the Danes, Fredericia and Alsen, remain unassailed, and, as far as any immediate operations are concerned, seem less likely to be taken now than they did six weeks ago. It is just a week since the Prussians opened fire upon the Dybbol heights from the batteries on the Wemming Bund.

If they go on at their present rate, there is no reason why the siege should not last as long as that of Troy. The whole brunt of the enemy's fire has been borne by battery No. 2, which lies near the southern extremity of Dybbol Hill. Why this battery should have been selected is not easily to be understood. There is no question that the left is by nature the weakest portion of the Danish line, and the one most exposed to the fire of an enemy advancing from Broagerland.

But if the object of the Prussians is to silence the batteries on the left flank, and then to force their way along the comparatively low neck of land on which these works stand, why is it that battery No. 1, the one next to the sea, is left comparatively unmolested? If there were any immediate purpose even of silencing the particular battery which is thus selected as a target for the Prussian artillery, how is it that no continuous fire is kept up, but that the enemy contents himself with sending a dozen shots or so in quick succession, and then ceases firing for two or three hours till the Danes have time to repair whatever injury the shells may have occasioned?

As it is, I can fairly say that hitherto the Prussians have made no valid progress towards the avowed object of their attack. We have had an artillery duel, and that is all, though it is doubtful whether the term duel can be fairly applied to a contest where one combatant only fires at rare intervals, and the other never fires at all. Happily, the casualties have so far been few in number.

The somewhat impressive and apathetic character of the Danish soldiers enables them to stand fire with singular coolness; and the risk from shells in the open air is not considerable if the men exposed to them are collected enough to seek at once the shelter of the earthworks. Though the soldiers working on the batteries of the contending armies are within easy range of each other, there has been but little rifle-shooting on either side; and therefore the bombardment has hitherto been a very bloodless one. Still, that this is the case is no merit of the Prussians. Every shell fired may produce the same loss of life as that occasioned by the one which fell into the block-house of battery No. 2. However, if the Prussians wish to do anything more than harass the Danes and cause the death of a few hundred men, they must pursue a different policy from that which they have adopted up to the birthday of their warlike king.

So much for speculation on the aspect of military affairs. Of actual events my budget is singularly barren. Every excitement fades after a time, and even the process of being shelled soon loses its first novelty. We—confining the plural pronoun to those who are mere lookers-on, like myself—feel ourselves personally aggrieved if any long interval passes without a shot being fired. I remember once being in a theatre where the curtain remained down between the acts for an unusually long time. A lad near me in the pit signified his disapprobation by stamping and shouting loudly. An old gentleman on the next bench turned round and asked the malcontent sternly whether he was not aware that the actors were a great deal more anxious to get the play over than he could possibly be himself. "Yes, sir," was the answer; "but then you see they are paid for their evening, and I pay for mine." Now I feel very much in the position of my turbulent acquaintance.

Prussian and Danish soldiers would be most heartily glad to have the battle over; but then, after all, it is their business to fight; and in some form or other they are paid for it. But I am only a spectator, and have a right, therefore, to grumble if things do not go on as rapidly and as smoothly as I was led to expect by the promises of the programme. I am aware that any exhibition of impatience must seem singularly brutal to my friends and entertainers here. The country lady who told George IV. "that the only thing she still wished to see in London was a Royal Coronation," was not guilty of a greater breach of delicate consideration than I should be if I expressed a desire that the bombardment might begin.

Nothing, however, I think, could disturb the good-nature or alter the civility of these kindly Danes. To many persons I am acquainted with here the capture of Alsen by the Germans means not only national humiliation, but personal ruin. In the event of a successful attack, their houses will be burnt down, their prospects in life destroyed, their families in all likelihood driven into exile; yet, from the calmness with which they discuss the subject, you would scarcely suppose that they were more nearly interested in the issue than I am myself; and this outward indifference, though due in part to an almost English sense of dignity and pride, is, I think, chiefly caused by the wonderful easiness of the national temperament.

At this very moment, when the town is being besieged, and when the enemy's outposts are not a mile away, there are German-speaking persons residing in Sonderborg, whose sympathies are known to be rather with the invaders than the invaded. Yet nobody dreams of molesting them. I have no reason whatever to suppose that these persons carry on any communication with the enemy, and I have little doubt the military authorities have reason to know that they do not; but still there is hardly another country in the world where popular feeling in such an hour would tolerate the presence of men whose wishes are in favour of an enemy so bitterly detested.

Much in the same way, I am daily astonished at the extraordinary courtesy with which our countrymen—or, indeed, strangers of any kind—are received. Correspondents like myself have some small return to offer for the kindness shown us; moreover, it is conceivable that the Danes may be gratified by the English interest in their concerns exhibited by the mere fact of our presence.

But, in addition to regular correspondents, we have had of late batches of English lookers-on—gentlemen estimable in private life, but whom not even a foreigner could suppose to have any political influence or power; yet these stray strangers, sometimes unprovided with any recommendation except their English looks and dress, are furnished with passes, billeted—if they have courage enough to ask for the favour—about the town, and given every facility which they could possibly desire. They wander about the works at unseasonable hours, astonish the natives with elaborate costumes after the fashion of the Alpine Club, ask unintelligible questions of everybody they meet, perplex the mind of sentries, and drive waiters to distraction; and yet they are treated as civilly as if they were bearers of the intelligence that England was coming to the aid of Denmark in a week.

March 23.

Yesterday, after all, was not destined to pass over without a sensation. It was getting dusk, when a rumour spread that the King of Denmark had arrived at Hörup harbour, the little port where all vessels to Sonderborg are now obliged to cast anchor. The royal visit was utterly unexpected, so much so that even the military and civil authorities of the town had no news of it until an hour beforehand. A number of open "chars-à-banc" were despatched in hot haste, and, about eight o'clock, as I happened to be strolling up the High Street, I came upon the royal procession. Except that the cars were filled with officers, I should have taken the "cortége" for a party of Alsen farmers coming into the town.

Of show, or military escort, there was absolutely nothing. It was a lovely moonlight night, though the air was as cold as a hard, clear frost could make it, and the occupants of the royal carriages looked tired and chilled. The hind seat of the first of the cars was occupied by the king and General Gerlach, while the front seat was filled by a peasant, who acted as driver, and a gigantic chasseur, with a cocked hat and plume, whom most of the few spectators about the streets took, I fancy, for the sovereign. No enthusiasm of any kind was displayed, and not a cheer could be heard; but then hardly anybody was aware of the king's coming, and his face is not yet well enough known in those parts to insure his immediate recognition.

The royal party drove through the town, almost without stopping, and passed over the pontoon bridge up to Dybbol. There the king was shown over the works, and visited those batteries which have suffered most severely. According to a report current here, a shell fell during the drive m unpleasant proximity to His Majesty. I have no reason to be sceptical about this story, except that I have invariably observed that, whenever crowned personages go anywhere near the scene of action, some remarkable incident of this kind is certain to occur for their especial benefit. Granted the fact, however, I am perfectly willing to endorse the truth of the accompanying report; that the king was delighted at the occurrence. Not even the bitterest political opponents of Christian IX. question his personal bravery.

And, if the gallant equerry—whose name we used to laugh so much about in London, when we read in the *Court Journal* during the period of the Prince of Wales's marriage that his Royal Highness Prince Christian was attended by Lieutenant Funck—was in the party, I have no doubt that he also vindicated the truth of the saying, "What's in a name?" After visiting the works the king and his suite returned to Hörup-Haf, where they slept on board the royal yacht.

This morning His Majesty went over to Augustenburg to see the hospitals, and has been in Sonderborg this afternoon paying visits to the principal personages of the town. I was seated at the dinner-table of my host, in company with a number of officers who are sheltered in the same hospitable mansion as myself, when a knock was heard at the door, and the king walked in unannounced, accompanied by a single equerry. We all rose in a hurry, and His Majesty, after bowing very courteously in return for our salutations, was shown by our host into the only vacant room in the house; from which the king made his exit, after a short conversation, by passing through an adjoining bedroom, encumbered with trunks and packages, over which he climbed laughingly. He looked a good deal older and more careworn than he appeared, according to my recollection, when his face was familiar to all London sightseers. But he had still that kindly good-natured smile which redeems a face in itself somewhat void of expression.

A crowd had collected round the doors, and gave His Majesty a hearty cheer on his departure. It is an easy thing, doubtless, for a sovereign to create a favourable impression if he seeks to do so; but still it is only fair to say that everybody who comes across the path of Christian IX. gives but one report as to the attractiveness of his manner. The royal visit is not likely to be a long one; and it is expected the king will take his departure tonight.

This glimpse of royalty is not, however, the sensation to which I alluded at the head of this letter—at least, not directly so. The one absorbing military question of the moment is whether the Germans are going to attack Dybbol; the corresponding one amongst civilians is whether the enemy will bombard Sonderborg. All the crowned heads in Europe might visit us without exciting much attention, unless their coming influenced the bearing of these two questions.

Shells are no respecters of persons; and, with the sound of cannon all day long dinning in our ears, we are not very curious about who comes or goes here, however exalted may be his rank. Our great "sensation" was a report, founded on the king's coming, that an armistice had been agreed to. The advocates of this hypothesis had a great deal to say for themselves. Why the king should have come thus unexpectedly, at an hour's notice, on the very day the grand onslaught of the enemy had been looked for, is a problem to which nobody has been able to find the clue.

The papers which arrived by last night's mail brought us telegrams from London and Vienna, announcing that an armistice was considered increasingly probable. Moreover, strange to say, at about two o'clock yesterday the enemy's fire ceased suddenly, and till ten this morning we had a complete respite, with the exception of the one shell which fell so near the royal carriage, the noise of whose explosion happened not to reach the town. When it was discovered in the morning that sailing vessels had actually re-entered the port of Sonderborg, which had been deserted since the beginning of the bombardment, it seemed certain that something must have occurred to suspend operations; and I was beginning to look forward confidently to a visit to Copenhagen, and the almost forgotten luxury of clean linen, when our dreams of peace were shaken by a vigorous recommencement of the bombardment from the Wemming Bund batteries. All day, up to the hour at which I write, the fire has continued with unexampled briskness, and with much shorter intervals of quiet than we have hitherto been accustomed to.

The night before last two deserters came into our lines from the Prussian camp. They complained bitterly of the hardness of their fare, and of the sufferings they had had to undergo, and said that the Schleswig peasants had shown no sympathy whatever for their German liberators. The men were both half drunk, and the only reason they assigned for their desertion was a reluctance to kill their fellowmen. One of them hiccupped out his view of the question with a comic gravity in words which I give as nearly as they will bear translation.

I was born, you know, without Schleswig-Holstein; I have lived without Schleswig-Holstein; and may the d—— take me if I see why I should die for Schleswig-Holstein.

Whether from ignorance, or from some faint remnant of honour, these two scampish philosophers professed themselves unable to give any information about the movements or numbers of the Prussian Army. "Nobody ever tells us poor devils anything," was the answer they gave to every question.

The Danish Government, with its usual frankness, has just published a statement of the Danish losses since the bombardment commenced. On the seventeenth day, when the Prussians captured Avn-Bierg, the loss was 300; while the total in killed, wounded, and missing, during the last week, has been double that number. The Prussian statement that on Thursday they did not lose 100 is received here with great incredulity, as several of the Danish shells were seen to fall in the middle of dense columns of men.

March 24.

The war, I am glad to say, is assuming a less sanguinary character than it bore at the first outset. The soldiers, on either side, have got tired of killing for killing's sake, and the rifle duels, which used to take place at every change of outposts, occur no longer. The lines of the two armies are now so close that the sentries can exchange words; and though the German soldiers speak no Danish, yet almost all the Danes can speak a few words of German. Friendly salutations are exchanged, and sometimes, I fancy, when officers are out of the way, the brandy flasks are passed to and fro from Dane to German.

In consequence a visit to the outposts is not now attended with any especial danger, so I availed myself of a temporary respite in the bombardment this morning to go round the extreme lines occupied by the Danish Army in the Sundeved. The area of King Christian's possessions on the mainland of Schleswig is now reduced to miserably small dimensions; and if the ground were clear and the path straight, a fast walker might easily walk all round this portion of his dominions in an hour. As I have often mentioned to you before, the position of Dybbol is nothing but a sugar-loaf sort of hill surrounded on three sides by the sea. The area of the base can be little above a square mile, and the broadest side of the irregular quadrilateral on which it stands—that stretching at the foot, from the Als Sund to the Wemming Bund—is about a mile and one-third in length.

I started from Battery No. 10, which stands close to the edge of the Sund; and five minutes' walk along the road to Aapenraa took me to the furthest sentry post on the Danish side. From there I had to turn to the left, and skirt the foot of the hill, directly under the Danish batteries, keeping always three or four hundred yards away from the hill. Every fifty yards or so along this line there was a rifle-pit, occupied by Danish troops. Two sentries at each were leaning upon the high bank of earth raised as a breastwork, with their rifles pointed across the mound, ready to fire at once in the event of an alarm.

In the trench at the foot of the breastwork, out of which the earth had been dug, some ten soldiers lay sleeping or smoking. Behind every hedge and under every available slope of the ground troops were stationed; and the whole country was dotted over with these little knots of soldiers, looking for all the world as if they had come out for a day's picnic. The Prussian line of sentries is not exactly parallel to the Danish. At the two extremities of the Danish cordon the Prussian outposts are full half a mile away; but near the high-road, which, as I have before stated, bisects Dybbol-hill, the Germans are so close at hand that I could distinguish their uniforms.

As far as I could gather with my field-glass, the enemy's advance posts are stationed along a line not far short of three miles in length. Commencing at Sand-Bierg, on the Prussian left, then passing through Rageböl and Dybbol villages, and terminating beyond Avn-Bierg on the Wemming-Bund, our road was a very broken one, as we had to make our way across hedges and ditches, and over the ruins of farmyards and gardens, and were naturally anxious to keep some prominent object between ourselves and the enemy's sentries, in case they should be tempted, by the unusual appearance of any one in civilian's dress at the outposts, to do us the honour of sending a bullet whizzing past our ears.

There were traces enough of the recent skirmishes in the ground over which we trod, and, if I had chosen, I might have carried away a boxful of broken bits of shells and bullets, and splinters. However, the only memorable trophy that I saw was a shell which had not exploded, and which was liable to the fatal objection that it might go off without a moment's notice. We had nearly accomplished our journey when, as we approached the most exposed part of our walk, the enemy began to fire at the batteries, towering above our heads. Unless for some unaccountable reason they had chosen to fire at the foot instead of at the crest of Dybbol-hill, we were in perfect safety, and we had the satisfaction of seeing the shells flying over our heads, and throwing up a perfect shower of dirt whenever they hit the earth-works of the Danish batteries.

Nothing would satisfy two young Englishmen in our party but rushing incontinently up the exposed side of the hill, in order to get inside the battery, which was then being shelled. I am certainly older than my friends, and, I trust, in this instance wiser; and, whatever form of death may be reserved for me, I never intend to allow my acquaintance the chance of saying, after I am dead, that I was a fool for getting killed. So I quietly gave the battery in question a wide berth, and made my way back to the camp under shelter of a friendly hill.

Going home, I met the one victim of the twenty shells or so I had just seen fired with unusual accuracy at the battery which the Prussians have tried so long in vain to silence. A poor Danish soldier had been wounded by the splinters of a plank roofing struck down by one of these shells, and was being brought home just as I reached the camp. Four of his comrades were carrying him on one of the army stretchers; and every five steps they had to stop, in answer to his prayers. The man was dying.

I have seen wounded men and hospitals enough, but of all battle sights the transport of the wounded from the front always seems to me the saddest. A quarter of an hour ago, this man, I could not help thinking, was full of life and strength, and now he was stricken down to die in agony. If he had fallen thus for any object, in obedience to any military necessity, his fate would not have seemed to me so cruel; but he had been sacrificed solely to a wanton and purposeless act of destruction. All things, I know, are fair in war, and if the Germans believe that they can facilitate the capture of Alsen by laying the town of Sonderborg in ashes, and shelling every hut beneath which the Danes can find shelter or refuge, they are justified in so doing according to all ordinary rules of hostility; but I cannot see that this dropping fire upon the works of Dybbol, this intermittent discharge of shells without aim or purpose, can even be supposed to serve any practical purpose.

It is incredible the Germans should be ignorant of the fact that their fire has hitherto done no damage to the security of the Dybbol position: it is absolutely impossible they should suppose that earthworks like those of the Danish entrenchments should ever be seriously affected by an irregular cannonade, interrupted daily for hours together, during which the Danes have ample time allowed them to repair any damage that their fortifications may suffer. The one sole purpose that can be served by the sort of warfare the Germans are now carrying on is to sacrifice the lives of a few hundred brave men uselessly and wilfully. Conducted as it has been for the last week, the war is a cruel and cowardly one. At a safe distance, out of reach of the Danish artillery, the Prussians amuse themselves by firing off shells against the Dybbol works, when the humour takes them. If they like to commence a regular attack, well and good; but, in the name of humanity, there should be a stop to this desultory warfare.

March 26.

Yesterday, as I told you, was one of the quietest days we have had since the bombardment commenced. The night which followed was still with an almost deathlike stillness; the sky was overcast, with low, hazy clouds, thick enough to shut out the light of the moon. Altogether, if ever there was a night which promised a respite from shells, a *relâche* of the pyrotechnic performance, it was that of yesterday. On this ground, I admit frankly, I resolved to avail myself of an invitation often given me by an engineer officer of my acquaintance to visit the batteries by night. I am not a glutton after glory; I am not, to use a Yankee colloquialism, "death" upon danger.

If I can see what I want to see, without coming unpleasantly near to shells or musket-shot, I am heartily contented. The civilian volunteers, who come here daily as aspirants for commissions in the army, are sent out at once to the front, to show how they can stand fire. The rule is an excellent one, and has my hearty approbation, but I am not an aspirant after a commission in this or any other army in the world. It is no part of an amateur's duty to get killed or wounded, and I think that any amateur who suffered such a fate would richly deserve the verdict of "Serve him right," that the Duke of Wellington is said to have passed on the only paymaster in the British army who ever got killed in action.

I make this statement in order to vindicate my character from any imputation of inconsistency with my professions to which the narrative of last night's adventures might expose me. In order to see the camp and the works by night—a sight which I felt sure was worth seeing—I chose the safest occasion that I could find; and if my path and the orbit of a shell happened to intersect each other, it was the shell, I can truly say, which sought me, not I who sought the shell. It was after ten when I left Sonderborg on my expedition.

The streets were already empty, the houses were closed, and well-nigh everybody was in bed and asleep. The dark waters of the Als Sund stretched out in the dim half-light like an inky lake; and the reflection of the lamps along the quay only served to make the blackness of the unlit expanse deeper by the contrast. The sentinel at the entrance to the bridge tried in vain to read our cards by the light of a flickering lantern, and finally, giving up the job as hopeless, allowed us to pass with a feeble protest.

So we proceeded across the long bridge of boats, beneath which the water rippled with a strange weird sound, and, climbing up the Dybbol hill, fell in with a Danish lad-soldier, toiling to the front beneath a heavy knapsack, who insisted upon accompanying us, not because he had any suspicion of our intentions, but because he felt lonely and wanted company. He was a boy almost in years, and complained greatly of the hardness of his life. For days, he said, he had not changed his clothes; night after night he was in the trenches, till five or six o'clock; then he had a long trudge home, and by nine he had to be upon parade.

And yet there was nothing of discontent about his complaints. It was all, he seemed to think, in the day's work. The inference that because there was something wrong, therefore there was somebody to blame, was one which apparently he had never thought of drawing. Whatever I have seen of discontent in the Danish Army is thus always of a passive, not of an active, kind. Over-worked, out-numbered, and ill-sheltered, these Danish troops still plod on manfully at their daily work, without much, indeed, of spirit, but with absolutely no thought of giving in. Our volunteer companion found it hard work, laden as he was, to keep up with our quick step; and so we soon left him behind in the darkness, and saw him no more.

There was no need of any escort, when we had once passed the bridge, or, indeed, much necessity for any permission. I am now pretty well known by sight throughout the camp, and vigilance is not the strong point of the Danish Army. If you walk boldly past a sentry, anywhere or at any time, the chances are that he will hesitate about stopping you. Even in the dark night our party was allowed to pass on unchallenged. No password is given out, and when a soldier has satisfied himself that the passer-by is not a person he ought to salute, he feels, I fancy, that he has done his duty. Sentry after sentry, wrapped up in his dark cloak, and looking in the dusk like a ghostly shadow, peered after us curiously as we went by, listened to the strange accents of our foreign tongue, and then walked back to his post, wrapping his cloak around him with renewed energy.

Through the camp itself we made our way unnoticed. Not a sound was to be heard; the white tents and the long deal-plank sheds—where the soldiers lay trussed, as it were, together in the hay—stood out against the dark sky distinct and clear. Everything was as quiet as if the same fate had fallen upon the Danish camp as that which befell the one told of in the Bible, where, when the enemies of Israel rose up in the morning, they were "all dead men." Then we groped our way across fields and ditches over the broken upland lying between the camp and the batteries.

Though I fancied I knew by this time every slope of the ground, yet it was hard work to find the path in this labyrinth of forts and earthworks. It was only by steering so as to keep the Dybbol windmill on my right, and the calm dark waters of the Wemming Bund on my left, that I could make out whereabouts we were wandering. The line of the Broager shore, on which stand the Prussian batteries, lay like a black cloud on the horizon, and not even the keenest eye could have distinguished the spot where their guns were placed. Along our path we came on all sorts of strange, shadow-like groups.

Sometimes we stumbled over a detachment of soldiers sleeping in the straw at the roadside, with their arms stacked beside them ready to advance at once, if the word of alarm were given. That any body of men could produce a sound by snoring in unison, so closely resembling the croak, croak of a chorus of Italian frogs, was a discovery I made then and there. Presently a relief party, with spades and pickaxes across their shoulders, instead of muskets, trudged slowly past us; next we were led out of our way by the smouldering embers of a camp fire, which every now and then flickered up with a dying flame, and threw a momentary light on the strange uncanny scene.

A train of empty waggons, which had brought earth to the front, flitted past us; the ground over which we trod had been ploughed into great holes and furrows by the shower of shells which had fallen on it days before. Gangs of soldiers were working silently at trenches and breastworks, sturdily throwing up the clods, scarcely allowed to speak for fear of disturbing the attention of the sentries who stood motionless beside them, watching for the flash which foretells the coming of a shell; and as we went by one of these trenches the alarm was given, the workmen scattered out of sight behind mounds and hedges like rabbits running into a warren, and the field seemed in a moment tenantless; but the alarm proved groundless, the men went back to their work, and all remained still and tranquil along the Prussian line.

Battery No. 2, the one which has suffered most severely from the bombardment, was the destination to which we were bound; but nobody we met knew its whereabouts. The common soldiers in the Danish Army know, if possible, even less than English troops of anything connected with the war in which they are not actually concerned; and I might as well have asked for the letters of the Hebrew alphabet as for the number of the different batteries.

The proportion of officers is so small in the Danish forces, that laree patrols and working parties are frequently under the orders of a corporal; and, at any rate, I could find nobody to show me the way. However, by trying battery after battery, in all of which, let me say, our party was received with the utmost courtesy, and the most unbounded confidence, I stumbled at last on the object of my search after an hour's wandering.

It is a strange spectacle, a battery by night. You cross a deep trench, surmounted with palisades; go through a narrow stockaded entrance, and find yourselves in an enclosure, more like a sawyer's sand-pit, magnified twenty-fold, than any other object I can call to mind. Great banks of sloping earth rise up on every side of you; the guns are pointed, with the gunners standing by them; at each embrasure the watchmen are stationed on the look-out for shells; groups of men are working hastily, throwing up fresh piles of earth over the rent and battered banks of the powder-magazines and blockhouses. On the ground there is a quaint confusion of broken planks, cannon-balls, powder-bags, spades, and muskets, everything being doubtless in its place for those who know where to look, though to a stranger the scene seems one of chaotic disorder.

Beneath the shelter of the earth-banks scores of soldiers lay sleeping, curled up in their cloaks, or covered over with empty bags. No talking was allowed, and the men who were at work scarcely made more noise than those who slept. Of the injuries the battery had received in that day's fire it would not be proper for me to speak; it is enough to say that, whatever they were, they were being promptly and completely repaired. We had walked all round the forts, had been told the calibre of all the cannon, and had had the damage caused by that day's shelling pointed out to us, and were about to leave, waiting to light our cigars till we had got clear of the powder magazine; when suddenly it seemed as if an electric thrill ran through everybody, and we heard the shrill cry, "Deck! Deck."

In a moment there was a stampede for safety. There was no time for courtesy or precedence. Hurry scurry, we all flew to the shelter of the sloping banks. Some of us rolled over on the ground, some jumped on the sleeping men, who woke up, fancying they had been struck by a shell; but, one way or another, on all-fours, or flat upon the ground, the whole party got under cover. Ten seconds, I am told, is the calculated time between the departure of a shell from Broagerland and its arrival at Dybbol. I know if this be the case that a vast amount of mental action can be crowded into a particularly short period. I had first to realise that a shell was coming; then, as I had got my back the wrong way, to turn round and look which side of the fort I ought to go to; then to see that the path was clear; and finally to crouch under the slope of the bank, squeezing as close into it as the resistance of matter would allow; and yet, after this, I know I had time to think the shell was very long in coming—to recollect a similar incident which had occurred to me at the siege of Gaeta, when a clergyman, who happened to be in my company, opened his umbrella with the view of breaking the force of the missile—and to speculate on the consideration, if two hundred and thirty shells had been fired the day before without hurting anybody, what were the chances against this particular shell hitting my individual self.

The calculation was proceeding in a decidedly unsatisfactory manner, when I caught the strange, cutting whirr of the shell, as it came flying towards us. I know it appeared to take an unusually protracted time in getting near. Then the whirr grew louder and louder, close above our heads. I glanced involuntarily upwards, and saw the shell strike the roof of the block-house some dozen feet beyond our shelter; then there was a flash, followed by a dull crash, as it struck and burst. A shower of earth was thrown up into the sky, and, fell down over our heads and shoulders. All was over; after a moment's pause the soldiers got up, shook the dirt off their clothes, and set to work stacking up the earth which the shell had scattered down.

Thus ended my experience of shelling, or rather of being shelled in a battery. It was one I was not sorry to have made, but which I felt no inclination to repeat. As to any exhibition of personal courage or the contrary, I saw scarce any occasion or opportunity for it. When once you hear the shell coming, there is nothing more to be done, unless you are goose enough to shriek or scream. You can hardly show that you are afraid; unless you are ass enough to jump up on the batteries and wave your cap, you will find it as hard to show that you are not afraid. Practically, if you keep your eyes about you, and have nothing to hinder you from seeking shelter at once, the risk, I take it, is very small, and one that no reasonable man would object to rim if he had any special object in so doing.

In spite, however, of all the calculations in the world, the sensation of hearing a shell whining towards you is not pleasant to my fancy. The Prussians, so I learnt from the officer who kindly showed me over the works, have been lately in the habit of throwing a shell regularly every two or three hours during the night, and the one with which we were favoured was the regular midnight allowance. These nocturnal projectiles are always aimed at the interior of the batteries; and if that in question was a fair sample, they are directed with remarkable precision. So we strolled homeward through the sleeping camp, and our party seemed to me to talk a good deal more cheerfully when the crest of Dybbol Hill lay between us and the Prussian batteries. Not a soul was stirring, and the sound of our steps and voices, as we tramped through the deserted streets, must, I fear, have disturbed the slumbers of many a burgher of Sonderborg.

March 27.

It is worthwhile to say something about the very important question what the Danes have done, or have not done, hitherto—what sacrifices and what efforts the nation is making or prepared to make in behalf of its national independence and the integrity of the monarchy. Let me remark in starting, that an immense deal of twaddle is always talked about the exertions that nations can make in modern days, in defence of their country. In semi-barbarous times, when every man was more or less a soldier, and when people hung much more loosely than they do now to their homes or occupations, it was possible for a *levée en masse* of a population to occur in fact, as well as in fiction.

Such a thing is not possible with the complicated wants of modern civilization; and, even in the most critical moments, all a nation can do is to spare an unusual proportion of her citizens and her treasure for the purposes of war. Men must be left for agriculture, railroads, shipping, commerce, and all the hundred demands of civilized society. Now, according to any reasonable calculation, Denmark has made a great if not an overwhelming effort. By the last published census the population of Denmark proper was one million six hundred thousand in round numbers, and that of the Duchies nearly one million. In a population of this amount the number of men capable of bearing arms would certainly not be over four hundred thousand.

Now the total of the Danish Army is estimated at some 50,000; and though I believe there has never been in the field anything like that amount by 10,000 at the very least, yet, when you make allowance for the immense number of non-effectives, of men scattered about in the little island garrisons, of soldiers on leave and in the hospitals, I think it possible that 50,000 men, or one out of every eight capable of bearing arms, has been taken from his ordinary pursuits to serve in the army; and in estimating the magnitude of this effort, it should be remembered that, for all military purposes, Lauenburg, Holstein, Schleswig, and the greater part of Jutland, are detached for the moment from Denmark.

The Danish forces, therefore, have to be recruited from a population of little more than one million; so that the ratio of men in arms to men capable of bearing arms in the actual dominions of King Christian is close upon one to five. Already great difficulties are found in getting labour to till the fields, and a prolonged continuance of the present effort would soon exhaust the country. If the common calculation is correct, the expense of this army is not less than 50,000 specie-dollars, or £11,200 a day—a sum which has now to be raised exclusively by the insular possessions of the monarchy. In ordinary times the total receipts for Denmark proper, including Jutland, were about four millions of specie-dollars, or £900,000 *per annum;* and therefore, at the present rate, the yearly expenditure of the country has been increased, speaking roughly, from one to five millions—a proportion as great, relatively to the resources of the country, as if our annual budget were raised from seventy to three hundred and seventy-five millions.

As far, therefore, as the State is concerned, I do not think any impartial person could expect Denmark to have done more than she has hitherto done. Every effort of the government has been supported by the voice of the country; and, with the exception of a small section of the party called the Friends of the Peasants, there is no political faction which is even supposed to favour pacific views. On the other hand, I do not see much evidence of intense individual enthusiasm, as distinguished from what may be called official and professional patriotism. It is very hard to judge of a foreign nation, especially of one which is eminently undemonstrative in its character.

I do not think, however, that the popular excitement is anything like that which would spring up in England in case Ireland were occupied by a foreign enemy, or even like that which I saw in America at the commencement of the Secession War. The existence of a general conscription paralyses the power of volunteering; but still it is strange to me how little there is of any individual action. Take this town for instance, whose defence is a point of national honour as well as strategical importance. There are hundreds of able-bodied young men about the shops and farmhouses, yet the very idea of a volunteer guard has never been entertained.

It may be said with some truth that Alsen is more or less impregnated with a German element; but even in the island towns which I have visited, where the population is wholly and exclusively Danish, there is no ardent enthusiasm outwardly visible about the campaign. Let me not be misunderstood as saying that the war is not popular in Denmark. All I mean to assert is, that I do not believe there yet exists in Denmark such a state of feeling as would make man, woman, and child ready for any sacrifice sooner than submit to the dismemberment of the country. As far as we can learn, it is only in the north of Jutland that the enemy has found his progress thwarted by the bitter personal animosity of the population.

If Fünen or Zealand were to be invaded, this, I have no doubt, would be the case also, only to a far stronger degree; but, so long as the war is confined to the southern peninsula, I think the resistance the Germans will meet—and have met—is that of a nation fighting gallantly, most gallantly, for its honour, not of a people struggling desperately for its very existence. So, in the same way, I feel confident that the Danish troops will fight on dauntlessly in defence of Alsen or Fredericia as long as there is any reasonable hope of holding their ground, but I question their fighting on with, the recklessness of despair when all hope seems gone.

The causes of such a condition of the public mind are intelligible enough. The sense of their own weakness operates very powerfully upon the Danes. They know only too well that, if Germany hold firm in her purpose, and the Western Powers continue firm to their want of purpose, the ultimate issue of the contest is beyond a doubt. Denmark knows that her only real chance of escape from her foes lies in some Continental complication, or some foreign aid. Men of education and cool brain may see that the possibility of such an occurrence has not disappeared, but the masses of the nation are growing hopeless by long waiting. The constant sickening expectation of some sudden turn of fortune is enough to wear out in some measure the ardour of the boldest of nations, and even the knowledge that all hope must be abandoned would prove less dispiriting than this state of prolonged suspense.

Moreover, Denmark labours under the fatal disadvantage, in a foreign war, of not being a homogeneous nation. Leaving her differences of race and language out of the question, her geographical position is alone sufficient to create a divergence of interests between the various members of her disjointed dominions. An universal dislike of foreign domination is the one common feeling actuating all parts of the Danish monarchy; but, otherwise, I should question any one of her provinces having exactly the same sentiments with regard to the war. A country made up of islands and peninsulas has not one patent and uniform national unity like that which pervades France and England.

The Danes of Alsen, though bitterly hostile to the Germans, wish to share the fortunes of the mainland, whatever they may be. "I am not only a Dane," a gentleman residing here, who hates the very name of a German, said to me the other day; "I am a Danish Schleswiger, and am bound to look to the interests of Schleswig as well as those of Denmark." So also Zealand, which lies close to Sweden, would probably be much more in favour of a Scandinavian union than Fünen, which lies scores of miles away from the Swedish coast.

Fünen itself must feel that the possession of Fredericia by a foreign Power would be so disastrous to its safety and independence, that the retention of Jutland by the Danes would be cheaply purchased by the loss, if it must be, of Schleswig and Alsen. Jutland, again, has a much closer personal interest in keeping the peninsula under one government with herself than the Danish islands can possibly have. And so on. I am not saying for one moment that in each of the different provinces there exists a party with a distinct policy. I wish alone to show that the existence of these individual and contradictory interests necessarily impairs the force of Denmark in carrying on hostilities.

March 28.

At last the war has begun in earnest. What causes may have decided the Prussians to commit themselves finally to the task of capturing the works of Dybbol, it is useless now to consider. Speculations have given place to fact; and the sword is to cut the knot which diplomacy, hitherto, has failed to disentangle. *Alea jacta est*—the lot has been thrown for war; and now there is no alternative open for the Germans except to enter Alsen as conquerors, or to retire from before Dybbol baffled and defeated. To a spectator this change from the monotony of a wearisome, purposeless bombardment to the brisk and rapid action of battle must needs be most welcome.

And it is with sincere and heartfelt pleasure I have now to record the fact that the first onslaught of the besiegers has resulted in a decided victory for Denmark. Your opinions about the abstract rights or wrongs of this complicated struggle may be what you like; your views of the expediency of continuing the war may differ from those current amongst the Danes; but I defy any man with blood in his heart, or living, as I do, amongst this kindly, gallant people, not to wish them God-speed in their death-struggle against overwhelming numbers—not to be glad with their triumph and sad with their disasters.

It was raining hard when I went to bed last night. The firing throughout the afternoon and evening had been unusually slack. I had heard, indeed, on my usual walk about the camp, that an attack was expected in the night; but my informant himself told me he had no faith in the report, which he had heard so many scores of times, and always in vain. About half-past three this morning I was woke up by the noise of heavy firing. The sound, however, has become so familiar to my ears, that I paid little attention to it, and lay dozing in my bed, speculating when the noise would cease.

Gradually it struck me that the sound was not that to which I was accustomed. It seemed to me in my half-awake condition that the army-undertakers, who pursue their calling on the open space before my windows, had begun their dismal work earlier than usual, and were driving nails into the deal coffins with unusual energy. All of a sudden the truth dawned upon me that what I heard was the rattle of musketry. In a moment I was wide awake and at my window.

There was short time for dressing, not to mention washing; but before I had hurried on my clothes, I heard the bugles sounding the shrill melancholy alarm-note through the town. Every door in the house appeared to slam at once, and I immediately heard the heavy tramp of troops moving down the street.

Meanwhile the noise of the bombardment grew louder and louder, and whenever there was a momentary pause, the quick, sharp ringing of the rifle-shot was borne on by the wind, like a treble accompaniment to a deep-bass symphony. Outside the house the spectacle offered was not one to be easily forgotten. The rain had been succeeded by a hard, clear frost; the moonlight shone placidly over the bay and the sleeping town, throwing the dark side of Dybbol Hill into deeper relief by the contrast between the silvery waters and the dull, dead earth. In the far east a pale white streak showed that the daylight was at hand. The Wemming Bund shores and the heights of Dybbol were enveloped in grey clouds of floating, shifting smoke. Soldiers were pouring out of every street and doorway. In front of every house facing the sea groups of people were collected, scanning eagerly the direction of the fire.

Dark masses of infantry were marching across the bridge, and winding their way slowly up the steep hill-side. Out towards Hörup harbour the iron-clad *Rolf Krake* could be seen getting up her steam and drifting, almost imperceptibly, towards the Schleswig shore.

The Wemming Bund batteries were silent: it was clear that the Prussians were moving up the hill, and that their guns had ceased fire for fear of mowing down the advancing columns. It was an anxious moment, I suspect, even for those who felt most confident of the power of the besieged to hold good their ground. All eyes were turned wistfully toward the crest of the hill, with a dread that a dark close line might be seen rising slowly above the brow of the heights, whose outline stood out clear against the blue, starry sky, pressing the Danish troops before them by overwhelming numbers. But still the fire of the Dybbol batteries kept on shaking the earth on which we stood, and deafening us with a jarring din which overpowered the sound of musketry, and rendered the voices of the bystanders scarcely audible.

Amidst the hurry and excitement, however, there was no confusion or disorder visible. Every regiment and every man knew his place, and the Danish troops marched forward stolidly, with a grim, stern look about their countenances, and no sound of any kind issuing from their tight-closed lips.

As soon as the night began to break I made my way through the town, and passed the bridge in company with a civilian attached to the army, who was a spectator like myself The long steep road I have so often described was covered with detachments of troops trudging up to the front. The camp was under arms; every battery and earth-work was manned; the cavalry was drawn up on the open "plateau" above the bridge, waiting silently for the order to advance. Under cover of the hill-slopes, batteries of field artillery were stationed, with the horses ready harnessed and mounted. Already waggons filled with straw were hurrying up to fetch back the wounded.

If the Prussians were to succeed in carrying the heights by storm, it was evident that a bloody resistance awaited them on this side the hill; but still the Danish batteries kept pouring forth showers of shells in ceaseless succession, and we could catch the rapid volleys of musketry, coming quicker and quicker from our side, in answer to the advancing fire of the enemy. So the minutes passed on like hours in the fullness of their excitement. As daybreak grew nearer the air became cold and chill, and a grey fog of mist and smoke spread across the western sky.

About five the fire grew slack for a time, and we thought that the attack was driven back, but no shell was fired from the Wemming Bund batteries; and till their fire opened, the retreat of the enemy could not be considered certain. The commander-in-chief, surround-ed by his staff, had taken up his position a few hundred yards below the windmill which stands upon the summit of Dybbol Hill. I could see, by the faces of the officers, that things, so far, were going well, and General Gerlach himself looked as bright and active as though the years which he could number were seventeen instead of seventy. I ad-vanced along the *chaussée* until the sound of spent rifle-balls dropping over my head told me that I had come close enough to the scene of action; and then walked slowly down the hill.

As I reached the bridge the fire broke forth again, in renewed and, if possible, increased fury. The whistling of shells, the crack of rifles, and the boom of cannon followed each other rapidly. The enemy was returning to the charge, making one more attempt to carry the heights by storm. In case the attempt should prove successful, or the result ap-pear even doubtful, I knew that the Danish reserves would be pushed up at once; so I took my station on one of the Sonderborg batteries, which commands a perfect view of the whole eastern hillside.

The day had now broken, and the sun was rising slowly behind the isle of Alsen. Suddenly a faint pink flush spread over the hill of Dybbol, and then the pink turned to rose-colour, and the rose-colour to red. In the dread solemnity of the hour the thought seemed strangely incongruous; but no one used to English theatres could have looked, I think, upon the spectacle without likening it mentally to the transformation scene in a Christmas pantomime, when the gorgeous glow of colour is poured upon the stage, and the Realms of Bliss open out to the wondering gaze amidst a halo of golden light. Illumined by the rays of the rising sun, the slopes of Dybbol were before us, as clear as if they were but a hundred yards away. The thick serried ranks of soldiers, the scattered sentinels, the snow-white tents, the yellow barrack-sheds, the bare brown fallow fields, were brought forth distinctly to view.

Beyond the hill there was a background of smoke from the villages, which the Danish shells had set on fire, tinged with the rich sunlight; and along the crest of the hill, where the battle was raging fiercely, the long straggling hedge of bayonets flashed merrily, as the sunbeams struck upon it; and, if it had not been for the ceaseless, deafening cannonade, one would have doubted whether a spectacle so exquisite could be one of bloodshed and death. The colour died away as rapidly as it sprang up, and the sun itself soon became obscured by the dull snow-laden clouds which the wind was bearing rapidly from the west.

It was now half-past six, and the battle still raged with little apparent abatement. Then I heard a cry raised by soldiers standing near me that the *Rolf Krake* was going into action. Slowly the unwieldy barge-like hull disappeared behind the headland of Dybbol Hill. We could hear the loud crash of her heavy guns, and then the batteries of the Wemming Bund opened fire, not, indeed, at the forts of Dybbol, beneath whose walls the Prussian columns were massed together, but at the gallant iron-clad. There was a long pause—so at least it seemed to us, waiting there—and then at length the *Rolf Krake* appeared from behind the headland, steaming fearlessly beneath the range of Prussian batteries which lines the southern bluffs, of the Wemming Bund bay.

Slowly she moved on, amidst a very hailstorm of shells from the cliffs above her. They splashed on every side of her, like giant porpoises playing around her keel. As the shots touched the water, fountains of spray and foam leapt up into the air, sometimes enveloping the vessel in a watery mist. We could see the rifle-balls fall into the water like handfuls of pebbles, and still her open deck remained crowded with the crew. Nothing touched her while she remained in sight, and, passing the batteries one by one, she steamed out into the open, till at last the farewell shots the Prussians sent after her fell so far astern that she was allowed to pursue her way in peace.

Then, as if in disappointed anger, the Wemming Bund batteries turned their fire full upon the crest of Dybbol Hill, and we knew that the battle was virtually won, and that the Prussians had retreated in despair. It was half-past seven, and yet to me it appeared as if not four, but four-and-twenty hours had passed since I was roused by the first opening of the fire. Leaving my post of observation, I hurried again across the bridge. The troops, who had been called out in haste, were now marching homewards, more briskly, but not more steadily, than they had gone forth to battle. The men wore their usual air of stolid indifference, but the officers were in the highest spirits. I was shaken hands with by every acquaintance and every acquaintance's acquaintance that I met, till my arm ached with the process.

Everybody was laughing; but of boasting or fanfaronade there was absolutely nothing amongst the officers I met with. Their tone about the whole affair was like that of highbred English gentlemen; they were proud of having done their duty, but they never thought of describing the battle as the greatest event of modern times, or of asserting their capacity to whip the Prussians single-handed. Meanwhile, the cannon growled on, though the shells were now few and far between.

Passing onwards, I came upon the dark side of the war pageant. Ambulance-men were carrying up the stretchers to the front, soaked and stained with blood. A long file of waggons were bearing back the wounded; and you could see the poor fellows writhe in agony as the springless carts jolted on over the rough stony road. To me, I own the sight of their pale haggard features was more painful than that of the dead men whose shattered corpses were carried past. Their pain, at least, was over, their anguish was still to come. Most of the wounded soldiers had been hit in the head, and many were scarcely sensible; but they all bore their pain silently, and answered cheerily enough when their comrades along the road gave them a word of kindly greeting. From the brow of the hill I could make out the retiring masses of the Prussians; but a dropping fire was still being carried on from Broager, and a couple of shells fell too near my path to render a longer stay desirable. From the hill I hurried back to the town, which was now swarming with troops, laughing and shouting with unwonted hilarity.

On my way homewards, I met twenty-two Prussian soldiers who had been taken prisoners during the engagement, to the great satisfaction of the Danes. They were, for the most part, young beardless lads, with fair, fresh German faces; they belonged to the 18th Regiment, and bore their capture with great apparent unconcern. Nothing could be kinder than their reception by the mob of soldiers who had collected to see them. The Danes shook them cordially by the hand, called them "*Camaraden*," slapped them on the back, raised bottles of "*schnaps*" to their lips, stuffed cigars into their hands, and bade them cheer up with a rough but not ill-bred familiarity.

The two officers taken prisoners were said to be extremely affected by their position, and held themselves aloof from any civility; but the men fraternised very readily with the Danes. At eleven o'clock the Prussians sent in a request for a two hours' armistice to bury their dead. I availed myself of the opportunity to visit the batteries which had been most fired at during the battle, and was surprised to find how very slight was the damage inflicted on them. In spite of nearly a fortnight's bombardment, Dybbol remains as strong as it was at the commencement, or perhaps even stronger.

During the armistice the Prussians sent several shells from the Broagerland batteries. The outrage, I must hope in charity, was due to some delay in sending tidings of the truce to the more distant batteries; but this breach of good faith, even if accidental, will cause the Danes to be more chary of granting such a favour on a future occasion. Towards noon a snowstorm came on, and the haze was so thick that the Wemming Bund shores became invisible from Dybbol. Probably in consequence of the mist, the Prussians have hardly recommenced their fire, and all remains quiet at the hour at which I write.

So much for what I saw myself of this battle. Let me add a brief statement of its main features, which I have gathered from officers who were in different parts of the field. The Prussians commenced their attack at half-past three in the morning by advancing in large bodies upon the centre and right of the Danish line of works; the chief assault being directed upon Battery No. 6. They failed to take the Danes by surprise, though, from their great proximity to Dybbol heights, they were able to advance very near the crown of the hill before the alarm was given. The Danish batteries opened at once upon the storming columns with a steady and well-directed fire, which seemed to do considerable execution amongst the enemy's works.

The Prussians fired steadily enough, but did not advance with any spirit after the first few discharges from the guns of Dybbol. Their officers were seen urging the men on, but without effect. To their repeated cries of "*Vorwärts! vorwärts!*" the soldiers replied with a hoarse "*Nein, nein;*" and the few detachments of Germans who pushed their way to the front were never in sufficient force to seriously threaten the works. The most convincing proof of this fact is, that the Danish reserve stationed in the camp halfway up the hill was never called into action; and the whole burden of the defence was borne by the four regiments who happened to be on duty along the line of works.

The Danes, according to all accounts, fought admirably, not only behind their entrenchments, but in the open field, when driving back the advancing columns on the hillside. Towards six o'clock it became clear that the Prussian attack upon the right and centre was a failure; and then the enemy commenced a movement upon the left wing, which is believed to have been intended for the principal operations of the day. The left is confessedly the weakest part of the Danish line, and it is against this point the bombardment hitherto has been chiefly directed, so that the Germans may very possibly have imagined that the fire of the lower forts was silenced.

Happily, the *Rolf Krake* came to the defence of the Danish shore batteries. Anchoring close to the low land which lies between Dybbol and Broager, she fired her guns into the columns of the enemy moving upon the Danish left. It is said that the troops were seized with a panic, and were seen to disperse and take to their heels. At any rate, the advance was effectually stopped. The *Rolf Krake* was struck by ten shells, one of which fell into her machinery, but the damage done to her was not considerable. The loss of the Danes is estimated by themselves at from 100 to 150 killed and wounded. From what I saw myself, I should be inclined to say it must be nearer two than one hundred. The loss of the enemy can only be surmised; but from the accounts of the prisoners, and from the observation of the soldiers in the Danish batteries, it is believed to be very heavy.

With regard to the ultimate influence of this repulse, it is almost too early to form any opinion. The Prussians have received a damaging defeat; and if it is as decisive as is supposed, they will not, I think, advance again to attack Dybbol by storm till they have got batteries much nearer to the hill than those of Broagerland. The effect of the victory has been most favourable to the Danish Army. It has raised the spirits of the soldiers which had been somewhat depressed by the capture of Avn-Bierg and Dybbol village, and has created a well-founded impression that, with even a small force like their own, the position of Dybbol may be successfully defended for a lengthened period.

Before I close a letter already too long, I wish to mention one event of the day, which will be of interest to your readers. There is here at present an English gentleman, the Hon. Mr. Herbert, brother of Lord Carnarvon, who has come over to see the siege. Contrary—I trust he will excuse my saying so—to the advice of his acquaintances, Mr. Herbert has been in every spot where firing was going on, and this to such an extent that the Danish soldiers declared he was an English Milord, who had got the spleen, and wished to get wounded in order to experience a new sensation. I have no great sympathy for civilians who thrust themselves into dangers which do not concern them, out of mere curiosity; but, if a man chooses to take a part in the actual fighting, I think he is deserving of the honour which is always due to bravery.

While our countryman was in one of the trenches this morning, a Dane fell wounded outside the works in a very exposed situation. There was some hesitation about bringing him in, when Mr. Herbert rushed out under a heavy fire of musketry, and bore the wounded soldier in his arms to a place of safety, amidst the cheers of the Danes. It was a gallant act done gallantly, and as such I have recorded it.

March 30.

There is a grim French story, whose name I forget, which proposes to describe the experiences of a man who lay for a long time under sentence of death. By a delicate refinement of cruelty, the condemned felon in a French gaol never knows what day is fixed for his execution. Any morning the gaoler may enter his cell and tell him to prepare to die. All he knows is, that, as the executions take place at an early hour, he is safe for the day as soon as six o'clock has passed over. Now, in the story to which I allude, the writer described with morbid detail how, the moment that the morning hour had passed, the condemned criminal, instead of feeling any relief at his respite, grew actually impatient for the long day to pass away, in order that he might know whether his life was to end next morning.

A somewhat similar state of mind exists at Sonderborg at the present day, (1864). We are, in one sense, under sentence of death. Whenever an attack comes, or the bombardment seems growing earnest, our hope and prayer are that it may pass over, and leave our existence unchanged. Yet the moment the danger has ceased, there arises a morbid desire that the enemy would recommence his onslaught, in order that we may know whether the next attack is to prove fatal to us or not.

Thus already the exultation at the victory of Monday is giving place to feelings of irritation at the inaction of the Prussians. Virtually the siege has been suspended since Monday morning. Both today and yesterday the fire has been slack in the extreme. Every couple of hours or so the Prussians appear to wake up, and throw some twenty shells over the brow of Dybbol Hill. Contrary to their former practice, these shells are not directed at the batteries, but are thrown a short distance beyond, with the view, I suppose, of dealing havoc amidst the soldiers in the trenches and encampments.

Happily, this desultory irregular fire has been productive of no effect beyond costing the lives of two or three men each day. It need hardly be said that the Danes have had ample time to repair whatever small damage had been done to the works, and I have no doubt that the position is as strong now as at any time since the siege commenced. When the real blow is to be struck, or whether it is to be struck at all, are still questions which everybody at Sonderborg is again discussing with a painful monotony.

Meanwhile the morale of the Danish Army has been visibly improved by their successes on Monday. All yesterday the troops were in higher spirits than I have yet seen them; and in the evening, when the Guards' band marched through the streets playing, they were followed by crowds of soldiers singing and cheering lustily. The weather, though inclement enough to English ideas, is still so much milder, that camp life has lost much of its hardships; the roads are excellent, and the men are improving day by day in soldierly gait and discipline.

They cannot yet be compared fairly with regular troops, but they have lost much of the raw militia look which distinguished them on my first arrival. Sonderborg itself is being gradually raised from a state of chaos into one of comparative order. New streets are being made to facilitate the passage of troops; signboards are placed all over the town, to point out the different quarters and cantonments; and it is very rare now that our main thoroughfare is subject to those inextricable blockades which used to be of constant occurrence. The state of siege, which has nominally existed for weeks, is at length being put into force, though to a very mild extent.

Police have been sent down from Copenhagen, and some slight supervision is exercised over suspicious characters; the local paper is placed under the censorship of the *burgomaster:* no lodging-house is allowed to take in strangers without a written permission from the military authorities; and regulations have been made to hinder the villages in the line of route between Sonderborg and the port of Hörup from being overcrowded by the influx of non-combatants leaving the town. Altogether within the last ten days the Danes can report good progress.

The Honourable Mr. Herbert—or Sir Herbert, as our paper, the *Danish Schleswiger*, designates him—is at present the hero of our English colony, for the gallantry he displayed during the engagement of Monday. He was cheered yesterday by the soldiers in the camp, and it is expected here that he will have the order of the Dannebrog given him for his act of bravery. If so, it will be well deserved. I suppose the tide of English visitors will set in with the spring, if this unhappy war should last long enough.

Our latest arrivals are two young University men, who brought velocipedes with them to Copenhagen, on which they intended to have made the journey through Alsen. Unfortunately—or fortunately, as you like to think—the velocipedes broke down a little way out of Copenhagen, and had to be left behind. I recommend the next adventurous Briton coming to see the war to bring stilts with him, which are less liable to break down, and will produce an equal sensation in Sonderborg.

April 1.

It is raining cats and dogs. To give Denmark its due, it is not a rainy country; at any rate, so far as my experience of it extends. Its climate has every other conceivable defect, and, therefore, this admission is one that should fairly be made. I attribute the fact of my being alive at this moment to the edifice of fur coats and boots and caps now in my possession, whose foundation was laid by the kindness of friends acquainted with the country, and whose successive layers have been supplemented by myself at different periods of my journey.

But the patent waterproof mackintosh, the oilskin cape, and splatter-dash leggings, which also form portions of my travelling wardrobe, have been more trouble to me than they are worth, and have hardly yet had an airing. If the Prussians should enter Sonderborg, and I should have to make my escape, leaving my belongings behind me, I shall waste no sighs upon my waterproof raiment.

It is the thought of the Pelz, the heat-containing, chill-and-cold-expelling, and richly-with-fur-provided overcoat, to quote its German description, which weighs down my mind whenever I contemplate the possibility of a Prussian occupation. Deerfoot himself, clothed in this cloak, would have been beaten in a foot-race by Daniel Lambert. There will be nothing for me but to follow the example of Joseph, and leave my coat behind me in the clutches of the Prussian Potiphar. This digression, however, will lead me I know not whither if I pursue it further. I have got a long way already from the fact I commenced this letter by stating, and so the best thing I can do is to come back to the point whence I started, and repeat that it is raining cats and dogs.

The whole country is covered over with a grey watery mist; the Prussian batteries, and the heights of Dybbol themselves are almost invisible from my windows, and I cannot restrain a feeling of regret that I have not followed the example of an imaginative friend of mine, and gone off to Copenhagen, in order to describe the siege of Sonderborg from what he happily terms a central position. I should see as much of the siege today from Copenhagen, or for that matter from London, as I do here at this moment. All last night we expected a renewal of the assault, and the weather would have been wonderfully favourable for a storming party, as no advancing force could have been seen till it approached close to the batteries, and no shot could have been fired from the guns with anything like precision. Nevertheless, the night went by without any alarm; and this morning we have only the usual amount of random firing. So as the day seems likely to be a blank, let me take the opportunity to describe some home scenes which I have witnessed lately in the interior of the island.

It is hard to get away from the war in Alsen. The roads for miles are filled with ambulances, powder-trains, and long files of waggons loaded with military stores. In every village, in every house almost, soldiers are quartered; the small white Dannebrog pennants wave in front of every large farmyard, and denote the presence of some officer in command of a company; the roadside hedges far and wide are being cut down in order to make fascines for the fortifications; while even in the most secluded spot you can hear from time to time the heavy booming of the cannon beyond Dybbol.

Thus, an atmosphere of war pervades everything, and renders more striking by contrast the peacefulness of houses that have become known to me during my sojourn here. I will try and speak of some of them to you, as I have seen them. I had always fancied that a country vicarage was an institution peculiar to England; you can find its very counterpart here in Denmark. Some three miles from the town, on the shores of the Augustenburg Fiord, lies a vicarage, where, had I been in holy orders, I should like my lot to have been thrown,—a long, low, one-storied house, whose windows look due south, and open upon a smooth well-mown lawn. Creepers cluster on trellis-work over the whitewashed front, and swallows have built their nests beneath the overhanging eaves of the high-crown thatch roof.

The climate is too cold for evergreens, and the summer too dry for turf, such as we have in England. But still, even in this tardy springtime, you may wander pleasantly enough amidst the flower-beds and bushes by the banks of the little fish-pond, up to the arbour terrace, where you look down on the blue waters of the Als Sund, and the dark woods of the ducal palace of Augustenburg. If you have exhausted the garden, you may go into the large paved farmyard court behind the vicarage, kept as neat and clean as the stable-yard of an English gentleman; pat the dogs, who sleep in sunny corners, upon the head; go into the great stables, where long rows of cows are tethered in their stalls, ruminating lazily; feed the pigeons in the wood-cots; smoke in the stables, where as nice a stud may be inspected as any parson with a taste for horse-flesh could desire to own; and then, entering the house by the hospitable doors, which stand always open, you are welcomed with a sturdy shake of the hand by a hale, portly gentleman, dressed much as an English country rector would be, who was above the weakness of straight-cut waistcoats and stiff-starched white ties, and whose manners had that stately self-possession which, I think, is only given to men who have lived long in the world, and lived therein easily.

You will be shown over a pleasant house, whose walls are covered with book-shelves and prints; the books written in every language, the prints taken from many countries. There are the recollections of vacation tours in foreign countries, we know so well in English homes; the miniature Swiss cottages, the vases of Bohemian glass, the views of Rome and Naples. Your host is too much a man of the world to object to speaking in German, a language as familiar to him almost as Danish; but yet, though all his fortunes are bound up with Alsen. though his stout espousal of the Danish cause will probably entail upon him the loss of his home in the event of a German occupation, he is the staunchest of Danes in feeling.

One of his rooms is almost covered with portraits of the celebrities in the war of 1848-50; his house is open to the army, and the officers and soldiers who get quartered there find that their lines have fallen in pleasant places. The one complaint the exquisitely neat, placid, English looking mistress of the house made to me was, that the officers stayed so short a time that as soon as you became acquainted with them they were obliged to go.

Buried yet deeper in the island is the capital—the *"Residenz,"* as Germans would call it—of Augustenburg. A sleepier little town cannot well be imagined, even in this war time. Its one street of straggling whitewashed houses leads up to the ducal palace. A century or so ago, some high and mighty Prince of Schleswig-Holstein-Sonderborg-Augustenburg must, I think, have either visited, or read an account of, the glories of Versailles, and resolved to imitate it on his own possessions. The large court which forms the palace has an absurd resemblance to the *"Grande Place"* of the residence of the Bourbon monarchs. Three sides of the square are occupied by a tall barracklike whitewashed building, with high redtiled roof; the fourth side is a range of stables and coach-houses.

In the centre of the main block of buildings there is a stone flight of stairs, leading up to the grand entrance, where the dukes used to mount and dismount amidst the bows of their handful of courtiers. Somehow these petty princes appear to me to have left a not unkindly impression amongst the inhabitants of their Lilliputian dominions. In spite of their treachery to Denmark, the common verdict seems to be, that the fault lay in their heads rather than their hearts; and that they were led into sedition by an unreasoning traditional faith, entertained for generations, that somehow or other they had been deprived of their rights by the reigning house of Denmark.

It is a curious fact, as showing how completely they were Germanised, that at the time when the prince (who calls himself Frederick VIII.) and his brother were children, a tutor was actually brought from Copenhagen to teach them Danish. However, the ducal regime is a thing of the past; the courtyard of the quondam palace is now filled with hay and straw; the long suite of reception-rooms is turned into a hospital; and the beds of the wounded Danes are placed in the halls where the banquets and revels were held in bygone times.

A pleasanter hospital I have never seen; the windows of the wards look out into the green forest park, and the stillness of the place is only broken by the sound of the distant cannon. The hospital itself is a perfect marvel of neatness.

Numbers of Swedish and Norwegian army-surgeons have come over to volunteer their aid, so that there is no want of medical assistance. As soon as the patients will bear moving, they are sent off at once to the hospitals at Odensee, to make room for fresh comers. At this moment most of the soldiers at Augustenburg are sufferers from fever, and in the wards I visited the other day there were but few cases of severe wounds. Even fever scarcely seems to make the Danish nature impatient or restless, and the sick men lay in their clean narrow cots almost without moving. Over every bed there stood the name and number of the patient, written on a slate; by each man's side there were books, and some charitable person had strewn the room with tracts, entitled, *"A Man Overboard; or, Where are you Going to after Death?"* a question which some of these poor fellows are likely to be able to answer before long much more completely than their interrogator.

The only want I could observe in the hospital arrangements was the absence of female nurses. The Danish soldiers are wonderfully kind; yet, in the place of the sick and wounded men, I would sooner have an unknown woman to tend me than the most intimate of my soldier friends. Still, the view of the trees and the water, and the stately avenues, on which the patients can turn their eyes when they are weary of gazing at the arabesques with which the walls of their wards are covered, would console me for the absence of Sisters of Charity.

Many times, I think, the exiled duke must have thought wistfully of the home that was standing empty in this pleasant Alsen island. I admit that he played his cards infamously, and lost the game by his own want of prudence and principle; but yet I cannot help owning that, if his sins have been heavy, his punishment has been heavy also.

Often, too, at Primkenau, in dismal Silesia, where his abode is fixed, the princely exile must think of the Hörup woods, through whose glades he has ridden and hunted so often in days gone by. There is a house there, belonging to the keeper of the forests, where, I doubt not, poor Frederick VIII. has lunched many a time. It nestles in the very heart of the forest, so that you may ride round it a dozen times without coming on it. A great oak stands before the door, which Christian II. is said to have planted three centuries and a half ago, when he was a prisoner at Sonderborg. If any traveller had come to this house, as I did some nights since, on a bright clear evening, he would have found it difficult to believe that a cruel war was waging not two miles away.

The great birch woods which stretch between it and the sea deaden the sound of the guns. In front, there is a garden where the children of the house were playing, and under the branches of the giant oak stands the house of the keeper of the ducal forests, now transferred to the possession of the Crown. Like most Danish country houses, it is low, one-storied, and thatch-roofed. Within, the rooms were bare, with whitewashed ceilings, sanded floors, half-covered, perhaps, with a patch of carpet; and iron stoves, which give more than the warmth of a coal fire, with much less of its cheeriness. There are officers stationed in the house—officers are stationed everywhere; and I fancy that the grown-up daughters, however much, as Danish girls, they may deplore the war, still feel the change from the ordinary solitude of their life not an unpleasant one.

Family life in Denmark is, to a casual visitor like myself, singularly easy of access; everything is so simple, and everybody is so kindly-hearted. In this, as in almost every house of well-to-do persons which it has been my good fortune to enter, there was not a lady of the family who did not speak English more or less, and German, and who could not play on the piano with some artistic skill, in so far as I am capable of judging.

The Danish ladies, I should say, are not strong-minded, and have certainly no idea of the rights of women. It is curious, and at first rather startling to an Englishman, to find that the young ladies, who have been playing and talking to you before supper about Bulwer, and Dickens, and Thackeray, and the Princess Alexandra—a never-failing topic of conversation—carry round the cups and change the plates; and, in fact, wait upon you instead of servants. I have no doubt they cook the dinner themselves, and mend the snow-white table-linen.

Then, when the meals are over—how the women get fed is a mystery to me—they come back into the drawing-room and resume their conversation with perfect equanimity. I do not know that I should like to live in the country in Denmark. I think it possible I might get tired of whist at farthing points, of eating brown bread and butter morning, noon, and evening, of going to bed at ten and rising at seven. But still the ordinary existence here is singularly easy and unpretending. And even in the throbs of a struggle for national being, the placidity of the current of daily life scarcely seems ruffled.

CHAPTER 8

The Bombardment

April 3 (3 a.m).

This morning was almost the quietest we have had since the siege first commenced. The Prussian batteries preserved a silence which in itself was ominous. But still there was nothing to indicate more than the ordinary briskness of fire which has hitherto invariably followed any interval of inaction. The day was clear and bright, with a cold east wind driving the clouds away, and the Wemming Bund shores lay distinct before us, as if they were scarcely half a mile distant.

About two o'clock the firing commenced, and gradually grew brisker. It seemed as if the Prussians were going to make up for lost time, and fire off their stipulated allowance of shells with greater haste than usual. I was riding in the island at the time, and paid but little attention to a sound which had become monotonous by repetition. Then, at last, the noise grew louder and louder, and the firing more close and constant; and I turned my horse's head homewards, feeling certain that something of more than ordinary import was going on. I was then three miles or so from the town; but before I had got many yards upon my road I heard the bugles sounding the alarm amidst the farms where the troops were quartered, and I knew that the war had commenced again in earnest. I galloped back, but found the town scarcely moved from its ordinary apathy.

Everybody at Sonderborg had got so used to the crash of artillery and the sound of shells, that a little noise more or less created no extraordinary alarm. The officers I spoke to assured me that the firing had only been a little more lively than common, and that no serious attack was apprehended. Only half satisfied by these assertions, I strolled out to the shore, and, as soon as the Dybbol Hill was clear in sight, I could have no doubt that something very different was going on from the halting, hesitating fire to which we have hitherto been accustomed. The shells were flying to and fro at the rate, as I counted them, of twenty-five a minute; the roar of artillery was incessant; and the sides of Dybbol and Broager Hills were covered with dense masses of smoke.

The alarming fact was that, amidst this tremendous fire, the Wemming Bund batteries were almost silent. The question was, whether this noise was created by the fire of our own batteries, or by that of the new batteries which the Prussians have been some time erecting on the range that passes from Avn-Bierg on the Wemming Bund, through Dybbol and Rageböl villages, to Sand-Bierg on the Als-Sund.

It was not long before I learnt that the latter explanation was the correct one. The Prussians had at last opened fire from the position they acquired so fatally on the 17th, and the works of Dybbol were being thundered at with such a discharge of artillery as I believe has not been heard since the days of the Redan and the Malakoff.

Suddenly, amidst the roar and din of the distant cannon, I caught the sound of a near distinct crash, and I saw a white puff of smoke rise up from the castle of Sonderborg, which stands at the very entrance of the Als-Sund harbour. The first shot was put down by the bystanders to the deviation of a gun aimed at the Dybbol bastion. But then, hardly at a minute's interval, shell followed shell more and more rapidly, and it became only too certain that the enemy were again bombarding the defenceless town of Sonderborg.

My own position was not exactly a pleasant one. The house where I have been so long and so hospitably sheltered looks, as I have mentioned before, straight upon the Wemming Bund, and stands on the edge of the sea, close to the castle. It was, therefore, exactly in the line of fire, and any return to it was for the moment unadvisable. So I worked my way through the outskirts of the town, trusting that the cannonade would slacken towards nightfall, and took up my position on a high hill, which rises at the back of Sonderborg. There I found a crowd of lookers-on collected, watching, like myself, the progress of the bombardment. The evening was coming on, and the light was fading in the west, but the constant discharge of cannon-shot kept on unabated.

The roar of the artillery is indescribable, except to those who have heard it. Not a sound seemed to pass without a flash and bang, and dull, deep rumbling. The whole western sky was covered with dark lurid clouds. Which was the smoke of cannon, which that of burning houses, it was impossible to discern. The centre batteries, Nos. 4 and 6, commanding the high road to Flensburg, against whose earthworks the fire was mainly directed, were enveloped in a mist of flame and haze. Every shot appeared to take effect. Great puffs, of earth-coloured hue, rose up towards the sky, as shell after shell hit the earthworks, and splashed the mud scores of feet into the air. But, though the fire was quickest against the centre, it extended all along the line from the Als-Sund to the Wemming Bund. Whether the Danish batteries were silenced—whether it was found impossible to man the guns beneath that pitiless, ceaseless fire—whether it was not thought advisable to respond—I cannot say.

This I know, that scarcely any response was made. The hail of shells and cannon-shot beat down mercilessly upon the Dybbol heights; and as the dusk grew on great blood-red patches of flame, like the lava-chinks on Mount Vesuvius, appeared on the hillside. Some barracks which had been run up to shelter the troops were burning, and the fierce cold winds fanned the flames into a devouring fire. Fancy Martin's picture of "The Last Great Judgment Day," coloured with the hues that Turner would have spread upon it, and you will have some notion of that weird, awful scene.

But I own that, for us, the bombardment of the town, though infinitely less terrible as a spectacle, had a much stronger fascination. The two Wemming Bund batteries, which stand on the extreme of the Prussian right, were shelling the lower part of Sonderborg with a cruel accuracy. Not an intimation had been given—not a warning of any kind—such as has been afforded of late in the most barbarous of wars. On the first bombardment of the 10th, we might charitably hope that the few shells thrown into the town were sent solely to clear the harbour, and not to destroy the dwellings of peaceful inhabitants.

No such excuse could be suggested at the present time. The bombs came whizzing towards the city with deliberate intent and aim. It is wonderful how soon you can tell the direction of a shell by its sound; and whenever a shot was fired in our direction the crowd of townsmen and soldiers amongst whom I stood cried out that the shell was coming long before it struck. we could see the dark puffs of smoke rising in dull succession from the houses near the port, and at last the smoke was followed by flame, and we saw that a house was set on fire.

With the fierce wind then blowing, it seemed probable that the whole city would soon be destroyed. Happily, the wind fell away suddenly, and the conflagration was extinguished. If the night were only here we knew there must be a lull in the shelling, but the night seemed endlessly long in coming.

At length, weary of waiting, I passed into the upper part of the town, where I had managed, luckily, to secure a shelter comparatively out of harm's way. The sight which met me there was sad enough in all conscience. The people were flying from the town, as the inhabitants of Sodom and Gomorrah may have fled from the accursed cities. There was little time to take anything with them in their flight. Women with scared pale faces, dragging little toddling children by the hand, were hastening away, God knows whither. Old men, bowed with age, were groping their way timidly up the long winding street. Some of the wayfarers had got bundles of bedding in their hands; others had articles of household furniture; long processions of carts, laden with every object that could be gathered together hastily, were rattling away as fast as the terrified horses could drag them; and the whole current of the population, which at this hour on ordinary evenings is coming homewards, was streaming out of the city. The wounded soldiers in the Caroline Amelia Hospital, which stands, or used to stand, close to the church, had been torn from their beds, and were passing in a file of carts up to Augustenburg.

And then, mixed up with the citizens and the soldiers, came in the wounded men from the front. No estimate can be formed yet of the loss beneath this afternoon's deadly fire, but it must have been a heavy one. Dead bodies, half covered with the blood-stained straw in which they lay, were carried by in a dismal progress. File after file of soldiers moved on, bearing their wounded comrades on stretchers through the streets, and the moans of some of these poor wretches could be heard for hundreds of yards away; others lay senseless, and, to all appearance, lifeless, with their wounds half bandaged, and with dark streaks of blood marking their heads and breasts. I have no wish to describe to you the horrors that I saw; men with their legs blown off, their bodies ripped open with shells, and their faces battered into a mass of shapeless flesh, are sights not pleasant to see, or to think of when seen.

Towards nine o'clock the fire slackened, and almost died away. There was breathing time for a moment, and I used it to make my way to the house where my luggage was lying. On my passage through the town I could see the damage that had been done. The room where the headquarters of the staff were placed had been struck by a shell, which had passed through the ceiling and the floor, and the whole staff had decamped at once to quarters higher up the town.

Another shell had burst through the coffee-room of the Holstein-isches Haus, where I had dined dozens of times, and the floor of a room in the same hotel, where I was playing cards last night, was covered with bricks which had been knocked down by the shock. A watchmaker's shop, by the town-hall, was shivered into fragments; and a house close to the *burgomaster's* was literally knocked down. The castle itself—at which the chief fire was aimed—had suffered comparatively little, though several bombs had fallen through the roof.

The casualties, as far as I can yet learn, have not been heavy, considering the fire. One shell hit a detachment of soldiers passing along the main street, and killed two, and wounded nineteen. At the house where my domicile has been fixed for the last six weeks everything was in disorder; the servants were crying, the officers' luggage was being brought hurriedly out of the rooms, and I had only time to pack up my bag, wish a hearty farewell to my kind host, and make my way back again to the upper town, before the bombardment commenced again.

It is now three o'clock while I write, and the bombardment still continues, though slacker than in the day. What damage has been done to these works it is impossible for us yet to learn. The Danish officers insist that no serious injuries has been inflicted; but it is certain that, from whatever cause, the fire of the Danish batteries has ceased for hours. Heavy rain has come on, which may possibly retard the expected attack of the Prussians.

Augustenburg, April 3.

The day was beginning to break when I closed my letter to you this morning. Sleep was almost impossible; the large guest-room of Reymuth's Inn, where I had found shelter for the night, was crowded with a motley company of persons who, like myself, had been shelled out of their abodes, and had come to the upper town as being comparatively safe. When my letter was finished, I laid down upon the floor, in the vain hope of getting an hour or two of rest. For some time I speculated on which side of the wall I should be safest in the event of a shell striking the roof.

Soon, however, I came to the conclusion that there were no data on which to argue the point; so I coiled myself up in my furs and rugs, and tried in vain to sleep. I suppose that I dozed, from the fact that every shell which struck the lower part of the town during the night woke me up with a start. But I heard the clock strike every half hour, and I was right glad when the weary night was over, and I got up, with every bone of my body aching, shook the dust from off my clothes, and prepared for the business of the day.

It is bad enough being in a bombarded town in the daylight; but it is nothing to the knowledge that shells are falling around you in the darkness. It was a strange scene on which I looked, as I threw open the window of the stifling room where I had passed the night. The population was flocking hastily out of the town; the troops, drawn up in the streets, were standing close to the walls in the hope of finding cover in case a shell should fall near them; dark masses of smoke were still rising from the side of Dybbol hill: for the moment, the fire was slack, and there seemed to be a temporary cessation of the merciless bombardment. It was clear, even if I had so wished it, that there was no stopping where I was. The headquarters, which had been already moved off to the very outskirts of the town, were being moved further into the country.

A shell had fallen into the garden of the inn; another some fifty yards higher up the street. Officers and civilians were alike quitting the doomed city; and the only persons stopping were those who were too poor or too helpless to find shelter elsewhere. The women who owned the hotel were in tears and hysterics, and would not have consented to stay another night in the house for all the guests in the world, if they had each been as rich as Monte Cristo. My difficulty was about my luggage, which was too heavy for me to carry, and which I was yet unwilling to leave behind.

In this dilemma I and a brother-correspondent of mine bethought ourselves of a kind friend whose company was stationed at a farm, some half mile distant, upon the sea-shore. To reach it we had to make a detour of nearly two miles, in order to avoid the range of the shells, which kept pouring into the town from Broagerland with fatal accuracy. When we reached the farmhouse, where we had often been hospitably received, we found our friend absent. Happily he had left word to render us any assistance we might desire, and we obtained the loan of a cart to convey our luggage to Hörup harbour.

The look of this quiet farmyard bore painful tokens of the presence of war. Scores of families had flocked in from Sonderborg, begging for shelter in the great barns, though even these lay but a little way beyond the range of the shells. At any moment the fire might be turned against the "*Laader Gaarde*" itself; and its landlord was fully aware of the dangers of his position. We advised him to fly, but he told us with truth that his whole fortune lay in the stock of cattle he had collected within his barns, and that until the buildings were actually in flames he and his wife meant to stick to them.

Yet, though the man was old, and the father of a large family, there was no look of fear about him. He spoke about the whole matter calmly, and with little apparent excitement. True to his Danish hospitality, he pressed us to stop and breakfast; but, tempting as the offer was to men tired out and hungry, there was no time to be lost. Every minute a shell fell into the town with a deadly crash, which could be heard for miles away. Smoke was already issuing from the houses near the port; and the rector of the town, who had just come in with his wife, told us that the flames were spreading rapidly. The cart was hurriedly got ready, and we then retraced our way, making even a longer detour than before to the back of Sonderborg.

We left the cart under the brow of the hill, and then pushed on as hastily as we could to the inn, which stands a short way down the long steep descent leading from the heights to the Als-Sund; the hotel was in utter confusion; there was nobody to ask for our bill, or to take our money. So we loaded ourselves with our luggage, and dragged it as rapidly as we could up the hill to our cart. In spite of the crowds which had left the day before, there was still a constant stream of women and children pouring out of the place; the truth is, that the poorer inhabitants have nowhere to go to, and flock back to their homes with a rabbit-like instinct whenever the immediate danger seems over for the hour. But now there could be no thought of stopping.

The Town-hall, the Holstein Hotel, the Post Office, and all the shops near this little knot of buildings, were in flames. Fifty-seven people—civilians, not soldiers—had been killed and wounded during the morning in this quarter of the town. The streets themselves were deserted, except by soldiers marching to and fro on duty; the air was heavy with the scent of gunpowder. At the brow of the hill a crowd of people were collected, watching the progress of the fire and the effect of the bombardment. There was not much speaking, and all faces were pale and anxious. The fire against the Dybbol batteries had almost died away, or at any rate, was reduced to comparative insignificance by the constant fire upon the town.

The soldiers themselves looked depressed by the danger which they had no means of resisting. No hesitation of any kind was visible in obeying orders; indeed, the men marched down the street towards the fire with their usual heavy tramp, but there was no singing to be heard, and their countenances bore no longer the stolid look so habitual to them.

Many friends of mine—men in whose company I have now lived daily for weeks—were amongst the crowd. There was little time for leave-taking or conversation. A warm grasp of the hand—a wish, heartily felt, I believe, on both sides, for each other s safety, and we parted company. Our luggage was heaped upon the cart, and we left Sonderborg amidst the crash of shells and falling walls. Our first step was to reach the harbour of Hörup, and there leave our bags and trunks. It was a weary trudge through the heavy roads, knee-deep in mire, especially to men who had not changed their clothes, or slept all night, or eaten anything in the morning. However, if we had been disposed to grumble, I think the sight of the groups we passed at every turning would have checked all inclination.

I had left neither family nor belonging in Sonderborg; my interest in the issue of the contest was only that of a spectator. I had plenty of money in my pockets, and strength to bear any hardships which might fall upon me in my flight; but these poor wretched families—fathers, mothers, children, grandchildren—were going forth from their homes ruined, destitute; with no knowledge where they would find shelter for their heads or food for their mouths, and yet they toiled on, sadly, if you will, but still silent and uncomplaining. God have mercy on all who can find no home in this cold, chill night! God forgive those who have wrought this cruel and wicked wrong!

At the little port of Hörup it was impossible to find even sitting room. It was only as an extreme favour that I could get permission to leave my bags in an outhouse. No steamer was lying in the harbour for Copenhagen; and even if there had been I should not have availed myself of the opportunity, as my intention is, if possible, to remain in Alsen until the fate of Dybbol is decided one way or the other. But this morning my prospect of getting any shelter whatever seemed of the slightest. Sonderborg was untenable; and the two thousand inhabitants, and some thousands of soldiers who were quartered there, were all scattered over the neighbouring villages. A civilian, at the best, had a bad chance compared with the soldiery; and amongst civilians a preference was very naturally and justly given to the personal acquaintances of the villagers.

We knocked at house after house, but with the same invariable answer, that no room could be obtained for love or money. I had been engaged that day to dine with the rector of Ulkeböl parish, an invitation which had passed entirely out of my recollection amidst the excitement of the last four-and-twenty hours. Of course all such engagements were cancelled by the events of the day, but still I resolved to keep my appointment, in the hopes that I might find some shelter for the night under the roof of the parsonage. I induced the cart which had brought my luggage to take me on to Ulkeböl, and was jolted for two hours over the vilest of roads, in the roughest of springless carts. It is in these conveyances that the wounded are carried from the field of battle to the hospitals, and I could form some opinion, from my own experience, of what must be the sufferings of these unhappy wretches.

When I reached the *Prester-Gaarde*, as it is called, tired, sleepy, unwashed, and ravenous, I found that the most I could hope for was an hour's shelter. The whole house had just been taken up for the residence of the commander-in-chief, General Gerlach, and his staff, and everything was in confusion. However, our host would not hear of our leaving till we had dined with him, and the proposal to men who had not had a meal all day, and had been stirring from early dawn, and saw little hope of getting a meal that night, was too tempting to be declined. I had the honour of dining in company with General Gerlach and his *aides-de-camp*, one and all of whom were as kindly and courteous as I have always found all Danish officers to be.

It was strange, though, to observe how completely military feeling appeared to have accustomed their minds to the incidents of war. The headquarters themselves had been bombarded; the city of Sonderborg was burning; and the crash of the shells could be heard in the far distance from the rooms wherein we sat. Yet everybody took it all as a matter of course. The conversation hardly turned upon the events of the day, but consisted of anecdotes about the respective merits of the quarters which the officers had occupied in the former Schleswig-Holstein campaigns.

In fact, it seemed impossible to a civilian to believe that the conduct of the war lay in the hands of the singularly quiet and nonchalant gentlemen collected round the pastor's board. Every house in the neighbourhood of the parsonage had been taken up for the business of the army, and I found that no possibility existed of finding a room anywhere in the immediate neighbourhood. Every officer expressed a fear that it would be impossible for us to procure quarters anywhere, and if I had listened to their advice I should now have been tossing about on board one of the little fishing-smacks which crowd the harbour of Hörup. I resolved, however, to make one more trial, and trudged on again to Augustenburg, from which place I now write to you. By a wonderful stroke of good fortune I secured a room there by the kindness of the correspondent of a Danish newspaper, and have got a table to write upon, and—what I care for much less—a rug to sleep in on the floor of the sitting-room.

I have spoken at length of these my personal adventures, because I believe they will give you a fairer idea of the practical working of the bombardment than any communication of hearsay reports. The moral result of this act will be, I think, to cover the Prussians with infamy. Without intimation of any kind, a murderous fire has been directed upon the town of Sonderborg, filled, as the enemy must have known it to be, with women and children.

A notification that the firing would commence after the lapse of some hours could have done no conceivable injury to the Prussians, and would have spared a fearful amount of needless and useless suffering and bloodshed. The Prussians have decided otherwise, contrary to the rules of war and the dictates of common humanity. Baffled in their assault upon the forts, they have consoled themselves by wreaking destruction from a safe distance on an unfortified and defenceless town belonging to the very country whose welfare they profess to be the object of their having gone to war. Deep and bitter is the indignation of the Danes; and, unless I err, this feeling will be shared in by Europe.

Laadengaarde (near Sonderborg), April 4.

The town of Augustenburg—and, indeed, the whole island of Als—was astir early on the morning which followed the bombardment of Sonderborg. Scant and wretched must have been the shelter gained by hundreds on that dreary night. Some idea of the crowd which spread itself far and wide in search of a roof to hide beneath may be gathered from one solitary fact. In the course of my own disconsolate wanderings I espied a fisher's smack of some five-and-twenty tons burden moored off the causeway which crosses the Augustenburg Fiord.

Seeing the fisherman on board, I asked him if he would let me shelter myself in the narrow hold of the vessel, where I thought it barely possible there might be room for myself and my two companions to crawl in. The man told me he should have been very glad to allow me, but that three families from Sonderborg had already crammed themselves into the hold, and it was impossible to find standing-room there for another human being. It was by the merest chance that I obtained quarters anywhere; and those quarters consisted of a cane sofa in a little room, which held three other inmates besides myself.

As a proof of the exceeding honesty of the people, it is worth while here to record the following incident. There was, as you may believe, hardly any conceivable amount, however exorbitant, which I would not have gladly paid to avoid passing the night in the open air. I made no bargain beforehand; when I asked for my bill in the morning—including, as it did, supper, bed, and breakfast—I was charged one shilling and fourpence altogether. My host, though an unmistakable Dane in look and manner, was, like most of the inhabitants of the ex-ducal capital, *Deutschgesinnt*, or German-minded, to a marvellous degree. He took in Hamburg newspapers, preferred talking German to Danish, and spoke of the Duke of Augustenburg as "his lawful sovereign." For the Prussians, however—the men who had bombarded Sonderborg—he expressed the utmost aversion, and said there was not a Schleswig-Holsteiner who would not sooner belong to Denmark than be annexed to Prussia.

As soon as I was up and dressed, my first impulse was to hurry on to the neighbourhood of Sonderborg to learn how things were going on there. The fires which rose from the town had pretty well died away during the night; the noise of cannon-shot had become very rare; and it was evident that, for some reason or other, there was a lull in the attack. The rattle of musketry had been heard just before daybreak at Augustenburg, and the bugles had sounded the alarm, so it was supposed an assault had taken place.

But, indeed, nothing could be known from the floating rumours of the place, and the few officers and officials I came across were too much occupied in the hurry occasioned by the general confusion to think of anything, except where quarters could be found for the service of their different departments. Happily the road was now comparatively clear, and the cold east wind had dried up the mud in a wonderfully short time.

It is, by the way, a mercy, for which the inhabitants of Sonderborg can hardly be grateful enough, that the inactivity of the Prussians did not permit them to commence the bombardment a month, or even a fortnight, ago. Had this been the case, the sufferings of the population, driven forth from their homes while snow was on the ground, and the roads were impassable from mud, would have been fearfully increased; they were bad enough as it was, but they might have been yet more grievous. The pause in the firing had caused hundreds of the towns-folk to retrace their steps towards the town. Two long files of waggons, going opposite ways, blocked up the high road.

Those coming from Sonderborg were filled with chairs, tables, car-pets, washing-stands, mirrors, pictures, and all the various apparatus of houses turned inside out. It looked as if brokers had levied an execu-tion upon the whole city. Everything had been thrown pell-mell into the vans, without thought for arrangement. Rosewood pianos lay in strange company with kitchen dressers, and fire-irons protruded from mahogany drawers in dangerous proximity to gilt-framed pictures. Every now and then a van had broken down beneath its load, and the furniture lay smashed and broken in the ditches by the roadside.

Alongside the vans there trudged men and women, carrying under their arms, or in great baskets slung on sticks, chimney ornaments, china ware, plaster images, and other little treasures of household life which had escaped so far unhurt. At the cottages along the road the vans were unloading their burdens, and the cottagers seemed ready enough to give such stowage-room as they were able; and in front of almost every house there were groups of children prattling and play-ing merrily. At that happy age fear is soon forgotten, and change of any kind is always a pleasure. The flitting was rare fun, and for them there was no thought of the morrow.

On the other hand, the file of carts going townwards were laden with living freights. Everybody was off to see what had become of what once were their houses—to save what salvage they might out of the general wreck. Soldiers, peasants, fishermen, housewives, and well-dressed ladies were huddled together in the straw spread at the bottom of the carts. Amongst the younger members of the fairer sex the pres-ence of the calamity had not extinguished the ruling passion of wom-ankind. It was odd to observe how, even in their sorry plight, they had contrived to dress themselves with some trace of elegance; how they squatted in the straw as gracefully as circumstances would permit; and what an obvious consciousness they betrayed of the fact that stolen glances were cast at them from time to time by the passers-by.

Amongst the elder females the one thought or care was about their furniture. Women, as a rule, cling to their household belongings with a tenacity incomprehensible to men; and the present occasion was not an exception to the rule. Living in a small community, in a time of excitement, as I have done for weeks, you soon form a speaking acquaintance with scores of people whose names are unknown to you.

Amongst the crowd there were hundreds of persons whose faces were familiar to me, and many were the greetings which I met with from the wayfarers.

Seated in a cart was an old lady, the owner of a house where friends of mine had lodged till the day before. When the bombardment began she refused to leave her dwelling, though it was one of the most exposed of the whole town. "No," she said; "she had seen every brick of it built; she had bought every stick in it by her own labour; and if the Prussians destroyed her furniture, they might just as well kill her too."

For four-and-twenty hours, while the shells were falling round her house like hailstones, she kept her resolution. It was only when the flames were actually spreading in the street wherein she lived that she fled, with a sick niece confined to her bed by illness. Strange to say, her house, and that of the *burgomaster*, where I had had my abode—perhaps the two most exposed buildings in the town—had not been struck by a single shell, though the ground near them was furrowed up with shot.

The old lady was hastening back to the town to carry off what she could save, and even her misfortunes had only increased her habitual loquacity. A little way on, my hand was shaken warmly by a man whose face at first I could not recognize, it was so changed from its usual aspect of good-humoured importance, so pale and haggard. He was the landlord of an hotel of which I had been a constant frequenter, and with whom I had many and many times discussed the progress of the siege. His house had been literally battered to the ground; he himself had escaped, with his wife and child, a baby in arms, but had saved nothing. The one treasure he was dragging back from the town was a baby's go-cart. In all likelihood he was utterly and helplessly ruined. A notorious German sympathiser, he could not expect much help from the Danish Government; while his chances of being indemnified by the Prussians were problematical in the extreme.

Alarm and misery seemed to have crushed the strength out of his mind and body; and though a young, vigorous man in years, he looked old and feeble. A few steps more, and I was curtsied to by the servant-girl of a family where I had been a daily visitor. The place was destroyed; the family were driven away to find shelter where they could; her situation was gone, and she was thrown upon the world, friendless. Her eyes were swollen with tears, and she could hardly speak for sobbing. "She was going," so she told me, "to leave the island at once—to get anywhere away from the shells; and then what was to become of her, God knew!" Poor child! she was young and pretty; and death is not the worst evil of which war is the guilty cause.

And so I might tell you dozens of such encounters I made upon my road. The poor people were glad enough to tell their misfortunes. I heard but few complaints, and little grumbling. The patient, kindly nature of the Schleswigers was hardly stirred to bitterness by the cruelty of their sufferings. They were ready enough to help each other; and carts and arms and shelter were placed freely at the disposal of all who needed them; but of passionate excitement there was no trace visible. As we approached the town we could see a dark column of smoke rising from near the water-side; but the batteries, both of the Danes and of the enemy, continued unaccountably silent.

The popular belief was that an armistice had been granted for a few hours; but on inquiring at headquarters I could find no authorisation for the rumour. However, between eight and half-past one, not a shot was fired. Whether the Prussian ammunition was exhausted, or whether, after thirty-six hours' shelling, the truth dawned upon the mind of the Prussian commanders that it was not humane or civilised to bombard a town without giving some time for non-combatants to escape, I cannot say.

Shells, as I have already mentioned, had fallen right beyond the town, and had even struck the windmills, which lie on the extreme edge of the hill, a mile away from the Als-Sund. As I have frequently told you, Sonderborg consists of one long winding main street, leading up from the shore of the straits to the summit of the hill on whose side the town stands. On either side this main street there is an irregular mass of buildings, terminating at a short distance amidst gardens and orchards; but I should think fully one-half of the houses in the town are situated in the High Street, as we should call it.

This thoroughfare may be roughly divided into three sections, of unequal length. The first section consists of a crooked narrow lane, rather than street, from the bridge to the town-hall; the second, of a broad, straight, even thoroughfare, from the town-hall to the military post-office, in which all the chief shops and dwellings are placed; and the third, of a steep, narrow, winding alley, passing from the post-office to the windmills and the open country.

The first and third of these sections had been comparatively untouched. The deadly fire of the Prussian cannon had been turned almost exclusively against the middle section, the Regent Street of Sonderborg. Until we had passed Reymuth's Hotel, where my last night in Sonderborg was spent, we could form no idea of the desolation that had been wrought.

Most of the windows in the upper town were broken, and there were great chasms in many of the roofs; but still the houses were open, and several of them were occupied by soldiers. It was only as we turned the corner, and gazed full down the street, that we knew what the bombardment really meant.

I saw Gaeta the day after the capitulation, when the dead still lay unburied on the sunlit hillside; I visited Palermo before any attempt had been made to repair the injuries occasioned by the Neapolitan shells; but in neither place, to my mind, was the havoc wrought comparable to that occasioned here. I know not how to describe the scene. I have walked hundreds of times up and down this little thoroughfare, till I could tell you well nigh the name of every shop in it, and the order in which they came. Yet I declare, if I had been placed there today, without knowledge of the event, I might have guessed for ever without finding out I was in Sonderborg.

The whole quarter was one mass of bare walls, charred rafters, and tottering chimneys, enveloped in a dim haze of smouldering smoke. The few walls left standing looked so near toppling over, that I felt as though the shock of one cannon-shot would carry the whole mass crumbling to the ground. The buildings here, one and all, are of poorly-made bricks, and lath and plaster; and every house by the roadside, almost without exception, was literally gutted. Many of the dwellings were absolutely indistinguishable.

I looked in vain for a bookseller's shop which had been one of my chief resorts. I could only tell that it might have been any one of the heaps of blackened bricks which encumbered the roadside. The bare walls of the town-hall were left standing, but the roof and flooring and rooms had disappeared utterly. The street was covered with fragments of shells and tiles and rafters; but the houses had fallen inwards, so that there was little impediment to one's passage. Crowds of people were poking amidst the ruins, to try and find something of their lost property; but a dead silence reigned about the place. Everybody was still, awe-struck with the destruction round them. At any moment the Devil's work might be begun again, and all ears were watching for the first whirr of the shell, so that they might scamper from the dangerous ground whose range had been obtained with such fatal accuracy. Fifteen hundred shells had fallen in this street, while those which had passed beyond its range might have been counted by a few scores. Of the number of casualties it is impossible as yet to speak with certainty.

******

The nearest approach to an official statement of the casualties I could ever find put them down at fifty-seven killed and wounded. Possibly half that number would be a truer estimate; but the guilt of the act does not depend on the amount of the casualties caused by it.

******

When I had given such a cursory glance as I could spare time for to the town, I passed through the side streets—by the hospitable house where I had lived so long, which now stood deserted and tenantless, with every pane in the windows broken, but still happily intact—and so out into the fields. Thence, in company with two gentlemen who have resolved to share their fortunes with me, I made my way to a farm-house some little distance in the country, where a friend of ours was stationed. There, thanks to his kindness, we found not only rations but shelter, and I have thus been fortunate enough to secure an abode, from whence I can command a view of the progress of the siege, with as little danger from shells as can be hoped for by anyone whose fate throws him in the path of active war.

As soon as we had thus billeted ourselves, we hurried off in search of the headquarters and the telegraph office. It was a long search and a difficult one, as everything was in the utmost confusion. At last we found our old friend the postmaster, wandering about disconsolately in a village some two miles inland, looking after quarters for the royal post-office. Half his mails, he told us, had been burnt in the destruction of the town post-office; and though he had been asking for a new office since daybreak, he could find absolutely nothing to serve even as a temporary shelter. Where the post-office was to be in future he knew no more than ourselves. Happily, he had a bundle of English newspapers, which he had put apart for us; and I read there the general expectations of a pacific solution expressed in leading articles written a week ago, with the smoke of Sonderborg full in view as a comment on the impossibility of prophesying.

April 6.

The gods—of whom Epicurus wrote and Tennyson has sung—would not, I think, have found such placid contentment in watching the thunderbolts roll beneath them, if there had been any chance that a stray flash of lightning might deviate from its course, and strike

Olympus instead of the terrestrial regions. And thus for me, living within sight and sound, and not altogether without reach, of the pitiless storm of shells which comes daily pelting down on Dybbol and Sonderborg, the affair has a personal human interest, not compatible with philosophical equanimity.

But for persons dwelling at a remote distance from the scene of action, I am afraid the narrative of each day's bombardment must seem uncommonly like that of the preceding or succeeding one. The frequenters of Jullien's concerts must remember the grand descriptive Army Quadrilles, which used to close the first part of his entertainment. The programme described was in that glowing language of which the Napoleon of conductors commanded the monopoly: we read with wonder how the enemy could be heard stealing forth from his entrenchments; how then the alarm sounded, every heart throbbed with manly vigour, and the gallant defenders of their country crept from their couches; again, the outposts are driven in—the skirmishers advance, and so on.

All this, or rather something of which this is the meagerest skeleton, was contained in the programme of the Promenade Concerts. We were supposed to be able to understand the progress of the battle by the strains of the music; but, speaking for myself, all we could perceive was a terrific crash of instruments, a deafening Babel of noise. Now, if I were to describe the siege as I see and hear it, I suspect you would know as much about it as you would have done of the storming of Sebastopol from hearing Jullien's Crimean Quadrille, without the assistance of his programme. Noise, smoke, and noise is about all the impression gathered from the spectacle. This afternoon I have been watching the progress of the bombardment for a couple of hours; and yet what I saw might be described in as many minutes. Standing by the sea-shore, sheltered from the cold bleak wind, I could see the career of every shell from its birth to its death.

The whole panorama of the war lay before me, and I looked straight up the Wemming Bund bay from the opposite coast of Alsen. On my left, across the calm, rippleless waters, were the cliffs of Broagerland, wreathed in a haze of smoke; on my right was the deserted city of Sonderborg; and in the centre, between these two boundaries of my horizon, stretched the hill of Dybbol. The fire was fast and furious. Sometimes it came from the Danish guns directed against Broager; then the crest of Dybbol hill was crowned with a belt of smoke; and one loud sharp report was all I heard of the course of the shells, falling as they did far away out of sight and hearing. Sometimes the guns of Broager returned the fire; then there was first a volume of smoke along the cliffs occupied by the Prussians, followed by a deep hoarse report, and succeeded after a minute's interval by a second and more distinct explosion as the shells struck the Danish batteries.

Sometimes the guns were turned from the Wemming Bund upon Sonderborg, and then I could hear the panting, whirring sound of the shells as they flew through the sky above our heads, growing louder first, and then fainter as they passed onwards, till it ended in a bang and crash as the bombs came bounding down upon the roofs of Sonderborg. And sometimes every battery began firing at once in every direction, till it was impossible to distinguish anything, or to say more than that shells were falling and bursting everywhere. Even of the injury done by the bombardment it is hard for an observer to judge, except by the indications of the smoke.

A shell bursts amidst the buildings of the town, a crash is heard, a pillar of smoke rises up into the air, and. then it is over. What walls have fallen, what havoc has been wrought, even the best of field-glasses will not inform you. It is only when the fire has ceased, and you can venture into the scene of the bombardment, that you can judge of its effect. Gradually, too, as the shelling goes on, the whole country becomes enveloped in a canopy of smoke; great banks of ink-black clouds gather about the horizon, against which each successive puff of white, new-born smoke stands out distinctly, till it floats away itself and is gathered into the darkness.

Today the one visible result of two hours' almost uninterrupted shelling is, that the town of Sonderborg has again been set on fire; the flames, however, do not seem to spread; and, indeed, a conflagration which cleared away the whole mass of ruins would now be no loss to the Danes. Apparently, the shells have been chiefly directed against the lower part of the town, that adjoining the Als Sund: the central quarter, as I stated in my letter yesterday, is entirely destroyed; and the upper part lies somewhat out of reach. No doubt the Prussians have already inflicted a vast amount of misery on the population of Sonderborg, and they may inflict more still; but, beyond this advantage, it is hard to see what practical result they expect from the manner in which they are conducting the siege.

I have commented often before now on the extraordinary character of their fire; today they poured what a French acquaintance of mine called a *"feu d'enfer"* upon the works for a couple of hours. Now they have stopped as suddenly as they began, and have thus given time for the Danes to repair their fortifications in peace. So it has been every day; the Prussians, in fact, follow the example of Penelope after a fashion of their own, and allow the web they have unwoven by day to be rewoven by night. Not only so, but the object of their fire is as uncertain as its duration. It is obvious to the most ignorant in such matters that earthworks, or even a town itself, cannot be destroyed by a few casual shells, but that the bombardment of any point, to be effective, must be sustained for a length of time.

Yet, in spite of this self-evident truth, the Prussians keep throwing their shells now at one place, now at another, with no apparent plan. For a quarter of an hour they will fire at the works; then they seem to get tired of producing no visible effect, turn their guns upon the town, and amuse themselves with knocking down a house. After this interlude of diversion, they try to concentrate their attention on serious business, but, like children, they grow weary of the task before it is completed.

Last night a purposeless engagement took place, in accordance with this indecisive system of action. Two companies of Prussians advanced from Dybbol village, drove in the Danish outpost, and occupied some of their rifle-pits. The alarm was sounded; the Danes turned out, expecting that an assault was at hand; and then the Prussians retired, being apparently satisfied with having disturbed the night's rest of their enemy.

The army is rapidly accommodating itself to the inconveniences occasioned by the sudden bombardment of Sonderborg. Considerable blame, I think, attaches to the military authorities, inasmuch as they had made no preparations whatever for an eventuality so extremely possible, if not probable. Had the Prussians assaulted the works of Dybbol while everything was in confusion during the height of the bombardment, they would have done so, to say the least, under very favourable circumstances. That this was not done is no merit of the besieged. However, the danger is happily past, and everybody is shaking down again into his place.

The misery of the hundreds of families driven out of their homes is perhaps only beginning in reality; but still, for the present, they have either got away from the island or found shelter in its more distant parts. Great numbers have fled across to Fünen, and the harbour of Hörup is half emptied of the vast flotilla of fishing smacks which lay at anchor there, with the white pennant floating at their masthead to secure them from the fire of the Prussian batteries as they tack across the bay. Riding over the island today, I met but few of the dreary processions of homeless families which were so frequent during the first two days after the bombardment. But two long strings of vans were still engaged in carting away furniture from Sonderborg.

The articles of value had gone first, and the loads I met were composed of the poorest and commonest household goods. The wonder was that a little town of four thousand people could have possessed such an infinite amount of furniture. The shopkeepers are opening new stores at Augustenburg, and the spirit of the army remains undaunted.

CHAPTER 9

Days of Waiting

April 8.

Never was there, I should think, a contest waged on more unequal conditions than that which is now being carried on between
the Danes and the Germans. I have no doubt that the Prussians before
Dybbol have some disadvantages peculiar to themselves. They have no
town close to their entrenchments, as the Danes had till the other day
at Sonderborg; and it is probable that a large portion of their army has
had to sleep habitually under canvas, or even in the open air. If any
faith whatever is to be placed in the reports of scouts and deserters,
the amount of sickness in the camp of the besiegers has been relatively
much greater than in that of the besieged. The Danes, too, are carrying on the war amidst a population which, if only passively friendly,
is certainly not hostile, while the Germans have found the inhabitants
of Northern Schleswig, if not actively hostile, assuredly not friendly
to their cause.

Both armies are well fed and clothed, and the Danes have doubtless
suffered less from the inclemency of the weather than their adversaries, who are not acclimatised to this most trying of climates. We are
now well on into April, yet the weather would be cold for an English
January. The sun is powerful enough, but the wind comes fresh from
the Arctic regions, without the chill being taken off. In the shade it
freezes all day long; the ground is as hard as iron under foot; the ponds
and ditches are coated over with ice; and every few hours a pelting
snowstorm comes on, powdering the whole face of the country with
a layer of snow.

Still, making all allowance for the difficulties under which the Germans suffer equally with, if not to a greater degree than, the Danes,
the balance of the account is heavily in favour of the Prussians. With

regard to mere numbers, the enemy, according to the lowest calculation, has four men in the field for every one of the Danes. He has behind him almost unlimited reserves, from which he can make good his losses; while the recruiting powers of Denmark are pretty well exhausted. If he could purchase the life of each Danish soldier by the loss of two of his own, the exchange would be an advantageous one as far as the prospects of the war are concerned. In arms, artillery, means of transport, money, and all the materiel of war, he is infinitely superior to his antagonist.

Even under the most favourable circumstances, the position of a besieger is always pleasanter than that of the besieged. The initiative, the power of action, the direction of the campaign—the *beau rôle*, in fact, of the drama—rest with the Germans. If the weather is inclement, or the ammunition has run short, or the men seem tired, the Prussians can virtually suspend operations, and wait till a more favourable conjuncture arrives. The Danes can have no respite of this kind: at any moment they are liable to be attacked; they must always be on the alert, always waiting for the blow to fall.

A cannonade a little brisker than usual—an apparent commotion at the outposts—is sufficient to disturb the whole army from its hard-earned rest. The same rule would apply, though in a less measure, to the besiegers, if they were exposed to the risk of sudden "sorties." I should be sorry to say that such an event were impossible, but still it has never happened hitherto; and though the Prussians must be, and doubtless are, prepared for its occurrence, the danger with them is a possible, but not a probable one.

Except on the two or three occasions when the Germans have chosen to force on an engagement, their troops are exposed to no constant danger. Their artillery is so superior, that they can fire at a safe distance, and can take the lives of their enemies without exposing their own. It would be folly to blame them for this, or call them cowards because they make the best use of their material advantages. War is not now—even if it ever was, which I greatly doubt—a matter of chivalry. If the Prussians can place their guns out of range of the Danish batteries, they are morally bound to do so; but there is no particular heroism in firing off guns from a position of safety.

Moreover, the Prussians have the enormous advantage of being upon the winning side. Given the present condition of the two combatants, the fall of Dybbol is a mere question of time. It is, I believe, an axiom of military science, that any fortress, whose garrison is unable or unwilling to disturb the besiegers by "sorties," must be captured sooner or later; and there is nothing in the position of Dybbol to make it an exception to this law. The utmost the Danes either can or do hope for, is to fight out a losing battle long enough for the chapter of accidents to come to their rescue. The soldiers have no prospect of victorious marches, of triumphant entries into conquered cities, of plunder, and spoil, and glory, to cheer up their spirits. All they have to pray for is to fall one by one, score by score, company by company, slowly enough to keep back the advance of the enemy for a few days or weeks, or it may be months longer.

It is not even in the open field, in the mad excitement of battle, that they can hope to fall; but behind trenches, and on the bare hillside, killed by an unseen enemy, whom they are powerless to assault in turn. Not a bright prospect, surely, to animate men on the eve of death. Unless you appreciate this fact fully, it is impossible to do justice to the courage of this gallant people. All that the Danish soldier has to do now is to lie in the trenches and wait for death. Every other evening, about dusk, the troops relieve each other at the batteries and along the various camps and posts on the eastern slope of Dybbol Hill.

The relieving companies have to march from their country quarters through the deserted town of Sonderborg, across the open bridges, and up the exposed hillside. From the moment they have crossed the summit of Sonderborg Hill they are under fire. This "*via dolorosa*," as it may well be called, extends for a matter of two long miles, up and down steep slopes, and over broken ground. With the irregular, spasmodic, wandering fire of the enemy, it is impossible to say at any moment when or at what point the shower of shells may begin to fall. It is difficult for the dense serried masses of soldiers to move at a rapid pace; it is as impossible for them to find shelter in such large numbers.

If the whirring sound of a shell is heard, there is nothing to be done except to march on stoically during the long-protracted seconds that elapse before its explosion, trusting that it may fall out of harm's way. Of course, the chances are immensely in the troops' favour as against any individual shell, and every possible advantage is taken of the undulations of the ground; but still the element of danger cannot possibly be eliminated. When at last the soldiers have readied their destination, they have to seek the comparative shelter of some mound, or trench, or hillock: there, for long hours of day and night, they lie on damp straw, or on the frost-bitten earth, hearing the shells whizzing over their heads or exploding round them, with no change to their monotony except when a killed or wounded comrade is borne past them from the front.

Weary with cold, fatigue, and watching, they wait out their appointed time, and then have to retrace their anxious journey back to the country quarters, where they arrive jaded, worn out, and yet still patient. It is the troops I have observed coming fresh from rest and marching into danger who shout and sing, not those coming home out of it. A harder trial to an enemy's courage cannot well be imagined; it could not be stood better than by these Danish soldiers. It would be easy for them to desert from the outposts if they were so minded, as the Prussian sentries stand within sight and hail; but deserters have been very rare hitherto, and the few there have been were almost exclusively South Schleswigers.

Whenever the time comes for departure, the men fall into their ranks steadily, if without enthusiasm, and march forward with a stout, firm step, never pushing on recklessly, but never loitering behind. Every day the number of men killed and wounded at the front and on the march to and fro, though not absolutely considerable, is still large enough to bring home the fact of the danger to every man in the army. But no hesitation is visible on the part of the soldiers: they look tired, and dirt-soiled, and weary, but it is their duty to advance when the order comes, and from that duty they never think of shirking.

It has been my fortune, within the last few days, to live in the close neighbourhood of some of the country quarters of the Danish Army. Troops quieter or better behaved than these peasant-soldiers no other nation could produce; whether they ever change their clothes I have reason to doubt, and tidiness is not their strongest feature. All night, and most of the day, they sleep in the straw; when they are awake, they smoke constantly, except when they are eating. Brown bread, fat pork, and milk compose the bulk of their meals, which they take hours in preparing, and hours more in eating. Drinking never seems to be carried to excess amongst them; and indeed the landlord of their quarters tells me that a great part of their pay is spent on the purchase of fresh milk, which to them is almost a necessity of life.

I cannot perceive, even, that they are addicted to the other frailty of most armies, or make hot love to the girls about the farm; they do not read much, and I have hardly ever seen them playing at cards; but then a great portion of their empty time—which, with eating and sleeping, is not long—is taken up in writing letters. These epistles are composed, as it were, in common; and every waiter appears to have the assistance of half-a-dozen comrades in suggesting what he should say, and how he ought to put it. Indeed, the correspondence of the army must be enormous. I was present this morning at a postal delivery, and, I should think, out of a hundred men, fully a third got letters. It was curious to watch the eagerness with which the lucky owners ran up as their names were called over by the sergeant. But when they had got their letters they proceeded to enjoy the pleasure with due deliberation.

They first looked at the superscription, and read it carefully a dozen times over; then they inspected the seal, and turned it round, so as to view it in every direction; and then, with extreme caution, they cut the letter open with large clasp-knives, taking care to leave the seal intact. When they had accomplished all these preliminary ceremonies, they placed the epistles in their pockets unread, till a more convenient opportunity should arrive for their perusal.

The officers have hardly much more to do than the men. Drilling never appears to have been carried on with much attention in the Danish army, and even if it had been, the men, while in country quarters, have too much need of rest to be disturbed unnecessarily. So the officers kill time as best they can; they read the papers, play on the piano, stroll a little—a very little—about the farm premises, sleep a good deal in bed, and doze still more upon the chairs and sofas of the sitting-room; talking occasionally, and waking up in earnest towards meal times. Even amongst them, as far as I have seen, playing at cards is rare, and gambling, in the real sense of the word, quite unknown. It is not a pleasant feeling, even to a comparative stranger like myself, when the time comes for the departure to the front.

Here are men you have been for hours living with, laughing with, and talking to as friends, and yet you know there is a chance—not altogether a remote one—that the cordial shake of the hand they give you in parting may be a farewell one for ever. As a matter of routine, they go forth to their duty; and when they come home, after the hours of service are over, they seldom talk about their adventures, but take them as things which need no comment. It is so, I fancy, more or less in every army, but more so in the Danish than in any other. It would be impossible to encounter danger with more outward indifference than is exhibited by the men amongst whom I live; it is not that they are indifferent to its reality, but that the sense of duty reigns paramount.

It is a strange life which we, the scant and few spectators of the bombardment of Dybbol, have now to lead. Any day, any hour almost, may bring things to a crisis. Every night we expect to be woke up, before daybreak comes, by the sound of the alarm; any morning we know it to be doubtful where we shall sleep at night. My bags are ready packed for immediate departure; when I undress myself before going to bed, I carefully put within reach the half-dozen articles I must needs carry away with me, if we should have to run for it at a moment's notice. But indeed it must be a short and sharp summons that would not give me time to gather up the few possessions which I still own in Alsen.

Most of my luggage "*went under*," as Yankees say, in my flight from Sonderborg: shirts, collars, linen of every kind had to be left to the mercy of the elements. If they have not been already devoured by the flames, they have certainly been drenched by the rain, which has pelted down through the shell-battered roof of the room wherein I used to dwell. At any rate, I shall see them no more; clean linen and I have bidden each other a long farewell; even my soap deserted me in the hour of need. I have one shirt left, and one only—that in which I write to you now—in which I have slept for so many nights that I am afraid to count them—in which I shall have to sleep for, I am still more afraid to think, how many nights yet.

My collars have been turned and re-turned till it is impossible to say which side is the least dirty. My handkerchiefs have ceased to be presentable; my boots are wearing out at the toes; and my coat is getting shaky at the elbows, ragged about the cuffs. If this goes on much longer, I shall have to wear my ambassadorial fur coat, and conceal by its outward grandeur the absence of all under-clothing. There is no possibility of refitting myself unless I leave the island. Sonderborg was the one emporium of Als, and Sonderborg is no more. Every shop is empty, most of the stores have been burnt, and what are left have been carried far away to safe quarters.

In all Augustenburg, ducal residence as it was, there is not a shop except an apothecary's and a pork-butcher's. By a fortunate meeting with an itinerant pedlar, I have managed to secure two pair of worsted socks, and a gorgeous, flaring pocket-handkerchief which would madden a drove of bulls, and bears upon it a pictorial representation of a railway train, a triumphal arch, and a galaxy of flags. These are treasures indeed; but the pedlar's stock is exhausted, and there is no prospect of its being replenished. Still, dirt is a calamity I am, fortunately, able to bear with philosophy; cleanliness is, after all, only a matter of comparison. In the kingdom of the blind, according to the French proverb, the one-eyed is king; and in a place where everybody is dirty, and ragged, and out at elbows, the possession of a pocket-handkerchief and a fur coat constitutes a relative splendour of apparel.

Everything depends upon the point of view from which you regard it. I find that a friend of mine, who was present with me the other day, when a shell struck the ground unpleasantly near to us, has described his own demeanour to his acquaintances as being that of dignified composure; to my eyes I recollect he bore the aspect of a stock-fish with its mouth open. So, in like manner, what you would consider dirt in London, I may be disposed to regard as elegance in Sonderborg.

As far as my quarters are concerned, I have no cause to complain. I am excellently fed—over fed in fact, for we breakfast at nine, have luncheon at eleven, dine at two, and sup at eight, and each meal is most substantial. In company with a friend, I occupy a room where I can read and write and sleep in quiet; the only objection to it being that, in order to reach it. I have to go through two kitchens and an outhouse, and have to stumble over a score of soldiers, who are always sleeping in the straw at the foot of the winding staircase which leads up to my abode. One special advantage of my quarters, which my kind landlord expatiated upon when he first showed me the room, is that, if the enemy should come in by the front door during the night, I can let myself down from the windows on to the heaps of farmyard straw which is piled outside.

But my real objection to our present mode of life is its exceeding monotony. I thought Sonderborg dull enough, but the unfortunate little town was a Paris compared with the farmhouse where I have been lucky enough to find shelter. There, at any rate, were always new faces about the streets, the sight of troops moving backwards and forwards, and acquaintances to speak to at any moment. But our tiny world is completely broken up. We are all scattered over the island miles away from each other, along rough cross-country roads; and the round to head-quarters, to the post, and the telegraph-office takes up the best part of the morning.

Yet I am better off in this respect than anyone else I know. The sea-shore lies within five minutes' walk; and if anything happens at the front, I can get a sight of what is going on from positions which command the maximum of view with the minimum of risk. In truth, the area over which I can wander is now sadly circumscribed. To cross the bridges is, as a rule, to expose yourself to an utterly useless danger, and the whole hillside of Dybbol is carefully eschewed, except by those who go there reluctantly on military duty. All day long, shells are cast haphazard, as it seems, from the enemy's batteries, over every part of the hill, and there is scarcely a spot where it is safe to stand out of cover.

Sonderborg itself is deserted. There is nothing to see in its bare walls, and roofless houses, and silent streets; and if you had a fancy for wandering amidst its ruins, you are very likely to be knocked down by the shells which come whirring from time to time across the bay from Broagerland, crashing the crumbling dwellings about your ears. At evening, when the fire almost always dies out, I sometimes make my way by a long circuit to the upper part of the town, where sundry officers of my acquaintance are stationed. Hitherto this part of the town, which lies on the further or inland side of the hill, has escaped any serious injury, chiefly, I suspect, because the elevation required to carry shells above the crest of the hill would subject the Prussian cannon on the Wemming Bund shores to a severer test than their gunners like to resort to.

In this "*Haute-Ville*" of Sonderborg the shops are closed, and the houses almost deserted. Still there are one or two pothouses, or "*be-vaertnings*" as they are called, kept open for the service of the soldiers encamped near the town; and there I sometimes come across old acquaintances loafing disconsolately about the half-closed tap-rooms. Inland, of course, I could walk or ride for miles; but in the present conjuncture of affairs it is not advisable to stray far away from the front.

Any hour the engagement might begin, and any hour it might become necessary to shift my quarters; so for the most part I hang about the shore, or the farm-yard where my tent is pitched for the time. There is too, within half a mile, a long beech wood, running down to the sea; there much of my time is spent. There are no leaves upon the trees, scarcely a bud yet upon the bushes; but the bare white trunks stand so near together, and the canopy of boughs is interlaced so closely overhead, that one is pretty well sheltered both from wind and rain. And here I stroll about the low sandy bluffs watching the white puffs of smoke as the shells dart to and fro between Dybbol and Broagerland.

Then I have daily to ride from ten to twenty miles in search of the letters and newspapers, without which our existence would be unbearable. Since the evacuation of Sonderborg the post has been flitting about in every direction. By one of those cumbrous arrangements due to a want of organising power, very conspicuous in all Danish arrangements, there are two places where letters are delivered: Augustenburg and Hörup-Haf; and in the former place there are two post-offices. Practically, our letters lie indifferently at each of these three depots; and as the two towns are five miles distant from each other and from the farm where I reside, I have to make my way in search of letters over a long stretch of ground.

Happily, I have got a sort of qualified ownership in a friend's horse, and my ride, as amateur postman, is not the least pleasant part of the day. If the weather were only warm, my life here would be tolerable enough; but then—nothing is perfect in this bad world—if the weather *were* warm, my shirt would be intolerable.

To understand at all our existence, you must suppose it to be passed amidst a constant accompaniment of shells. The first sound I hear when I wake in the morning, the last before I go to sleep at night, is the boom of cannon. We talk of nothing else and think of nothing else, except whether the shelling is faster or slower than usual, and what progress the enemy is making. Every day, and often many times in the day, we have arrivals at our quarters of officers just come in from the front, and from these I hear constant accounts of the state of affairs. I cannot think that particulars of such a nature can be of any interest to non-Danish readers. Whether the name of the corporal who lost his arm yesterday was Hansen, or Petersen, or Rasmussen—one of the three it is almost certain to have been—or whether the gun whose muzzle was knocked clean off stood in battery A, B, or C, are not matters of importance, as far as the outer public is concerned.

It is only, therefore, of the broad features of the siege that I wish to speak. This much may be justly said, that the final struggle seems growing daily nearer and nearer. The Prussian fire has improved in accuracy, or, at any rate, the ranges of the different positions are now better known; the circular chain of batteries which is to surround the foot of Dybbol Hill is rapidly approaching completion. There are now fourteen, or some say sixteen, batteries, in position at different points between Avn-Bierg on the Wemming Bund and Sand-Bierg on the Als-Sund.

Yesterday afternoon, we had two or three hours of the heaviest firing we have yet known; the roar of cannon was almost continuous; and its severity may be judged from the fact that upwards of 1,500 shells were thrown close round Dybbol windmill, with the object of setting fire to the farm-buildings which surround it. At last the attempt was successful, and a dense cloud of smoke rose from straw-roofs, and covered the whole crest of the hill. Strange to say, the windmill itself, though its sides are thatched, did not catch fire, and still stands erect in defiance of the enemy. The centre batteries suffered more severely than they have done yet; but, fortunately, the fire was much slackened after nightfall, and the Danes have been able to repair the injuries inflicted.

Today the fire has been much less constant, possibly because the whole country is covered with a rainy mist. But the belief amongst all the officers here is that the attack cannot be much longer delayed.

April 10.

Will the Conference be followed by an immediate armistice? This is the one political question that occupies the thoughts of all persons here who trouble themselves to think of anything but the immediate occurrences of the hour. Before this letter reaches you, the question will have been decided. I trust, most sincerely, in the affirmative.

If it were thought possible to hold Dybbol with security, the idea of any armistice which left the Germans in occupation of what they now possess would be rejected with indignation. When I first came here, the belief in the practical impregnability of Dybbol was very prevalent. Having seen the resources of both armies, it is an impression which I never shared; and I have not hesitated to express the conviction that, whenever the Germans choose to exert their overwhelming superiority in real earnest, the capture of the Danish position is a mere question of time.

This impression has of late made way rapidly amongst the more moderate of the Danes, officers as well as civilians. This change of sentiment is certainly not owing to any shortcomings on the part of the Danish soldiers; on the contrary, these peasant levies have shown a courage, a patience, and a power of endurance, of which the best trained troops of any nation in the world might well be proud. What has weighed down, what is weighing down, and what must weigh down, the besieged army, is its immense inferiority in numbers, and in the efficiency of artillery. The Latin poet says:

It is not a quarrel where you beat and I am beaten!

It is not a battle where one party fires and the other is fired at; yet such is virtually the contest which is being waged between Germany and Denmark. Short as the line of Dybbol is, its defence requires all,

229

and more than all, the troops which the Government of Copenhagen can place at the disposal of General Gerlach. There are not soldiers enough to assume the offensive: to act on the defensive is all that the Danes can do, or hope to do. Strange to say, the Prussians are allowed to pursue the erection of their trenches, and parallels, and batteries, with but little molestation from the besieged. I know, indeed, that orders not to fire upon earthworks in course of formation within range, and full in view of Danish batteries, have created much wonderment, not to use a stronger term, amongst the officers.

But the general impression seems to be that the whole resources and energies of the Danish Army must be reserved to repel the enemy whenever he attempts to carry the works by storm. There must, however, be at last an end to a conflict so unequal. Every day that passes weakens the Danes by casualties in the field, and still more by the constant watching and hardships to which their soldiers are exposed. The amount of sickness in the camp is very great, and for another month there is no prospect of any lasting improvement in the climate.

Under these circumstances the Danes are fighting a losing battle. How much longer they can hold out is a question about which it is impossible to form an opinion: so much depends, not only on the accidents of war, but on the vigour with which the Germans prosecute the siege, and on sacrifices they are prepared to make for the accomplishment of their object. When I was in Flensburg ten weeks ago, the German officers were confident that three days would not elapse before Dybbol were in their possession; yet the works remain untaken, and are undoubtedly stronger than they were at the commencement of February. It is, therefore, idle to predict how much longer the defence may not be maintained. Enough already has been done to vindicate the honour of the Danish Army, and the question is now one of political expediency, not of professional military dignity.

Meanwhile, if the Prussians are, as their newspapers stated, to enter the Conference as the conquerors of Alsen, they must make haste about their work. Today an assault was confidently expected, and this morning the bombardment was very brisk for a couple of hours. It has died away again, however, and no forward movement is yet reported.

8 p.m.

The firing from the new Prussian batteries has been carried on all the afternoon with great vigour. At one time the number of shells averaged fifteen a minute. The Danish batteries have replied but little.

A dense fog has set in, so that it is impossible to see anything or even to distinguish clearly the quarter from which the sounds come. We could discern, during an interval, when the fog partially cleared off, that Dybbol windmill has at last been struck down, but its stump still remains erect.

April 12.

In ordinary years, these two last days ought to have been glad ones in this island of Alsen. The long, dreary winter has broken at last, and the spring has burst upon us in all its freshness. We may have snow-storms yet, and the ponds may be frozen again, as they were three days ago, but the winter tide is on its ebb, and the summer well-nigh at hand. How delicious is the first sensation of warmth, you must have shivered for months in a northern winter in order to understand.

The fire is out, and I am writing by an open window, breathing in the fresh, soft air; the sun is shining brightly; the birds are chirping merrily; the young lambs have been turned out for the first time from their winter shelter, and are bleating in the fields. The dogs about the farmyard are basking sleepily in the sunlight; and the bushes underneath my window have covered themselves, as it were in a single night, with festoons of green leaves.

Yet, though all nature is glad, this outburst of spring brings no gladness for the defenders of Alsen. Never during the siege have I witnessed so much depression in the army as during the last three days. The dispersion of the camp at Sonderborg has in itself operated unfavourably on the spirits of the soldiers. As long as the little town remained the headquarters, the troops were cheered by each other's company, and by the consciousness that they formed part of a force which, however small compared to that of its enemies, was still considerable in itself. Now that the whole army is dispersed in small detachments over the country, these sources of encouragement have vanished.

The men hang about their dull quarters, waiting listlessly for the time to come when it is their turn to go under fire, and brood constantly upon the forlornness of their position and the dreariness of their prospects. No army could be subjected to such a trial without injury; the wonder is that that injury has been, as yet, so trifling. The Prussians have at last adopted a plan of action, and have stuck to it with dogged pertinacity. That plan consists in hurling a continuous shower of shells on the Danish batteries, and on the eastern slopes of

Dybbol Hill.

For the last forty hours especially the fire has been incessant. Even at the moment when I write, the sound of the shells is like that of an axe striking a tree with continuous blows. Stroke follows stroke with monotonous regularity. If there is a moment's interval of quiet, it is followed by a cannonade of redoubled violence, till lost time has been made up for, and then the firing subsides into its wonted order.

The whole base of Dybbol Hill is encircled with a range of batteries, and every day the number is increased, and the chain more tightly drawn. Thus the different lines of fire intersect each other at every angle, and the shells fall like hailstones over the whole width and breadth of the Danish encampment. At first the number of shots was noted carefully; but now that the fire has become continuous, all count has been lost, and only a vague surmise can be formed of the rate at which the bombardment has been carried on.

This morning, at a period when the fire seemed more slack than usual, I counted a hundred shells in a little under a quarter of an hour, and during the hottest part of the engagement, I have no doubt that as many as a thousand projectiles were thrown from the Prussian batteries in the course of each hour. I have spoken before now of what seemed to me the apparent inaccuracy of this never-ceasing fire; and though the Danish officers are astounded at the excellence of the Prussian practice, it is still evident to me that, in reality, the precision with which a shot can be directed against a given object falls far short of what it ought to be by the theory of gunnery.

As I mentioned before, I think, fifteen hundred shells had to be thrown before the enemy could succeed in knocking down a windmill on the very crest of the hill; and the injury done to the batteries, prominent as they are, has been comparatively slight; the shells constantly bury themselves in the earth without exploding, and even when they explode against the breastworks the quantity of earth displaced is seldom very great.

Unfortunately, to dismount the guns, or silence the batteries, or to remove the obstacles in the way of storming the works, does not appear to be the present object of the enemy. His plan is to make the hillside utterly untenable, to render access to the front from the island so dangerous as to be impossible, and to force the Danes to abandon their position and retire from Dybbol. How far this scheme is likely to be successful, it is hard to say, and as yet I fancy the military authorities of the army are as ignorant on the subject as I am myself. All I can say is that the test to which the courage and perseverance of the Danes are put is one which human strength or resolution cannot, I think, endure for long.

At the risk of repeating myself, I must, in justice to the Danes, impress upon you what are the conditions they have now to struggle against. "Submit" would perhaps be a more correct word than "struggle," for the worst of their lot is that it is entirely passive. There is nothing, literally nothing, they can do; they are not numerous enough to make a sortie; and, brave even as the soldiers are, they lack that dash and discipline combined which would enable them to charge the enemy with much prospect of success.

Their own batteries are perforce almost silent. If a single shot is fired, it is answered by a perfect torrent of shells from the Prussian guns, and the mere fact of firing indicates with fatal accuracy the position where the Danish cannon are placed, and entails a certain retaliation. Practically, the only thing to be done is to reserve the fire for the decisive moment, whose speedy advent every Danish soldier prays for eagerly. Nothing can be worse than this resistless cannonade. Extreme accuracy of aim is no object to the Prussians now; the more widely their shells are strewn over the whole hillside, the better for them. The enemy is so close at hand, that if he chooses he can advance to the attack with but a few minutes' warning.

It is essential, therefore, for the Danes to keep a very large force within easy reach of the batteries, in addition to the troops required to man the long chain of earthworks. In other words, as long as the crest of the hill is the Danish line of defence, a great portion of this small army, and almost all its artillery, must be kept on the Schleswig side of the Sund, that is, on the slopes of Dybbol Hill. Now the object of the Prussians is to make every man in that force feel that at no time and in no place is he safe from destruction. That object has been pretty well attained. There is not a field, or house, or hollow where shells have not fallen.

As soon as the different stations can be reached, the soldiers shelter themselves behind trenches, and slopes, and hedges, and there they are in comparative safety; but the safety is only comparative after all. There these gallant fellows lie patiently for long dreary hours; they have to wait there till the alarm sounds, or till a shell comes crashing in amongst them; then the mangled bodies of their comrades are carted silently away, and the survivors crowd closer together, waiting for the next dread summons.

It is not a battle, but a slaughter, a "*battue*" of human beings. It is impossible to sleep or walk about, or to stir from shelter, till at last the hour comes for the men to be relieved; and then they have to march homewards over the bare roads, across the open bridges, and up the narrow streets, along a line of route shelled upon constantly from the enemy's batteries. The march to and from the front is more perilous than the sojourn there, but the mere fact of movement more than compensates for the additional danger. Of course, the chances are immensely in favour of each individual soldier escaping without injury—if not, the maintenance of the position would be impossible; yet the casualties of each day are as great as those in a serious engagement, and constitute no slight loss for so small an army.

Without excitement, without warning, without power of firing a shot or striking a blow in return, man after man is knocked down, maimed, or killed. When a shell bursts, the fragments explode far and near, carrying death with them. What the actual numbers of killed and wounded on any one day may be, it is impossible to tell as yet; but, from what I hear, I should put it down as not less than a hundred. There is one field-battery, with which I am well acquainted, which has just passed four-and-twenty hours at the front. One man and two horses killed, two men severely wounded and one slightly, and two cannon out of eight destroyed—this is the list of its casualties, and I have no reason to suppose it to be an unusually heavy one.

I have this moment heard that the officer in command of the field-battery which went out to replace the one I have mentioned was struck by a shell on his way to the front, and is severely wounded. The mode, too, of death is singularly horrible to the bystanders. When a man falls in battle struck by a rifle shot, there is little beyond the fact of death to shock the nerves; but here it is different: men are literally blown into fragments, and disfigured in the most awful manner. A shell fell yesterday amongst a party of five men standing near a bridge. Three escaped unhurt: but according to their statement, the two others had disappeared, and all they could find was a number of limbs scattered in the bushes round. The story may be—probably is—exaggerated, but it is not impossible.

Yesterday morning, as the fire was for the time directed solely against the works, I ventured into the town, and happened to be by the church as they were bringing the dead bodies in from the front. The dreary procession was almost over when I reached the spot, but still there was one waggon as yet unloaded. The carts drew up at the entrance of the churchyard, and there men were waiting with stretchers, which they placed alongside the conveyance. A couple of soldiers got into the waggon, and threw out, one by one, the knapsack, the musket, and the powder-flask of the dead man, which were carried off to the depot; and then they took up roughly, though not irreverently, a bundle, so it seemed, of charred clothes and discoloured flesh and clotted blood, and, swinging it by the head and legs, lowered it upon the stretcher; then an arm and the stump of a foot followed piecemeal, and the ghastly burden was earned into the church.

As the stretcher passed me I caught sight of the man's head. That the head of a human-being, alive but a few hours before, could look like what I saw, I could not have believed. The features were utterly indistinguishable; the skin was that of a mummy, thousands of years old, smeared over with blood; and yet, in spite of the disfigurement of the face, there was upon it an expression, so it seemed to me, of unutterable terror, which has haunted me ever since. Fancy the effect that such an object must have produced, carried through ranks of men who know that the same fate might await them at any moment, and then remember that such spectacles are of hourly occurrence.

In defiance of all this, the Danish soldiers still go forth dauntlessly to take their place at the works. There is not much of singing now; but the men march forward silently and resolutely. I saw yesterday some soldiers freshly arrived, who were quite excited at the prospect of going under fire. "Oh," said an officer to me, by whom I was standing, "after a couple of days they will lose all their gaiety, but they will go on just the same."

So it is: there is to me something touching and grand in the aspect of these Danish regiments as they move on boldly towards their appointed place. As they pass their comrades returning homewards and greet them with a cheer, they might repeat with truth the saying of the old Roman gladiators, the famous "*Morituri te salutant*." They are going "*into the jaws of death*"—going to be slaughtered helplessly by an unseen enemy—and yet hitherto no reluctance to advance has been manifested. Their courage does not spring from the passive obedience of the Russian, or the fatalism of Eastern nations, or the reckless daring of French soldiers. They go out to die, much as Englishmen might do, because it is their duty to obey, without murmuring, but not without questioning.

Amongst the officers the wisdom of exposing the army to this helpless slaughter is gravely questioned. On Sunday a council of war was held, at which it was determined to hold Dybbol to the last; but if this fire should be continued, no courage in the world can hold out indefinitely. Each day the danger of the position grows greater. Already officers state openly that the army is being sacrificed to the wilful obstinacy of the populace at Copenhagen. Much of this talk, no doubt, simply represents the impatience of the moment; but it also indicates a feeling which may ultimately influence the fate of the campaign.

The almost universal belief entertained, or at any rate professed, by military men here, is that Alsen can be defended after Dybbol is captured or abandoned. It is a belief I have never shared; and my own opinion is that if an armistice could be obtained by which the Prussians took Dybbol, while the Danes were allowed to hold the island, it would be the best prospect that Denmark could hope for. Before, however, you receive this letter I fancy that, one way or other, the question must be decided; the present conjuncture of affairs cannot last for many days longer.

April 13.

All last night the firing was incessant. So ceaseless was it, that I, one of the soundest of sleepers, was constantly woke up by the dull, heavy booming of the artillery. According as the fitful wind shifted, the sound faded away, or grew so loud and distinct that it was difficult to believe shells were not bursting close to the house where I was sheltered. About midnight, a gentleman who shares my room with me roused me up to say he was certain a shell had fallen in the farmyard, and proposed that we should go out and see what was the matter. However, as it was pitch dark, and not a soul was stirring in the house, it seemed to me that we had much better lie still and wait till we heard somebody else moving.

It turned out that I was right, and that the noise we—or rather he—had been startled out of sleep by was occasioned by the explosion of a powder magazine in one of the Dybbol forts. This morning the fire has been comparatively slack, and what there was has been directed against the town. A building close to the parish church was set on fire, but the conflagration has not spread. It is strange how difficult it seems to be to burn down the town. As all the houses are built with woodwork frames, and many of the roofs are of thatch, I should have thought beforehand, that a conflagration once kindled would have laid all the city in ashes in a few hours' time.

This has not been the case, though we have now had a dozen large fires in different parts of Sonderborg. The explanation I take to be, that there are numbers of open spaces, gardens, orchards, and yards between the houses, and that the streets are too broad, and the dwellings too low, for a strong draught of air to be created. At present, the destruction of the deserted place by fire would be rather a gain than otherwise to the Danes. As I am speaking of the bombardment, I may as well say here that some of the English papers, while condemning most justly the conduct of the Prussians, appear to me to spoil their case by confounding two completely different issues.

It is absurd to blame the Prussians for bombarding the town at all. Assuming that they are justified in making war, they are authorised to carry on the war in the most efficient manner; and there can be no question that they have materially improved their position by shelling the Danes out of a town which was of extreme value for the defence of Dybbol. Much in the same way, I do not condemn them for re-commencing the bombardment from time to time, so as to hinder the Danes from returning to their quarters.

The one fact for which I hold them guilty of the gravest condemnation is, that they bombarded a city filled with women, children, and non-combatants of every kind *without the slightest notice or intimation.* Six hours' delay could not have entailed the least damage to the besiegers; they are not even able to plead the excuse that they intended to storm the position during the confusion created by an unexpected bombardment of the city. The only attempt at palliation of the offence I have heard put forward is, that the Danes had previously declined to accede to a request of the Prussians not to bombard Dybbol church, which was used as a hospital for the German wounded soldiers.

I have not been able to ascertain whether there is any foundation for this story; but, even if true, the excuse is a most impotent one. The church stands directly in front of the Danish batteries, and is surrounded by earthworks the Prussians have themselves thrown up. If the Germans deliberately chose to use a building for an hospital lying at the foot of the Danish batteries, while they have scores of villages in the rear completely out of range, they could not reasonably expect the Danes to cease from firing at a spot from which a cannonade was being directed against Dybbol.

So, in like manner, cruel as I feel the system of warfare recently adopted by the Prussians to be towards the Danes, I cannot blame the Germans for it. If they believe they can shell the Danes out of Dybbol from a distance, without risking the cost of an attack by storm, I think they are right in sparing the lives of their own soldiers. There is no heroism in firing shells when you are safe out of harm's way; but also there is no cowardice in so doing, if you can effect the end of war by such a process. Still, in spite of one's better reason, there is something less revolting in ordinary acts of war than in this cold-blooded manner of dealing out death blindfold. The amount of the Danish loss each day is kept secret, but it must certainly be very heavy.

Yesterday an officer who visited the works told me he saw six men killed by one shell, close to the spot where he was standing. A Danish major was struck dead this morning, while writing in his tent, by the explosion of a shell; two guardsmen working at the trenches were severely wounded. These are only a few accidents of the night's work I have heard accidentally on my rambles today. I give them merely as samples of a score of similar events that are narrated as each division of troops returns from its duty at the front. I happened, when riding out early today, to meet the train of sick and wounded who were being brought down in carts to Hörup-Haf, in order to be shipped to Fünen or Copenhagen. I counted at least forty carts, averaging four soldiers in every cart.

I am told a similar train comes daily from the hospitals at Augustenburg. If you add to the soldiers well enough to be removed the number of killed, and of men too severely wounded to bear removal, you will see at what a fearful rate the Danish Army is being weakened by this murderous fire. Eight hundred men have arrived today from Fredericia to make up for the recent losses; but I am afraid that any reinforcements Denmark is in a position to send can only serve to prolong a hopeless struggle. The Danes are too brave to be used up as mere food for powder; and yet this is the only purpose that they now can serve.

The intelligence that the meeting of the Conference is adjourned for ten days has been received with bitter disappointment. The reasons for the delay may be solid enough; but to men like the defenders of Alsen, fighting a battle becoming day by day more hopeless, each day's delay in the conclusion of an armistice is not only a protraction of their agony, but almost a death-blow to their prospect of escape. They receive the news with much the same feelings as Bluebeard's wife might have heard from Sister Anne that the brothers spurring to her rescue had stopped upon the road to bait their horses.

It is, I believe, impossible that the next ten days can pass without creating some material change in the present position of affairs at Dybbol, and that change one unfavourable to the Danes. This belief, at any rate, is the one entertained by the Danish officers. To add to their disappointment, they are gravely informed that, by the beginning of next June, Sweden will have her army encamped in her southern provinces. I recollect once being present in a company when the question was discussed; What would be the best thing to do if you saw a man drowning in a river? A sententious acquaintance of mine said:

The one thing is for the man immersed to keep his head cool; so I should stand upon the bank and endeavour to divert his attention from his danger, by starting some indifferent topic of conversation.

This, it strikes me, is the course of policy pursued by the bystanders toward Denmark in her death-struggle.

April 14.

One shell is very like another, and each day's record of events differs little from that of its fellows, except inasmuch as the number of shells is greater or smaller. The part of the besieged is now an entirely passive one; the troops can do nothing except lie behind the trenches, where they find an imperfect shelter, and wait till the Prussians can summon up resolution to complete their work. I calculated, the other day, that since Sunday last not less than 10,000 shells a day had been thrown from the enemy's batteries.

According to an official statement now published at Copenhagen, the number amounted to 12,000. This estimate, however, is infinitely smaller than that given by the German papers. Last week, according to these reports, the position of Dybbol was bombarded by 18 field batteries, with eight companies of heavy artillery, and each of their guns fired on an average 500 shots a day. There are eight guns in each Prussian field battery, and probably double that number in each company of heavy artillery; so that, if this statement be correct, 136,000 shots would have been discharged daily.

This calculation is so palpably absurd, that I am disposed to think there is a mistake in the figures, and I take the real German account to be, that each gun was fired on an average fifty times in a day. If so, the Danish and Prussian estimates would agree tolerably well together. The Danish batteries have practically ceased replying. A score or two of shells have been fired daily, to show that the guns are not silenced, and the losses of the enemy amount daily to some half-dozen men.

I quote these facts to show how completely the contest is a one-sided one. Not only the initiative in the conflict, but the whole dictation of its progress, rests with the Prussians. To spectators on the island, the advance of the enemy appears vacillating, unsatisfactory, and slow. I doubt, however, whether it seems so to the troops engaged in the deface at the front. For the last two days the fire has been much less frequent, and the common opinion is that the Prussians have exhausted their ammunition and are pausing for fresh supplies.

This is a mere surmise, and one the truth of which I am inclined to doubt. The enemy has achieved the first object of the bombardment, that of reducing the batteries to silence. What actual damage has been done to the fortifications it is difficult to ascertain. Considerable injury, however, has been inflicted on the works on the left and in the centre of the Dybbol line; and what is more important, these injuries cannot easily be repaired. The Prussians are now so close, that they can see every movement of their enemy; and the moment working parties are discovered, such a shower of shells is poured upon them, that the attempt has to be abandoned. Under these circumstances, a cessation of fire is of little benefit to the besieged, except in as far as it revives the spirits of the army.

In the night of Wednesday to Thursday the Prussians drove the Danes out of the rifle-pits in front of Battery No. 2, and an attempt to retake them was made without much energy, and was not followed by success. The loss of the Danes on this occasion I have heard variously estimated at from 75 to 200 killed, wounded, and missing. In the last bulletin received here from the War Office in Copenhagen, the amount of loss on the previous day is not given, but is only stated in vague terms to be relatively less than on previous occasions; a statement which in itself is ominous.

The Prussians are said to be erecting new batteries under cover of the captured rifle-pits, only four hundred yards distant from Fort No. 2, which hitherto has stood the brunt of the attack. Yesterday the chief fire of the enemy was turned against the Danish right. The newly-erected batteries of "*Sürlokkegde*" shelled the northern side of Sonderborg and the approaches to the bridges, while those of Sand-Bierg fired across the Sund and burnt down the farmhouses that constitute the hamlet of Rönhave.

The truth is, that the Prussians are pursuing the Anaconda strategy which General M'Clellan designed to carry out in the invasion of the Confederate States. The difference is, that, while the Federals had to surround in their coils a vast continent, the Germans have only to encircle a hill some couple of miles in circumference. The issue cannot, I think, be doubtful; and the marvel to me is, that the victim has struggled so long and so successfully against the gigantic force of his destroyer.

Councils of war have been held daily, at which the question whether a new and superior line of defence should not be adopted has been discussed eagerly. Up to this time, however, the decision has been in favour of a determined resistance. About the wisdom of this decision it is not for me to judge. The evacuation of Dybbol involves, in my opinion, the probable surrender of Alsen; but, on the other hand, an attempt to hold out against overwhelming odds entails a fearful and useless loss of life, and is merely a protraction of the nation's agony. As to the heroism of the resolution, there can be no manner of question.

Meanwhile, for observers and narrators of the siege like myself, there is nothing to be done except to wait wearily. Yet the minor incidents of this struggle are not undeserving, perhaps, of record. It is curious to note how not only the ordinary course of nature, but the ordinary tenour of daily life, goes on with but little alteration.

Seed-time has come round, and the labourers are ploughing and sowing the very fields in which shells fell yesterday, and over which armies may trample tomorrow in their advance or retreat. Great masses of smoke and flame on the right of the town spread over all the island the news that the farmhouses along the Sund have been burnt down by the enemy, and yet the inmates of the dwellings on the left, which are equally exposed to the fire, go on with their wonted duties, as if the time was one of complete peace and quiet. The great farm where I am quartered at this moment stands on a sort of debatable land between peace and war. Four hundred soldiers are stationed here, and the house is crowded to its very cupboards and closets with guests, amongst whom I and two brother correspondents are the only civilians. The house lies somewhat sheltered by the cliffs of the sea-coast, and there is no obvious reason why the Prussians should fire upon it.

Still there is no material reason why they should not shell it if they think good; and their previous conduct has given little cause to hope that any consideration of humanity will restrain them from so doing. If the heights of Dybbol are taken, and if any attempt should be made to defend Alsen, even long enough to allow the Danes to make good their retreat, then the doom of this large farm, its vast barns and stables and cowhouses, will be the same as that of Rönhave, which is now a mass of blackened ruins. Any moment a shell may be sent flying in our direction, and the signal may come for instantaneous departure; and yet, in spite of all this, the work of the farmyard goes on, hour by hour, much as usual. The young children, it is true, have been sent away to a neighbouring village; but a little bright-eyed thing of two years old is still kept in the house, because her mother cannot bear to part with her.

Today, too, two little twins of this numerous family are to come over and see a newborn kid that has been promised them for months as their especial property. The dairymaids and women-servants keep on working about the premises, with a sublime indifference to the constant roar of cannon, though I am afraid their work is somewhat interfered with by the courtship of the soldiers, who idle all day long about the place. The ladies of the family go on with their household duties, cook the dinner, wait—I am ashamed for the gallantry of the Danes to say—at table, and sew in the rare intervals of rest, as if the thought of danger had never crossed their imagination or disturbed their nerves.

Even our host himself, whose property may be destroyed any day, seems to have no anxiety, except how to make us comfortable, and secure our having a great deal more to eat and drink than the small amount he has consented to receive in payment can be possibly supposed to cover. Otherwise one would not suppose from his manner or conversation that he had anything more than a casual spectator's interest in the question, whether his house and stock and property are to be destroyed or not. He is not a solitary instance of this to me almost inexplicable philosophy.

I met yesterday a farmer who was going to see whether a fire visible in the distance did not arise from his own farm-buildings. Yet he stopped on the road and talked to our party, with perfect apparent equanimity, about the progress of the war and the rate at which the bombardment had proceeded. Not a day passes that I do not come across one or more of the shopkeepers of Sonderborg, whom I used to know as a customer, and who have literally been burnt out of their dwellings, and have had all their stock-in-trade destroyed. They have nothing to do, and idle about the neighbouring villages, ready to chat with anybody they can come across.

They all express a strong desire to have the war finished, and assert that enough has been done for the nation's honour, but of their private losses they talk with outward unconcern. 1 believe that almost all the householders in Alsen are insured against fire; and, moreover, there is a general belief that they are likely to receive compensation from any government which obtains possession of the island after the war is over.

Still, any pecuniary indemnification they could possibly hope to obtain cannot make up for the loss of their business and the destruction of their trade connection. As much as I can understand the matter, I believe the causes of this extreme apparent indifference to be partly a strange stolidity of temperament habitual to the Schleswig character, and still more a strong sense of personal dignity, which creates a more than English dislike to any exhibition of sentiment. The animals themselves in Alsen bear the noise of the artillery with a wonderful composure.

The storks, knowing that summer is at hand, have come back in flocks to the island, and are taking up their old quarters in the houses where they have been sheltered so long. The dogs about the farmyard never bark, even at night, however loud may be the crash of the shells bursting in the town; our horses, which shy at any stone along the road, never exhibit the slightest alarm at the thunder of the cannon; and the sheep browse in the fields, near which shells are falling, without paying the slightest attention to the sound.

I have seen but one animal which betrayed any consciousness of danger, and that was a stoat, which was carrying off to its hole in a ploughed field a dead rat nearly as large as itself. The cannonade was brisk at the time, and every time a shot was heard the stoat dropped its prey in guilty terror; then the moment the sound had died away it clutched up the rat again, and crossed another furrow in fear and trembling.

The Mohammedan who was furtively drinking a glass of spirits when the thunderstorm came on threw the contents of the glass upon the ground, saying—so the story goes—"*Allah, Allah!* what a deal of noise about a little drop of brandy!" But the stoat, thought he evidently entertained a similar belief that all this discharge of thunderbolts was intended to deprive him of his spoil, stuck firmly to his booty, and finally carried it off in triumph, in defiance of the angry gods. It is not perhaps in accordance with the dignity of history that I should tell you this incident, which I observed the other day; but I am weary of hearing guns, and of writing about parallels and bastions and angles of elevation. It is pleasant to get away into the woods and watch the symptoms of returning summer, and see how nature is constantly restoring the resources which men are destroying.

Yet, even if you could get away from the sound of cannon, the mere love of natural beauty brings the observer back, strange to say, to the contemplation of the war. Anything lovelier than the view from the hill at the back of Sonderborg, on one of those bright spring evenings, when the sun is setting behind Dybbol in a cloudless sky, I have never seen out of Italy. The air is so clear, that you can count every house upon the hills opposite, and the cliffs of Broagerland look so near at hand, that you fancy you could throw a stone across the bay.

The smoke from the burning cottages is tinged with red by the rays of the setting sun, and over the eastern slopes of Dybbol Hill, deep sunk in shadow, the white puffs of smoke keep springing up in spiral pillars, as shell after shell comes crashing down, far and near, in quick succession. As the sunlight fades away, and the darkness comes on, the stillness of the air grows almost oppressive; the red flashes of light become clearer and clearer as the shot darts from the cannon's mouth, and the fiery trail of the rockets may be watched through the air as they fly down upon the Danish batteries. The spectacle is a grand one, but then it is impossible to lay aside the thought of the men who are lying killed or wounded on that bare hillside, standing forth so clearly against the dark, starlit sky.

April 17.

A sort of reprieve has been given to the Danes. Yesterday a messenger came in with a flag of truce from the Prussian lines. The exact tenour of his message has been kept carefully secret. All that has oozed out at present is, that he was the bearer of a summons from General von Wrangel for a surrender of the position within eight-and-forty hours. Of course there is a host of rumours current about the terms under which the surrender is proposed; but the only thing as yet certain about it appears to be that the Prussian commander-in-chief considers the game in his own hands, and that, unless his proposal is acceded to, tomorrow will not pass over without some attempt to drive the Danes yet further out of the entrenchments they have held so long and so gallantly.

The officer who brought over the message said that all the enemy had done hitherto was mere child's play compared with what he was now in a position to do. All this may be mere gasconade, like Prince Frederick Charles's proclamation after the skirmish of Missunde; and the object of that peremptory summons to surrender may be to intimidate the Danes, and to strengthen that section of the army which considers enough has been done for the honour of Denmark, and that further resistance is futile.

Personally, I am inclined to fear that the proposal is made only too seriously. It is all important for the prestige of Prussia that Dybbol, if not Alsen, should be in her hands before the assemblage of the Conference on Wednesday next; and the progress made by the enemy within the last fortnight is sufficient to convince him that if the attack is to be made at all, it should be made speedily. The message, whatever it may have been, was communicated at once to Copenhagen; but nobody anticipates an acceptance of the terms offered, and there is little question but that the Danish Government will adhere to its policy of resistance.

It would be difficult for any ministry to surrender the last stronghold of Denmark in Schleswig on the very eve of a conference, which it is hoped will lead to an armistice within an early date. It is a bold game that King Christian and his ministers are playing, as the capture of Alsen by storm would involve not only an immense sacrifice of life, but the loss of all the artillery of Dybbol and the probable destruction of the Danish Army. However, the boldest courses of action are sometimes the wisest, and I trust they may prove so in the present instance.

Meanwhile, since the arrival of the "*Parlementaire*," the Prussian fire has been much slackened. The forts, indeed, have been rained upon day and night with shells as usual, but the hillside and the town have been spared. Indeed, there has been something ominous in the silence that has reigned for a considerable portion of the day. Another farmhouse burnt down on the Alsen bank of the Sund is almost the only incident that has occurred upon our right. On the left, I am afraid that the twenty-four hours have not been so barren of result. Sixty Danish soldiers were surprised and taken prisoners at the outposts.

The officer in command of the detachment and his servant made good their escape; and it is thought that if there had been equal zeal on the part of the soldiers they might also have effected a retreat. The Prussians are now so close at hand to the left of the Dybbol line of forts that the outposts have been drawn in behind the entrenchments. I have not been able to discover the losses of the besieged during the last two days, but I fear from the tone of conversation amongst the officers, who are acquainted with the facts, that they have not been below the average.

Under these circumstances it is difficult to take a sanguine view of the Danish prospects; and if I, who have no personal interest in the matter, can hardly escape the depressing influence of the prospect of affairs, it is natural that the soldiers, whose lives are at stake, should feel cheerless enough. I am obliged to dwell upon this point, because I feel that it must be understood thoroughly for anybody to appreciate the magnitude of the efforts the Danes are making. If ever men deserved the success they are unable to command, it is these Danish soldiers. To say that no reluctance has been shown to advance to the front, or that the ardour of the first days still remains amongst the troops, would be an idle perversion of the truth; but this much I can truly state, that the army, so far, has endured a trial of unparalleled severity with a courage and patience to which there have been but few and rare exceptions.

However, it is little use speculating on what the morrow may bring forth. In the present instance it may be truly said that sufficient unto the day is the evil thereof. We have had one bright sunny day at any rate. The wind is fearfully cold and cutting; but in sheltered spots, out of the wind's way, the air was so hot that an overcoat was almost unbearable. I took advantage of the lull in the bombardment to wander through the upper part of the town. Very probably it may be my last walk in that portion of Sonderborg.

Yesterday, before the flag of truce came in, a shell was thrown from the batteries on the Schleswig side of the Sund, which struck a mill in a line with the windmills at the top of the town. So, if the attack begins tomorrow in earnest, probably the whole northern part of the town will be reduced to the same state as the lower part. From the Broager batteries, I believe this portion of Sonderborg cannot be reached with much effect, but it lies fearfully exposed to a cross-fire from the Sund. The town itself was even emptier than on former days. I went into the great inn of the place, which has still been untouched by shells, and found the house in charge of one servant-girl, who has stopped there all along with really remarkable courage: the cellar was exhausted, with the exception of a few barrels of beer; the rooms were all shut up, and the only inmates were half-a-dozen soldiers, loitering about the tap-room, and paying court to the barmaid, whose love of admiration exceeds her fear of cannon-balls.

The street was deserted, and below Reymuth's Hotel I could not see a single person moving about. The only sign of life in the place was—if the bull may be excused—the manufacture of coffins. The military undertakers have been driven out of the open space before the castle, and now carry on their trade in a sort of sand-pit, close to

the high road, at the brow of Sonderborg Hill. There a lot of army carpenters were hammering away busily at the great deal coffins; while
others were painting them a dull deep-black colour. The demand has
evidently exceeded the supply; and the stock in hand was very low.
Though it was Sunday, the work went on unabated; and if the attack
should come tomorrow, I am afraid there will be many a poor Dane
who will have to content himself with a much more rough-and-ready
receptacle for his bones than these elaborate and cumbrous boxes,
whose contemplation, the authorities here appear to think, will be
such an encouragement to the troops on their way to action, that the
coffin-building establishment must be in the most conspicuous position possible.

CHAPTER 10

The Fall of Dybbol

On board the *Haderslev*, Hörup-Hav.
Near Sonderborg, April 18.

The end is come; and with it, amidst great sadness, it has brought this much of consolation, that I can at last speak freely. I have known for the last ten days that the army was becoming rapidly demoralised by the fearful trial to which it was exposed; that day after day the losses were at the rate of from one to two hundred *per diem*; that the troops were more and more unwilling to go to the front; that on more than one occasion regiments had refused to cross the bridges, and had only been induced to obey orders by the promise that they should speedily be led into action; that desertion had become common; that the forts most exposed to the fire had been completely silenced, and their guns dismounted and destroyed; and that, in the opinion of nine officers out of ten, the position was utterly untenable.

The necessity for concealment no longer exists. No reticence and no outspokenness can alter accomplished facts, and therefore I am now enabled to assert that the order sent from Copenhagen to hold Dybbol *à l'outrance* was bitterly unwelcome to the army of Alsen. I stated in a letter written three weeks ago, while summing up the character of the struggle, that the Danes, in my opinion, would fight on gallantly for Dybbol as long as there was left a shadow of hope, but that they would not fight on with the recklessness of despair when all hope was gone. The event has exactly corresponded to my anticipations. Yesterday passed gloomily enough. The end was felt to be close at hand; and nobody who knew the facts of the case could doubt what that end would be.

But yet towards evening, as the fire died away, there was a kind of reaction, so at least it seemed to me, in the feeling of the men I lived amongst. Another day had passed after all, and the meeting of the Conference was drawing very near. There was a rumour that the Prussian ammunition was exhausted, and time itself seemed to be fighting on the side of Denmark. The wind had gone down; the air was warm and still; and the moonlight night was so peaceful, it was impossible to believe that the final struggle was to come on the morrow.

However, a rumour arrived at our quarters before I went to bed that the Danish Army was to be withdrawn during the night, and in consequence I slept in my clothes, having given orders to be called if anything unusual occurred. In the morning I got up somewhat earlier than usual, had breakfast with the family of the house where my abode has been fixed for the last fortnight, congratulated them on the night having passed so quietly, and then rode out to look for letters. The fire, though extremely brisk, was directed entirely against the forts of Dybbol Hill; and the universal belief was that the Prussians would shell the hillside, the bridge, and the fortifications for several hours, and then possibly attempt a storm when the Danes were worn out; so I rode leisurely about my business, sauntering along through the pleasant lanes and wood-paths of this Alsen island.

Riding homewards, towards headquarters, I met orderly after orderly galloping hastily along. Something was evidently stirring, and the whole face of Dybbol Hill, and the banks of the Sund, were now covered with smoke. I set off galloping towards the coast; but I had not gone many steps before I met a Danish gentleman, resident at the same house as myself, who told me that the Prussians had already captured Forts No. 4 and 5, and that "all was lost." There was no time to be wasted.

The "*Laader-Gaarde*" farm, where I was stationed, was a position sheltered enough from any fire, either from Broager or from any of the batteries on the further side of Dybbol, but utterly exposed in ease the enemy was once in possession of the crest of the hill. The moment I reached a position from which I could see the hillside, it was clear that the battle was lost; the centre batteries had already been turned against the town, and the shells followed each other so rapidly, that their sound was like that of a steam-hammer striking constantly. The *Laader-Gaarde* itself was surrounded by spiral columns of smoke rising into the air, and then dying away into the clear blue sky, as shell after shell struck the ground in its neighbourhood.

The *Rolf Krake*, which was moored almost opposite our dwelling, was being fired at fiercely by the enemy's batteries. Great waterspouts sprang up on every side of her, as the shot fell in showers about her; and every now and then there was a fearful crash heard above the roar of the cannon and the constant crack of musketry, and we could tell that a shot had hit her iron sides. It was no pleasant work making my way back home. To ride was simple folly, so I led my horse across the fields, taking such little shelter as the roadside hedges could afford me; and, watching anxiously the direction of every shell—a practice in which experience soon makes one perfect—I got at last up to the great farmyard.

At the gate I met the servant who attends to our horses on the look-out, to tell us that we must be off without a moment's delay. I had always looked upon this groom as the idlest and most arrant humbug in the whole island of Alsen; but on this occasion, to do him justice, he showed a coolness for which I had not given him credit. He proposed to go and fetch our luggage from the farm, while we waited outside at a safe distance. This, however, I would not consent to. No one is less partial to putting his head in the way of a shell than I am myself; but still I could not reconcile it to my conscience to allow a man to go into danger for the sake of fetching my luggage, which I was not willing to undergo myself. So I sent the man off with the horses, and then made a bolt for the house.

I suppose, while shells are falling round you, the open air is decidedly safer than the interior of a dwelling; but it is impossible to resist the impression that it is an advantage to have a roof over you under the circumstances. Inside the house everything was in confusion. The officers whom I had left sleeping at breakfast-time were all away in the battle, prisoners, or wounded, or killed, for anything we could tell; the few wounded soldiers who were stationed at the farmyard had been ordered out; and the only people left were the family and servants of the farm. The rooms were being rapidly dismantled; but yet I found that my belongings had not been forgotten. With that marvellous kindness of the Danish nature, the first thought of our landlord, amidst all the terror and confusion of the unexpected bombardment, had been to place in safety the property of his foreign guests.

A cart was standing before the door, and the luggage was already being brought out of my room. It was but a couple of minutes I spent in packing; I had been prepared for such an event long ago, and it needed but a moment to close my bags and throw them upon the cart. Then there was a hasty leave-taking with my kind host, one warm grasp of the hand, and a hasty dash across the farmyard, till I reached the shelter of a hedge, which followed the direction I was about to take; and now I was practically out of danger.

As soon as I had reached the outskirts of the wood which stretches along the shores of Alsen, between Sonderborg and Hörup-Hav, I fastened up my horse and made for a point whence I could command a view of the scene of action. It must then have been about the fiercest moment of the short and disastrous conflict. From four to ten the enemy had shelled the batteries and the whole face of the hill with pitiless accuracy; the outposts had been drawn in; not a sentry even stood between the redoubts on the left wing and the advance posts of the Prussians, scarcely a stone's throw away.

Suddenly the Danish soldiers, crouching as best they could under their battered trenches, heard a shout. With one rush the Prussians swarmed into the batteries, and, in ten minutes from the time the alarm was given, the Prussian flag was planted on the bastions of Dybbol. Forts No. 1 and No. 2, which defended the extreme left, had almost ceased to exist five days ago; indeed, twelve out of the sixteen guns of the latter battery had been dismounted, and not replaced These redoubts were, I believe, deserted when the Prussians occupied them: the weak garrisons of Nos. 4 and 5 were taken by surprise, and overpowered by the overwhelming numbers of the enemy.

Thus the whole of the left wing of the position was carried by storm, and the Prussians pushed on at once to the forts on the right, carrying all before them. The second line of entrenchments, which the Danes have been throwing up during the last fortnight, were also occupied at once. By this time, however, the Danes had rallied from the surprise, and made one last effort to recover their lost ground. They charged the Prussians with the bayonet, and drove them back with shouts from the inner line. Their triumph, however, was shortlived. The columns of the enemy came pouring over the hillside, bearing down all before them by their dead weight of numbers, and then it was felt that all was over, and the order was given to retreat.

It must have been about this period that I took my post of observation on a ridge commanding a full view of Dybbol Hill. The facts that I have mentioned were not known to me then. All I could tell was that things were going badly for the besieged. The brow of the hill was lined with dark masses of troops too close and too serried to belong to the Danes. With my field-glass I could see the Prussian flag waving gaily from the heights; and it was clear, from the crowds of soldiers standing on the bastions of Fort No. 4, that there, at least, the fighting had ceased.

Along the broad, bare, shelterless roads, leading from the brow of the hill to the bridges, dark lines of infantry were retreating hastily, and their columns were raked constantly by shells thrown from the field batteries, which the Prussians were bringing up with all speed to the line of Dybbol. It looked to me, standing there, as if their own guns had been turned against the Danes, but this I behlive was not the case, as very few of those guns were left in a state to fire at all, and those few were spiked before the Prussians could enter.

Meanwhile, the scene itself, apart from the interest of the struggle, had about it a strange beauty. On the face of Dybbol Hill, looking eastwards, the morning sun shone brightly. To the right, along the Sund, vast columns of smoke rose straight into the air from the burning cottages of Ulkeböl Westermark. On the left the cliffs of the Wemming Bund shores were enveloped in the haze caused by the ceaseless puffs of snow-white smoke which were belched forth by the Broager batteries. From the crest of the hill a belt of flame flashed constantly; and the clear blue sky overhead and the still blue sea underneath encircled the whole of this picture of fire and flame and smoke in a gorgeous setting.

The noise was fearful, greater even than I ever yet have heard it. As the Danes retreated down the hill, the Prussians turned the whole force of their fire full upon the bridges and the streets through which the retiring troops would have to pass. The Danish batteries on the Sonderborg shore opened fire to cover the retreat, and with some effect. The immediate result, however, was to bring down upon them the fire of Broager with fearful accuracy. The windmill battery, which stood on the left of the town—about a quarter of a mile from the farmhouse I had just quitted—was silenced in a few minutes. One shell came crashing through the thatched windmill, and in a moment it was in flames; the fire spread to the houses between it and the town, and a vast cloud of smoke rose up, obscuring the view of the hill behind it.

Every now and then the whistling of the shells through the air ceased suddenly, the cannon were silent, and I could hear the sharp ring of musketry and the hoarse shouts of the combatants; after which the cannon burst forth again, drowning all in an avalanche of sound. But with each pause the fire of the musketry grew fainter, and the shouts more distant. The *Rolf Krake* had steered slowly away, beaten off, and severely injured by the fire from Broager. It was clear that the day was lost; the one question was how much was gone; and there was no possibility of discerning this by merely gazing upon the smoke-covered hillside.

So I mounted my horse again and worked round through the woods to the back of Sonderborg. Except that a great battle had been fought and lost, nobody whom I met knew anything. All the symptoms of an approaching rout were clearly visible; detachments of troops were marching gloomily from distant country-quarters, in obedience to the alarm that had been sounded, but without knowing what point they were to make for. The roadside fields were full of scattered groups of soldiers, haggard, powder-stained, and dust-covered, wandering about without their arms, or gazing anxiously from any eminence which afforded a glimpse of the distant heights of Dybbol.

The roads were already choked up with long lines of carts, bearing the wounded anywhere, so it was away from the field of battle. I went on to the headquarters and found them utterly deserted, except by a score of orderlies waiting for the orders that never came. I passed on to the Parsonage, of which I have so often written, where the commander-in-chief resided. General Gerlach had been confined to the house for some days, owing to a severe accident, and I thought that there, possibly, some intelligence might be learnt; but the place was deserted by everybody except the pastor and his servants.

The general had gone out early, and no tidings whatever had been received, except a vague rumour that things were going ill. From the high-road hard by I could see large bodies of troops retreating hastily from Sonderborg. It seemed as if no time could be wasted. If the Prussians succeeded in crossing the bridges with the Danes, and thus entering the town, our retreat was liable to be cut off at once. So, in company with the brother correspondent whose fortunes I have shared hitherto, I resolved to make the best haste I could to Hörup-Hav, and there, at any rate, secure a shelter for the night.

It was hard work urging on our tired horses, but there was no time to think of mercy to beasts. For some way our progress was stopped by the increasing press of waggons crowding towards the harbour. At last, however, we got ahead of the train, and galloped on as fast as the rough cross-country roads would allow. When we reached Hörup, the soldier who had charge of our horses was not forthcoming, and it was impossible to find a place where we could even tie them up. So, trusting to past experience, I rode on another long weary mile to the house of the pastor of the village, with whom I was previously unacquainted, feeling sure that I should not ask a favour in vain. I was not disappointed in my expectation, and, after having got stabling for the horses, and being welcomed with that frank, kindly hospitality which is so natural to the Danes, that, even on a day of national disaster and personal peril, their first thought is how to make a stranger comfortable, I walked back to the harbour of Hörup.

The water-side, the roads far and near, and the wooden piers which have been hastily knocked up for the retreat, were already crowded with wounded soldiers. An immense steamer was moored along the pier, waiting to receive them. Even the most fearful of spectacles loses its effect after a time; and I have seen so many wounded for the last few weeks, that I have become somewhat callous to the sight of suffering which a mere spectator has no power whatever to relieve. But still the scene was terrible. As the carts jolted down to the wharf, soldier after soldier was borne out on stretchers and placed on the deck of the ship. The men were well wrapped and covered up, and their wounds seemed to have been all attended to carefully.

Bad, however, is the best at times like these. Some of the men lay so quiet, that you could scarcely tell whether they lived or not; others tossed from side to side constantly in the restlessness of pain; and others literally writhed with agony as the carts swayed to and fro. In more than one case, which I observed in the course of a few minutes, the occupant of the cart was found dead when the bearers came to remove him, and his body, instead of being taken on board ship, was replaced in the straw and covered over with a soldier's coat. In this one vessel 600 wounded men were carried off, and seven other steam-packets were lying in the port waiting to receive their dismal freight.

My business, however, was not with the dead or dying. Officers whom I knew had come down to the pier, and from them I learnt that the whole of Dybbol was lost; but that the bridges had been blown up in time, and the advance of the enemy arrested. Forthwith I set out again on my travels, and trudged over the four long miles which lie between Hörup Pier and the *Laader-Gaarde*. There I felt pretty sure I should learn something. At any rate, I should hear the fate of the family, for whom I was deeply alarmed, as a rumour had come in that the farm had been burnt down an hour after I left it.

Happily, the story proved not to be true; I found the house standing still intact; the children had been got away, but the farmer himself was there with his wife, alone in their dismantled house. I tried my utmost to persuade them to leave, as any moment the Prussians might shell the place from Dybbol; but to no purpose. Our host said that as long as he lived he would stop by his farm-buildings; and his wife said that where her husband stopped there she should stop also. There was nothing to be done, and so I parted company with my kind, simple hosts—God knows, unwillingly enough.

The town of Sonderborg was in flames, and the bombardment was continued without ceasing. The smoke, however, concealed the view of the hillside. Thence I went to a neighbouring dwelling, whither a few of the officers who had lived with us at the *Laader-Gaarde* had. as I heard, gone for shelter. There I found a friend—a captain of artillery—and learnt with extreme pleasure that the whole of our late companions had escaped so far unhurt. He himself had no orders what to do, and it was clear that as yet no plan had been formed either to defend or evacuate the island.

Major Rosen—an officer from whom, in my character of a correspondent, I have received constant civility, and who was the chief of General Gerlach's staff, and, it was whispered, the real commander of the army—had been wounded and taken prisoner; and no orders had yet been communicated, even to the troops. Under these circumstances I resolved to return to Hörup harbour and spend the night there, leaving my further course to be guided by the news of the morrow.

I was fortunate enough to secure a sofa in the little Assens steamer, with whose captain I had a speaking acquaintance. An hour's row about the port in search of the vessel, lying *perdu* amidst the host of shipping, has at last brought me to my destination; and here, after fourteen hours spent almost without pause, either walking or riding, I am writing as best I can by one flickering candle.

It is too early to attempt to estimate fully the import of this disastrous defeat. The loss must have been fearful. My suspicion is, that of the Danish troops who were on the hillside of Dybbol not half made good their retreat. The bridges were blown up early in the day, and the Prussians were too close upon the Danes to render it probable that any great portion of the retreating army could have got across before their pursuers. The *tête-de-pont* on the Schleswig side held out valiantly, and delayed the advance of the enemy till there was time to destroy the bridges.

The soldiers who manned this post were brought over in boats, after spiking their guns. Three thousand captured, killed, or wounded, is the lowest estimate I have just heard of the Danish loss. Three regiments are said to be completely cut up. Of the 18th battalion not a single officer has returned. General Duplat, the commander of the first division, is amongst the killed. The Prussian loss I suspect to be comparatively small. The Danes had not time to fire their cannon into the advancing enemy; and I believe two companies of field artillery alone took part in the action on the Danish side. The Danes fought gallantly, but the battle was lost from the first; and the only aim was to make good a retreat which should have been made a week ago. The main question is now. Can the Prussians cross to Alsen?

Hörup-Hav, April 19.

I have not much to add to my letter of last night. As the details of yesterday's battle become more fully known, the general result of the conflict is even more disastrous than I was at first led to suppose. General Duplat, six colonels, and forty officers in all are dead. The number of killed, wounded, and missing is now estimated at from 3,000 to 4,000; and the whole of the cannon on the Dybbol heights has fallen into the possession of the enemy.

Today some 400 or 500 missing soldiers have come in from different parts of the island, but the muster-roll of the lost and absent is still a fearfully heavy one. It would, I think, be of little interest to you for me to repeat the names of the officers who have fallen. To me, who have now lived in this camp for months, and to whom most of the leading ones here were known, either personally or by sight at least, the dead list has a very painful attraction. One incident, however, let me mention, as that of a brave soldier's death. When General Duplat was struck down on the slopes of Dybbol Hill his soldiers wanted to carry him away.

"Leave me alone," said the general, "it is all over for me, and you have other work to do." "Bravely done!" he shouted again, as a young officer pressed forward in obedience to his orders, and with these words on his lips he died.

Major Rosen fell by the side of the general, mortally wounded, and today his dead body was brought back into the Danish lines. This gentleman, the real head of the army at Alsen, was a Holsteiner bred and born, whose family have adhered throughout to the side of Denmark. Two days before his death, his brother's farm at Ravnhavn was burnt down and destroyed by the Prussian shells from Rageböl.

Another young officer I was slightly acquainted with, who is now amongst the dead, had married but two months ago, and had to leave his wife—a girl of nineteen—three days after their marriage, to join the war. So I might record instances by the score of sad private histories, whose fatal issue is wrapped up with that of this great national disaster; but the figures, I think, speak for themselves more powerfully than any statement of mine could do. Four thousand killed, wounded, and missing!—what words can add force to this simple fact?

It seems that the Danes were completely taken by surprise. Somehow or other, they had made up their minds that the Prussians would not attack before the evening, and at the moment of the assault the men stationed within the forts were sleeping or eating, thinking that a few hours' rest lay before them. The forts on the right were evacuated as soon as it was clear that those on the left and centre were in the hands of the enemy. The retreat of the Danes from the right was effected with extreme order and regularity, and the troops passed the bridges without the least tumult.

The Danish loss was almost entirely upon the left; the artillery officers in the redoubts were taken without exception. So complete was the surprise, that the intelligence of the attack was not received at headquarters at Ulkeböl till the position was in the hands of the Prussians. The Guards, who had been relied upon to check the advance of the enemy in the last resort, did not reach the bridge until too late to take part in the action, and their loss was extremely slight, comparatively, only eight men being killed. At the *tête-du-pont*, which was defended with great gallantry, the chief fighting took place. I am informed by Danish officers that the Prussians fought splendidly in their repeated assaults upon this last entrenchment.

Today has passed gloomily and quietly. At two o'clock the Prussians offered an armistice, in order to bring over the bodies of the Danish officers who had fallen in the battle. The offer was accepted at once, and thirty bodies were brought across in boats. I regret to say that the corpses of these gallant men had been rifled of their buttons, their shoulder-straps, and even of their boots; the insides of their pockets were turned out, and the rings—so I am told— were taken off their fingers.

Of course, such things will happen on all hard-fought battlefields; but to the Danes, who have an extreme personal respect for the bodies of the dead, the incident was very painful. After the armistice was over, the Prussians recommenced shelling the northern side of the town, but only slackly. Their advance on the island is expected tomorrow.

The headquarters are moved tonight to Hörup, close to the port.

CHAPTER 11

After the Battle

Hörup-Hav, April 20.

My letter bears the date of Hörup-Hav, where my residence is fixed—if a man can be correctly said to reside in a place where he shifts from boat to boat at night, and has no roof to shelter him throughout the day. But at this moment I am writing from the hospitable farmhouse where I lived till the capture of Dybbol. I little thought when I left it last Monday that I should ever see its inside again; still less that I should write there ill perfect peace and quiet. Such, however, is the case. I should hardly know the place, it is so changed from its normal state during the time I had my abode here.

The Dannebrog flag is taken down from the doorway; the soldiers quartered here, who filled every nook and corner of the house, are scattered miles away over the island; the officers, who formed our society, have taken up their quarters further inland; the family and children are gone; the house is dismantled of its furniture; and nobody is left except a few farm-servants. The place is so wonderfully quiet, that it has a charm for me at this moment which you must have lived for weeks amidst din, and noise, and bustle, the clashing of swords and the roar of cannon, to understand thoroughly. Passing by the place on my way home from Sonderborg, I turned in to see how my kind host was faring; and, finding the room empty, I am writing in the apartment which used to be the headquarters of the officers.

I have this moment returned from wandering over the town—a visit which I had not expected to pay, if at all, for many a day to come. Since daybreak not a shot has been fired on either side. No formal armistice has been concluded; but it is clear that the Prussians are not for the hour disposed to commence the attack, and until they do, the Danes will certainly not hurry on an assault by random firing. Thus for the present we have perfect peace. Any moment it may end, and the shells may be hurled against the ruins of the town and the remnant of the Danish garrison; but meanwhile there is time to breathe, and for that we have cause to be thankful.

As soon as I learnt that the fire was suspended, I made my way from Hörup-Hav to the outskirts of Sonderborg, where I fastened up my horse and set out for the town on foot. In all enterprises of this kind, it seems to me there is no harm in discretion. If the Prussians should recommence firing, as is quite possible, without notice, my luck would be very bad indeed if I could not creep under shelter of walls and hedges to some place of safety; but to be on horseback in the middle of a narrow street, where shells are falling about you, is by no means a position that I covet.

Moreover, on a morning like this, it is a pleasure to wander alone on foot through the quiet country fields. The day is one of exquisite warmth and beauty. Not a cloud is to be seen in the sky; not a puff of smoke rises from the cliffs of Wemming Bund or the heights of Dybbol; the houses and cottages which were set on fire have burned themselves out; the air is so still, that the windmills with which the country is studded stand with their sails motionless; not a musket-shot is to be heard; the one sound which breaks the perfect stillness of the day is the singing of the birds, who have come out in force to greet the advent of summer.

So, on this lovely spring morning, I strolled across the fields to the town of Sonderborg. I worked my way behind the hedgerows, now covered with the first tinge of green, for fear that some Prussian rifle-man might think it advisable to try the accuracy of his needle-gun upon my person. Even the fields near the town were deserted, and the labourers have been driven away by the dread of the bombardment. Only on what we should call the parish-ground of Sonderborg, where the poor have each a plot of their own, a couple of peasants were still digging away on their small patches of land. Shells are bad enough; but to the poor want is even a worse danger than death.

I passed over a common where there used to be barracks; the sheds were burnt down, and the land was literally furrowed with shells. In a space of some twenty feet square I counted as many holes, surrounded by mounds of earth, which the balls had thrown about them as they buried themselves in the soil. I walked on through the orchard gardens which stand on the southern side of Sonderborg. They too were deserted. The little cottages which face the fields, where the poorer part of the inhabitants lived, were now at last empty of their owners, who had stuck to them with a mussel-like tenacity. They were so slightly built, that wherever a shell had struck the whole building had come tumbling down; but fortunately their roofs were very low, and most of the bombs directed against this part of the town had flown over the roofs into the open country.

Through the lonely gardens, bearing already that indescribable air of neglect which creeps so soon over places where man's care has been daily given, I walked on to the house of the *burgomaster*, which had been my home till the town was bombarded. Most persons in their lives must have felt the pang occasioned by the sight of a dwelling where you have lived and had friends and been kindly welcomed, whose doors are now closed to you, and whose rooms are occupied by strangers. But here the house had not changed its owners, but stood tenantless. I climbed over the garden wall; not a soul was to be seen; every window was broken; the little room in which I had slept was still intact; but there were great chasms in the roof, and in the wall there was a hole so large that I could have crept through it easily. Whatever may happen, the house will have to be rebuilt before it can be again inhabited; and, amidst the changes which this war must bring about, it is little likely that the present officials of Alsen will be retained in their places.

So I bade a last farewell to the house, standing so prettily on the island shores, where I had spent so many happy days and had received so much kindness. I looked into the bare, deserted rooms, plucked a few of the primroses and crocuses which had sprung up in the little garden, and then moved onwards up the winding streets I had traversed so often. I stood for a few minutes on the open space commanding a view of the Sund. Dybbol Hill lay before me, but little altered in look from what I had known it hitherto. The soldiers wandering about the roads and encamped, upon the fields were Prussians instead of Danes, that was all. With my field glass I could see that the uniforms were different, but to the naked eye one body of troops appeared very like another.

The number, indeed, was strangely magnified, and the whole army of Alsen if collected at one moment on Dybbol Hill would have seemed small compared with the masses who were already quartered on the bare slopes so gallantly defended, so easily lost. Yesterday Prince Frederick Charles and all his staff came down to the *tête-du-pont* by the Sund to inspect their newly-acquired territory; but today, as no armistice was declared, the lower parts of the hill were apparently not visited by curious observers. Large bodies of troops were employed upon the redoubts, engaged, I suspect, in removing the cannon; but otherwise there was no sign of activity.

The Prussian sentries were pacing up and down, close to the water's edge; the trenches were crowded with riflemen; the cannon visible on the slopes were turned towards, not away from, Sonderborg; and the bridges were broken by a long gap between the ends still jutting out from either shore. Between myself and the castle not a human being was to be seen. The Danish soldiers stationed by the banks of the Sund were partly under cover of the *schloss*, partly behind trenches which have been hastily raised up close to the shore. The care with which the men kept their heads under shelter of the earthworks showed that there was still danger of hearing a rifle-shot whizz past you; so I turned backwards to the town.

It is strange, I may mention here, that the castle itself has received but little injury. The shells have struck its immense stone walls time after time without penetrating them; the roof has been destroyed; but the grim prison-like *schloss*—about whose date there is no tradition left, so old is it—has survived all the younger buildings of the city. What is more odd, too, is that the wooden barrack sheds, which the Danes ran up just before the bombardment began, though roofed over with thatch, remain unhurt.

An English officer, who visited the works some weeks ago, remarked to me on the folly of placing such sheds in their present position, where the first shell would set them on fire. Every building, however, on the hillside has been burnt, but the barracks have escaped—were not even set fire to by the Danes on their retreat, and are now occupied by the Prussians. "*Sic vos, non vobis*" should surely be the motto inscribed upon their entrance.

Then I moved onwards, through narrow winding alleys, into the main thoroughfare, which was so completely *the* street of Sonderborg that, alone amidst its compeers, it has no name whatever. A scene of such utter desolation I could scarcely have conceived. When I saw the town last, directly after the bombardment, there were plenty of people about the streets, and the volumes of smoke and flame which rose on every side gave it a sort of ghastly animation. But now all was quiet as the grave—silent as the tomb. I went through street after street, passed house after house, and met nobody. Every building was more or less injured, but the luck which attends all mortal things had bestowed

261

very unequal measure upon the different dwellings.

One house would be literally pounded down to the ground; another would be a mere mass of blackened ashes; while a third would remain intact, except for its shattered roofs and broken rafters. The doors and windows had been burst open by the mere concussion of the noise. There was not one I could not have entered easily if I had liked. Small articles of household ornament, flower-pots filled with plants withered for want of water, pictures hanging crookedly from the walls, looking-glasses broken to a thousand pieces, might be seen through the open windows. There was not much, indeed, to steal, for most of the dwellings had been burnt to their bare walls by the fire; but what there was any one might have taken. Not a soul, however, was to be seen.

On entering the main street, up which you can look for nearly a quarter of a mile, I could not see a person moving. The deathlike silence was absolutely oppressive; my own footsteps seemed to awaken all sorts of ghostly echoes from the gaunt, blackened walls; the mere crash of a shell would have been welcomed for the moment, to break the painful stillness. There is nothing grand about the ruins of a small town like this, with not a building in it, except the castle, of about a hundred years of age or more than two stories high. The remnants of these comfortable Danish *burgher* homes had no grandeur in their desolation. The one thing impressive was the perfect unbroken solitude.

In my hour's wanderings over a town which numbered four thousand inhabitants but a fortnight ago, I met only six persons, all of whom appeared to me to be country farmers, attracted thither by curiosity like myself. The upper part of Sonderborg was now as empty as the lower. The day was overpoweringly hot; I was half parched with thirst; but even in the outskirts I could find but one house of any kind where water was to be obtained. As far as I could see not a single dwelling was inhabited, if I except half a dozen which lie on the other side of the hill. The camp by the windmills at the back of the town is itself deserted; and, except the soldiers on duty at the batteries, the pigeons on the housetops, and a stray spectator, there may be said not to be a living thing in the whole of the dead city.

The place must be altogether rebuilt, if ever it is to become again the chief town of Alsen: my own. belief is, that Sonderborg will never recover its importance, but will remain for many years to come a mass of ruins. It was a relief to get back to the open fields. On the verge of the town I met an old stork poking disconsolately about amidst the ruins of the adjoining houses. Its nest had probably been destroyed, and it stood there as a fit emblem of the desolation the war has brought upon this ill-fated city, sacrificed to the maintenance of Teutonic nationality.

I have just heard with great regret that Lieutenant Jaspersen, of the *Rolf Krake*, was killed during the affair of Monday. He was a bright, cheerful lad, who had been much in England, and was one of my earliest acquaintances in Sonderborg. I have had many a warm shake of the hand from that frank, open, gallant sailor. Poor fellow, his death was instantaneous. A shell struck the *Rolf Krake* full upon her deck— wood, by the way, not iron—pierced right through, and exploded underneath, killing the lieutenant, wounding six men round him, and causing much injury to the vessel.

April 22.

The day after a battle, I suspect, is always dreary; how much more so are the days after a defeat! Very dull, at any rate, and weary have been the hours which have gone by since the capture of Dybbol. The Danes are drinking, as it were, the dregs of their disaster. It is not so much, I think, the actual personal grief for the loss sustained, the misfortune which has fallen upon Denmark, that depresses the minds of the soldiers and civilians still left on Alsen.

I have been in many countries at great moments of a nation's destiny, both for evil and for good; and it has always struck me before, as it strikes me now, how small a portion public affairs, whatever may be their magnitude, occupy in the lives of individuals. After all, the personal interests of private people take up the chief part of their thoughts. As far as I could observe, London went on after much the same fashion on the day when we received the news of the Battle of Inkermann, and on that when we heard of the massacre of Cawnpore. So it is here.

Though Dybbol may be fallen, and Alsen may lie at the mercy of the Prussians, and the greatness of Denmark may seem to have passed away, yet meals must be cooked, and fields tilled, and newspapers printed, just as if a victory had been won. No sensible man would ever accuse the Danes of want of patriotism, because there is not mourning or weeping in every house you enter. Many homes, indeed, have been made desolate by this battle; many families widowed of one dearly loved; and there the sorrow is not soon to be forgotten or speedily to pass away.

But for those whose private fortunes have not made shipwreck in the general disaster, the first impression caused by the battle seems already to have died out. Men whose homes, or estates, or pursuits lie in the island of Alsen have many things to think of besides the welfare of Denmark. Ultimately their fortunes must be shared with those of Schleswig—not of Fünen or of Zealand. The longer I live in Alsen, the more I see that the nationality of its inhabitants is very composite. Already I fancy I can perceive a not unnatural tendency on the part of the residents in the island to describe themselves rather as Danish Schleswigers than as Danes. People seem to me to talk German a good deal more readily than they did some weeks ago; and complaints are made about the extent to which the welfare of the country is sacrificed to the obstinacy of Copenhagen, which I had not hitherto heard.

I am told that Zealand has suffered nothing by the war; that, on the contrary, the Copenhageners have been making money fast; that the Duke of Augustenburg has always been regretted in Alsen; that the lower class of Danish officials were not men whom the Schleswigers could respect—and so on. There is little importance in these vague grumblings by themselves; they serve only to show in which way the wind is setting. The defeated as well as the absent are always in the wrong, and the Alseners would not be human beings if they were not beginning to perceive that there is something to be said for the new proprietors, "I am a Dane myself," a farmer here said to me the other day, "and wish, if possible, to belong to Denmark; but I fear there can be no permanent peace for Schleswig, if a separation does not take place." And I suspect this feeling is now a common and a growing one in Alsen.

Even amongst the soldiers themselves, I think I can perceive that the prospect which this defeat gives of an early termination of the war is not without some shade of consolation. The peasant recruits cannot but be anxious to get back to their homes and families; they have suffered long privations and hardships; they have done enough for the honour of Denmark; and if at last they have been worsted in the conflict, they have fought against overwhelming odds and have held their own manfully.

There is no unwillingness amongst them, now that the first hour of depression has passed away, to go on fighting, and if the order should come they will, I have no doubt, fight on gallantly, but there is no eagerness to continue the war; and the announcement of an armistice would be received, to say the least, without any general dissatisfaction.

Besides, the result of Monday's battle has come home to the army more than it has to the inhabitants of Alsen. There is not a soldier who has not friends, comrades, kinsmen, amongst those who fell upon the field, or are lying in the hospitals, or are in the hands of the enemy. A retreat, too, is always dispiriting, and virtually the Danish army is retreating from Alsen.

The headquarters will be removed today or tomorrow to Assens, in the island of Fünen; every day troops are embarking; the great bulk of the army is scattered over the island, in readiness to move; and the harbour of Hörup is crowded with vessels, lying at anchor for the reception of the soldiers in case of need. There is little at the moment for the troops to do; the Prussians have scarcely fired a gun since Monday, and have made no attempt as yet to pass the Sund; the long processions of soldiers and waggons which used to block up the roads leading to Sonderborg have almost disappeared; and most of the wounded have been removed from the island. In fact, it is difficulty when you wander about the neighbourhood of Sonderborg, as I have done for the last two days in every direction, to imagine that one army was still besieging, and another still defending, this Danish stronghold.

The truth is, that our present position is one which I suspect has few parallels in the history of warfare. I have been sometimes in a theatre where the audience were uncertain whether the play was at an end and the curtain about to drop, or whether there was still one more last scene to come. Everybody was getting up, some had already left the house, and nobody exactly knew if he ought to follow their example or sit down again till the drama was terminated. Now this is exactly the condition we all are in now. Is the curtain to drop on the capture of Dybbol, or is the closing scene to be the entry of the Prussians into Alsen?

Yesterday the Germans sent in the body of General Duplat with a military escort. The officer in command said he was desired to express the hopes of the Prussian army that the dead soldier would be buried with the highest honours, and to state that two wreaths placed upon his bier had been laid thereon by the hands of Prince Frederick Charles and Field-Marshal Wrangel, in honour of a brave man's memory. This sort of sentimentalism is not very much to the taste of Englishmen, or, for that matter, of Danes, but the trait is worth mentioning as a well-meant act of courtesy. I have always endeavoured to do justice to both combatants, and never saw any advantage in exalting the merits of the Danes by representing their enemies as cowards or barbarians.

The bombardment of Sonderborg is bad enough, without adding to the sins of those who perpetrated it offences of which they are not guilty. For this reason, I think it right to state that I can discover no adequate foundation for the charges of having outraged the persons of the dead, which have been brought against the Prussians by the Danes. Yesterday I visited the church of Ulkeböl, where the bodies of the dead officers were laid, in order to ascertain for myself what truth there was in these rumours.

The scene was strangely impressive. Out of the hot air and the bright sunlight, I passed into the little church of Ulkeböl. Like all Danish churches, it is simple almost to bareness. One long, low nave, with white washed walls and wooden roof, constitutes the whole of the edifice; the floor is filled with high wooden pews, separated by a broad passage up the centre. At the east end is the wooden altar-screen with the crucifix above it, and the unlit candles standing on the communion table before it.

A sentinel was placed at the door to keep away curious idlers; and as I entered I found myself alone with the dead. The sunlight struggled feebly in through the dust-stained windows, and the only sound to be heard was the chirping of the birds underneath the eaves. The dead did not lie all together: even in their last resting-place above the ground the rules of military precedence were still kept sacred. In the porch were placed the bodies of the non-commissioned officers; behind the altar those of the captains and lieutenants; and in the little vestry, apart from their fellows, were the colonels who had fallen.

Very silently and slowly I picked my way amidst the corpses which lay around me. About their aspect there was little horrible; none of them were much disfigured; and on only two or three faces was the blood still left unwashed away. They were all clad in their uniforms, and laid upon their backs, with straw beneath their heads, as though something was still needed for them to rest upon without uneasiness. On their breasts were pinned pieces of paper, stating their name and rank.

Many of the corpses had already been buried or sent away at the request of friends. But still there were some fifteen officers left, and about as many corporals and sergeants. The wounds were all in the face or breast, none, as far as I could see, in the back. They were all, too, apparently inflicted by rifle-balls, and not by shells—a fact to which I attribute the absence of any great disfigurement. Almost without exception, the expression of the faces was that of men in deep, heavy sleep, after hours of wakeful weariness. Very peaceful and calm they looked as they lay there awaiting burial.

The presence of death had already given a sort of refinement to the features, not common in Danish faces; and the fixedness of the usual Danish expression was toned gently down amongst the dead. I saw men with whom I had chatted, and dined, and laughed but a few days ago. Many were young; all were in the prime of life; and had families and friends, and kinsmen. Yet, by a strange coincidence, the last person probably to gaze upon their features before they were lowered into the grave was a casual acquaintance, with whom they had passed a few hours in company.

The time for the funeral was approaching, and I had scarcely left the church when I could hear the salvoes fired across the newly-made graves. I wonder to how many Danish wives and mothers that burial-ground of Ulkeböl will long be a place of pilgrimage! Close to the church there is a farmhouse, which a Swedish lady has bought that she might be near the cemetery of Sonderborg, where lies the body of her husband, who fell in the campaign of 1848. If her example should be followed, there will soon be gathered round about Ulkeböl a sad colony of widowed wives and childless mothers.

However, I must state that the corpses which I saw bore no traces of any unusual desecration. In every case their boots had been taken off, and the rings removed from their fingers: in only one instance had any part of the dress except the boots been pulled off, and there were no cuts visible upon their hands. Of course, I cannot say positively there is no truth in the Danish story that the fingers of officers were cut off for the sake of their rings. I have not seen all the corpses brought back: all I can say is, that I saw no trace of it myself.

I am afraid there is no army in the world in which there is not more or less plundering of the dead after the battle is over. If there is, it is the Danish one; but even that I doubt. Personally the feeling on the subject has always seemed to me exaggerated. If a man shoots me dead, I do not feel that he increases the wrong done me by wearing my boots and rings. But I know that robbing the dead on the field of battle is considered a disgraceful act, according to military codes, and therefore it is fair to say that the Prussians, in my belief, are not worse in this respect than their neighbours.

On board the *Haderslev*,

I write this on board the steamer which is now carrying me away from Alsen. Whether it may be my lot to visit it again in the course of my journeyings, I cannot surmise. Day after day has passed since the fatal Monday—which now seems an age ago—and each night I have expected to be awoke by the alarm that the Prussians were coming. But still nothing has occurred to break the uniformity of our daily life. Copenhagen had become the centre of political action, and Fredericia seemed to be the place where future fighting, if it occurred at all, was likely to come to pass. Under these circumstances, either the capital or the stronghold of Jutland appeared to be more eligible quarters than the half-deserted island of Als. But still I was unwilling to leave the place where I had stayed so long till I had seen the matter out to the end. There was a chance that the Danes might make a last desperate struggle for Alsen; and so I lingered from day to day, meaning each night to go the next morning, if nothing had happened meanwhile, and still waiting on.

However, yesterday evening I heard that the Prussians had sent the greater part of their army before Dybbol, and the whole of their siege artillery northwards in the direction of Fredericia. I learnt also that the Danes were transporting the remnant of their troops as fast as possible to Fünen; and that the headquarters were to be removed this morning without fail to Assens, a little sea-port town on the western coast of Fünen. Moreover, I needed no information to assure me that the Danes had abandoned all idea of seriously contesting the passage of the Sund. I walked over the whole of Sonderborg yesterday, and satisfied myself that no preparations were making to defend the town. The utmost that can be expected from the troops still stationed on the banks of the Sund and on the neighbouring heights is that they should delay the advance of the enemy across the straits long enough to allow the bulk of the army to make good its retreat. Be the cause what it may, the Prussians have shown no sign of pushing on their success with vigour. The whole conduct of the war, as I have often had occasion to observe before, is to a looker-on inexplicable. There is no doubt that the Prussians might have crossed over to Alsen without difficulty on the day of the capture of Dybbol. Their entrance on any one of the days immediately following would scarcely have been attended with greater difficulty; and the inevitable result would have been the capture of what was left of the Danish Army.

Yet the Danes have been permitted to remove their troops in sight of the enemy without molestation, and no apprehension, as far as I could learn, was ever entertained by the Danish commanders about their retreat being cut off. At this moment it is asserted by officials, who ought to be well informed, that the Prussians have no intention of crossing the straits at present. It is said that, as long as the Germans remain upon the Schleswig side of the Sund, they oblige the Danes to maintain a force in Alsen, the loss of whose services can be ill afforded; that if, on the other hand, the Prussians move on into Alsen itself, they will be forced themselves to keep a large army there, and will be exposed to the risk of constant assaults by naval expeditions disembarking troops upon the island. At Dybbol they are in perfect safety from any attack, and, as they can cross over the Sund whenever they think good, they are as much masters of Alsen as if they were quartered amidst the ruins of Sonderborg.

Whatever might be the justice of these calculations, it appeared probable that I might have to wait for days or weeks on the island, seeing nothing except the movements of a few Prussian troops, crowding in and out of the Dybbol forts, like ants burrowing in a sand-hill. Even if the Germans should make up their mind to a sudden advance on Alsen, there was no great probability of any further fighting, and there was a great likelihood that I might be taken prisoner without warning, and be detained till the Prussians had satisfied themselves of my nationality; so I resolved to follow the example of the commander-in-chief, and leave Alsen with what haste I could.

It was late in the evening when I accomplished that most difficult task of making up my own mind, and there were many kind friends to be said farewell to before I left the island. If it is the advantage of a roving life that you make many friends, it is the disadvantage also that you have many partings. The community of sympathies, the close intimacy of a life whose days were necessarily spent together, and, above all, the participation in some measure in a common danger, had made many of the acquaintanceships I had formed in the island very like friendships; and, as I parted company with those who had sheltered and befriended me so cordially, it was impossible not to feel that our paths in life were scarcely likely to cross again.

There was little, too, cheering in the prospects of those to whom I bade farewell. National humiliation, the loss of their country, and the ruin of their private fortunes, were the lot to which most of them had to look forward. All I could do was to utter a heartfelt though unavailing hope that better times might be in store for this kindly, honest people, and with this hope we parted.

It was early morning when I was on foot again on my way to Hörup harbour. The cold dry east winds which had been blowing for weeks had at last disappeared, and the deep-blue skies had vanished with them. The heavens were covered over with dull black clouds. The trees were still bare of leaves, and the wind moaned fitfully through the great birch forests across which my road lay. It seemed a fitting day for the retreat from Alsen, and, in fact, the removal of the headquarters to the island of Fünen, on the other side of the Belt, was a confession that the battle was over.

Ten regiments, I was told officially, were to be left in Alsen; but I knew that these skeleton regiments probably averaged little over five hundred men apiece, and that many of them were under early orders to leave. Even though there was no alarm, the scene at Hörup harbour was one of extreme confusion, and it was easy to judge what it would have been if the Prussian cavalry had been seen coming out of the forest glades which surround the one harbour of Alsen now that Sonderborg is lost. Carts jammed up the narrow roads and the slightly-built piers which had been hastily run out into the sea. Steamers, fishing-smacks, barges, and rafts were all dovetailed in together, in an inextricable puzzle. The landing was crowded with officers of the staff looking hopelessly after their horses and their luggage. The large Swedish steamboat which had the honour of carrying General Gerlach and his staff was to have sailed at nine; but two hours elapsed before it could be got away from its moorings.

A great number of scattered troops were collected about the quay, waiting for transport on the different sailing-vessels, but there was no cheering as the general embarked, followed by his staff. Little was said by anybody, except a few hasty farewells, and not a shout was raised. Indeed, ever since the defeat of Monday, the Danish troops have been wonderfully silent, and I have never once heard the "*Tappre Landsoldat*," whose strains used to be so familiar. There is no heart, indeed, for singing now.

Very shortly the steamer got under weigh, and moved out to sea, the officers crowding her paddle-boxes to get one last sight of Alsen. As the ship came out of the port, in sight of Dybbol and Broager, the "*Dannebrog*" was raised to the fore, and the military band struck up an air, which, I suppose, was patriotic, but which sounded strangely mournful. I question whether the ship was within reach of the Prussian batteries; at any rate, they vouchsafed no notice, and the staff of the late army of Alsen made good their retreat, with no need for undignified haste. They had stopped for five full days after it was clear that Alsen was untenable; and to stay longer would have been simple folly. But, inevitable as it was, the mere act of retreat was still a painful one.

The packet by which I sail started immediately after the war steamer, which we have already left far behind: the low bare heights of Dybbol and the wood-crowned slopes of Alsen are no longer visible; and to Sonderborg itself I have said what seems likely to be a last farewell.

CHAPTER 12

Copenhagen

Copenhagen, April 26.

Copenhagen, I trust, is not destined to be my Capua. Yet I own frankly, that I never felt so much sympathy for Hannibal's soldiers as I do at the present moment. If their campaigns through Italy bore any resemblance to that of Alsen, I cannot find it in my heart to blame them if they did linger in the first habitable city it was their fortune to enter. Sieges are all very pleasant to read of, and bombardments look well in print. But I doubt whether—with the exception of the sieges which Uncle Toby conducted with the help of Corporal Trim, and which the Widow Wadman look at from behind the arbour—anybody who ever took part in a siege, as besieger, besieged, or non-combatant, derived much satisfaction from the spectacle. I know that, as Als faded out of sight, the one predominant feeling in my own mind was that of personal satisfaction. If Sonderborg had laid in the Isle of Wight instead of that of Als, and I had left the enemy in possession of an English city, I am afraid my feeling would have been much the same.

After three months of dirt and discomfort and danger, the prospect of clean linen and good beds and the luxuries of civilised life over-weighed all other reflections. It was some comfort to me to see that even my Danish fellow-travellers were influenced by a like feeling, and that their spirits rose visibly as we got fairly upon our way. That it should have been so may have been very wrong. If so, I can only say, with Mr. Pecksniff, "*Poor human nature!*"

As it was, the long dreary journey through the night across the is-land of Fünen, the chill passage of the Great Belt in the grey morning dawn, and the dull, dusty railway ride from Korsor to Copenhagen, were rendered endurable by the thought that every hour was bringing me nearer to the haven where white shirts and warm baths and sleep undisturbed by shells awaited me. The reality, contrary to the ordinary rule of life, fulfilled the expectation. When Faust sold his soul to Mephistopheles, he made a bargain that the fiend should never claim his own till his victim had tasted such a complete sense of gratification that he could not even desire a change in his existence.

The Devil, as all readers of the life-drama are aware, tempted Faust in vain with every seduction of beauty, wealth, honour, passion; and it was only at last, when the lover of Gretchen and Helena was seated one day, after dinner, dozing in an armchair in the warm sunlight, that he felt every longing gratified, and uttered the expression of perfect beatitude which was needed to complete the contract. That Goethe had a profound knowledge of mankind I had always known; but how deep the truth of this lesson was I had never appreciated till the other morning, when, on my return from Alsen, I sat down at the breakfast-table of the *Hôtel d'Angleterre* at Copenhagen, with a pile of English newspapers before me, clean, washed, shaved, and warm.

Pleasant, however, as Copenhagen is to me now by the force of contrast, I should doubt its being a lively town at any time. It has the indescribable look of a city which has outlived its past greatness. Of all times, too, the present is probably the least favourable for seeing the capital of Denmark. An air of general depression is visible everywhere. The disaster of Dybbol has brought the war home to the Copenhageners, as I suspect it never was brought before.

Yesterday, for the first time, an estimate of the loss on the 18th was placarded on the walls; and that was in the form of a statement from a German newspaper, according to which the total Danish loss, in killed, wounded, missing, and prisoners, was five thousand five hundred. Now this loss, great in itself, is all the more important from the smallness of the country. The Danish Army is raised from every class; and between five and six thousand men cannot be taken from a little kingdom, numbering in its present limits not more than a million and a half of inhabitants, without the blow striking with more or less force upon every family in the land.

The whole life of Denmark, too, is centred in the metropolis to an unfortunate degree, and therefore every man of any station in the army, wherever his home may have been, is certain to have had relations with Copenhagen. Even amongst the small circle of acquaintances which I, as a stranger, have now in this city, I cannot go anywhere without hearing some story of a private grief or sorrow caused by the great national calamity. There is a sad monotony in the details

273

that I am told.

The poor young lieutenant, of whom I wrote to you the other day, who was killed on board the *Rolf Krake*, has, I find, left a widowed mother, now childless, to mourn his death. Major Schau, who was reported dead, is still alive, but has just had his leg amputated, and lies dangerously ill. This officer, whom I have met constantly at Sonderborg, was the last of seven sons, whose parents still live. Five were killed in the former war, one in the present campaign, and the last now lies maimed, wounded, and, it may be, dying. So I might repeat to you story after story of like import; but it is the same in all wars; and there are German homes left desolate, doubtless, as well as Danish ones.

I have been present today at the funeral of Major Rosen, whose name I must have often mentioned to you. My acquaintance with him was only that of a stranger. I had occasion many times to interrupt him, on matters connected with my duties as a correspondent, at periods when I have no doubt he was overpowered with the pressing cares of his office. Let me bear testimony to the uniform courtesy and consideration with which he received me, as I believe he did every stranger who sought his assistance. His pale, worn, somewhat stern face, with the clear marked features, and the scanty brown hair falling loosely about his high narrow forehead, rises before me as I write. He was a man, I think, few would have ventured to take a freedom with, and none would have hesitated to ask for a kindness.

Everybody respected him, and those who knew him loved him. A Holsteiner by birth and breeding, he was faithful to the losing cause; and the same unselfish loyalty was the cause of his death. On the 18th, in obedience to his duty, he was in a place of comparative shelter on the hill-side of Dybbol. When, however, he saw from his shelter that General Du Plat had been struck down, he rushed out upon the open road to lift up his fallen comrade, and fell instantly by his side, wounded to death. A large crowd of soldiers and citizens assembled yesterday to witness his funeral at the Holmen's Kirke. Of spectacle there was very little. The Danes have even less power than we have ourselves of organising imposing processions; but there were crowds of mourners, and many tears. His coffin, decked out with garlands of the first flowers of that spring he had just lived to see, was carried through the streets of Copenhagen, preceded by a company of soldiers, and followed by a long train of carriages.

In the quiet cemetery outside the town the procession ended its sad journey. There, by the newly-dug grave, the flowers were taken from the hearse, the sword and crosses and medals were removed from the velvet cushion, placed upon the top of the bier, on which they lay, and the coffin was lowered into the trench dug for it. The solemn words were said; the dust was thrown upon the coffin, and struck it with the dull, hollow sound which, once heard, is not soon forgotten. The chief mourner, the late major's son—a child of some six years old—was led up to the bank, and peeped down timidly and wonderingly into the grave; and then all was over. Tomorrow there is to be a military funeral, at which the different trades unions of the city are to assemble; and for many days to come such spectacles will be familiar to the streets of Copenhagen.

April 28.

I once had the honour to meet a great Italian exile who had just returned to his country after long years of absence. I asked him, I recollect, about his future plans, and whether he intended to take up his home in the land of his birth. "No," he answered; "I want to get away as soon as possible, for on my return I see nothing but graves on every side." So, I think, a Danish soldier, coming back to Copenhagen at this moment, might well hurry away again, saying that he also saw nothing but coffins here. Every day witnesses the burial of soldiers who have fallen in the war, and the sight of the long sad processions marching through the dull quiet streets has become so common a one, that it attracts but little notice.

Sir Walter Scott's father, whose great delight was to attend funerals as an amateur mourner, would have been in his element at Copenhagen. For my own part, I cannot work upon my feelings so as to get affected about the death of individuals whose very names were unknown to me. I see that other foreigners, who knew, if possible, less about the dead than I do myself, are affected at these ceremonies even to tears; so I suppose the absence of emotion is some defect in my moral nature.

An American gentleman who was present at one of the recent public funerals in Copenhagen remarked to a friend of mine that, "when he saw people crying, he did feel somehow as if he belonged to another congregation;" and in this respect I agree with his sentiments. As a rule, therefore, I keep away from spectacles of this kind, and yesterday I contented myself with seeing the great procession, which accompanied the bodies of the officers fallen at Dybbol to the

275

grave, defile past the windows of a house where I had obtained standing room, without following it to the cemetery. I do not know that I missed much by so doing, except that I should wish to have witnessed the scene which concluded it.

The king, as I think I mentioned to you, walked at the head of the procession, close behind the flower-clad coffins, bowing slowly from time to time in answer to the silent salutations which greeted him along his path. After the coffins were lowered into their graves, he spoke a few words of sympathy to the chief mourners who followed the different hearses, and then was about to leave, when he caught sight of a poor woman in deep mourning standing by a common soldier's grave, and weeping bitterly. He turned round at once, left his suite, took the woman, after the German fashion, by both her hands, held them in his, and asked her name kindly, while the tears poured down his own cheeks.

There could be no doubt about the genuineness of his emotion, and the dense crowd which surrounded the place of burial made way at once for the king, and greeted him, as he passed out, with a respectful silence, more eloquent, I think, than any cheers. His Majesty looked worn, sad, and prematurely aged; and all who come into contact with him tell me that the events of the war have agitated him deeply. At his accession he was not popular in Copenhagen. The faults of Frederick VIII. were of a nature which a people pardons easily; and his merits were of the class to be valued, perhaps, above their real value. Christian IX. is not a soldier-king like his predecessor; he has not the rough simple frankness of manner which made Frederick VIII. in very truth, and not in courtly phrase, the "*well-beloved*" of his subjects; and, above all, he was more than half a German in the eyes of the people who had accepted him reluctantly as their sovereign.

But, during the troubled months of his sad reign, the conviction seems gradually to have forced itself upon the Danes that he is faithful and honest, at any rate, to the cause of Denmark, and that he has made their country, their fortunes, and their cause, his own. The community of calamity has already endeared him to the Danes; and I believe his hold upon the nation is stronger now than when he first ascended the throne of Denmark.

But, apart from the constant spectacle of these funeral processions, the aspect of the town of Copenhagen is very gloomy at the present day. With the approach of summer the self-imposed mourning for the late king has been laid aside, and coloured dresses and ribbon-be-decked bonnets are again to be seen about the streets. Unfortunately, the public loss has been succeeded by a thousand private ones, and the number of people you see wearing mourning in Copenhagen is fearfully large. In private society there is naturally no great gaiety.

The theatres are open nightly, and are well attended. The *Bier-Kellers*, too, and *Cafés Chantants,* the Vauxhalls, and Walhallas, and Alhambras, and Tivolis, for which the city is famous, are opening for the summer, and seem, if their placards may be believed, to be doing a good business. But otherwise, amusement there is none.

How much of this dullness is due to the circumstances of the hour, how much to the normal condition of the city, I cannot judge. My impression is that at the best the capital of Denmark is not a lively residence. It is not, I should think, what advertising builders call an "improving locality." I see but little building going on anywhere, and the town already looks too large for its population. From the window of the room where I am writing I look out upon the great central square of the town, the Kongen's Nytor. The broad, open space, though this is the busiest time of the day, is only dotted over with half-a-dozen carriages and a hundred or so of foot passengers. Street railway cars, which look as if they had been imported direct from New York or Philadelphia, run across the square; and even the most obstinate of Copenhagen Conservatives could not, I think, object that there is any traffic for them to interfere with.

The docks and quays are but poorly filled with shipping; the fashionable quarters of the town are so lifeless, that the streets of Belgravia in the deadest season of the London year would seem crowded in comparison. In the commercial parts of the city there are people enough going to and fro; but the number of carts or carriages is still very insignificant. The shops are small and shabby, and have that nondescript *omnium gatherum* character which in other countries is only visible in provincial towns of little importance. Every article you see exhibited for sale is either imported or of second-rate quality. Money, I think, must be burning very hotly indeed in your pockets to induce you to spend much of it here.

The foreign residents in Copenhagen whom I have met with complain one and all that there is little society at any time, and that, to such as there is, access for strangers is impossible. Personally I have found the Danes so wonderfully hospitable, that I doubt the truth of the latter assertion; and, moreover, I have observed that a similar complaint is always made in every capital it has ever been my lot to visit.

The former statement I can readily believe.

During the last fifteen years Denmark has been going through a social revolution. The free institutions introduced by the late king transferred the government from the hands of the aristocratic classes into those of the *bourgeoisie*. Since that time the old ruling class has lived apart in dudgeon, while the new one has not yet accommodated itself to its altered position. Very much, too, of the social life of a little capital like this depends upon the court The peculiar tastes and the matrimonial relation of Frederick VIII. practically put a stop to all court society; while the new dynasty has entered on its career amidst circumstances which have in themselves precluded all idea of such entertainments.

April 29.

Another day has passed, and still we have no news that the hoped-for armistice has been concluded. Yet we seem to be drifting towards peace. This morning I received intelligence that the evacuation of Fredericia and Alsen had been definitely decided upon, and that the decision was being carried out as fast as possible. This evening, small handbills hawked about the streets informed the public that Fredericia had been abandoned.

For the last three days the evacuation of this fortress has been carried on with much secrecy, and finally only a small garrison was left in the place, under the command of Colonel Nielsen, who had instructions to quit the position as soon as an attack was apprehended. Yesterday afternoon the Germans appeared in force on the shores of the Belt, and drove in the Danish outposts. As it seemed probable the assault would have been made today, Colonel Nielsen resolved to withdraw the garrison, and at half-past eleven last night the Danes finally evacuated the fortress, without being disturbed in their retreat.

It seems doubtful, from the official account, whether the guns were saved. We are told in vague terms that "the most important part of the war material was carried off, the cannon spiked, and the ammunition either removed or destroyed;" from which statement, I suspect that much of the artillery must have fallen into the hands of the enemy. It is not known positively that the Germans have occupied the deserted fortress, but there can be little doubt that this is already the case. The intelligence has cast an additional gloom over the city; but, so far, there has been no exhibition of any popular indignation. The night is, fortunately, cold and rainy, so that few people are about.

278

The month of May opened with a heavy fall of snow, which has only slowly melted away beneath the hot sunlight of midday. The climate is obviously uncertain whether it ought to consider itself summer or winter, and the country is equally uncertain whether it is to regard the condition of affairs as one of peace or war. The truth is, that Denmark—not, I grant, by her own fault, but by the necessities of her position—has fallen into that state of mind immortalised by Wilkins Micawber, when a man lives on for years, amidst increasing embarrassments, trusting always that something will turn up.

Persons whose lot has thrown them into contact in private life with men inspired with this belief, must have observed with what an unreasoning faith its devotees cling to the idea that some unforeseen stroke of fortune is to relieve them from their difficulties, how resolutely they refuse to look facts in the face, and how confidently they trust that somebody or other must be forthcoming to pull them out of the ditch.

I was once acquainted with a gentleman who, having a good deal less than nothing, married a lady whose pecuniary assets were likewise represented by a negative quantity. When remonstrated with on the imprudence of his conduct, he remarked, after deep reflection, that there must be somebody amongst his connections who could not let him starve. Now, it is the curse of small States that they necessarily look to others for support. Denmark has shown vigour and energy and resolution enough of her own. She has helped herself; but, contrary to the French proverb, Heaven has not helped her in return.

In what I say, therefore, I must not be understood as imputing want of manliness to the Danes. All I say is, that, being by the force of circumstances dependent upon others, they have learnt to entertain an indefinite faith that something will be done by somebody to help them at the last moment. Had it not been for this belief, their gallant but useless resistance would never have been undertaken. Were it not for this delusion, there would be no prospect of the war being still carried on now that all hope is lost. That such a prospect does exist is, I fear, possible.

In a military point of view, the fortunes of Denmark seem well nigh desperate, and it is hard to see how the Danes can reject any terms on which an armistice may be offered them. The war party here seem to be hardly alive to the real position of affairs, and talk as if it were still in their power to carry on hostilities, and reduce Germany to reason by the pressure of a blockade.

Even supposing that the blockade of half a dozen Prussian ports could really do much damage to a great inland country like Prussia, whose commerce finds its chief exit through Hamburg, the Rhine and Belgium, I do not think the Danes could be allowed to carry out their purpose. Prussia now holds Jutland, the wealthiest of the Danish provinces, in her possession; and if she chooses she can cross over into Fünen. Should it come to a question of exhaustion, the occupation of Jutland and Schleswig, not to mention Fünen, will wear out the Danes much more rapidly than the blockade of Konigsberg or Stettin will wear out the Prussians. These reflections are so obvious, that the good sense of the Danish people cannot fail to perceive their force. The war-at-any-price party has already brought calamities enough upon the country; but I doubt its having the power, if it have the will, to force on the government to an insane continuance of a hopeless struggle.

At this moment the only thing which can save the country is an armistice; and the conviction that this is so is a very general and growing one. With the fall of Fredericia the curtain has, it appears, dropped upon the last act of the Schleswig-Holstein campaign. Denmark may say, with the French king after the Battle of Pavia, "*Tout est perdu hors l'honneur.*" Her honour is indeed safe, and with that barren consolation she must, I fear, remain contented for the present.

May 3.

Most persons, like myself, who have been in the United States during the Secession war, must have been struck with the fact how very little the immense extent of the country isolated one State from another. At Chicago or Philadelphia, at Boston or St. Louis, separated as these cities are by hundreds or thousands almost of miles, you knew as much or as little about the progress of the war. Here, on the other hand, though the whole area of the war is not larger than that of one of the smallest of the American States, you are surprised at the extraordinary degree to which the different provinces are separated from each other.

Nobody in Alsen knows what is going on in Jutland, or *vice versa*. Zealand is hardly aware whether Fünen is invaded or not; and even here, in Copenhagen, the knowledge of how the campaign is faring in the different provinces of the monarchy is of the scantiest. In spite of telegraphs and railroads and steamboats, Denmark is still a confederacy of disjointed states, rather than a homogeneous country. It is necessary, I think, to bear this fact constantly in mind, to understand the nature of the war. Zealand is divided from Fünen by a channel as wide as that of Dover.

Fünen, again, except in its north-west corner, is separated from Jutland by straits nearly as broad. Jutland is cut into halves by a broad inland fiord; and the islands of Alsen, Œroe, Langeland, Lalland, Falster, Moen, Femeren, and the series of minor ones which stud the Baltic Archipelago, are divided from Zealand and the mainland by wide tracts of sea. Thus the communication between the different parts of the monarchy is most imperfect, and community of race and language is the only tie which preserves the integrity of the kingdom.

Where this tie is wanting, as in Holstein; or only exists imperfectly, as in Schleswig; the bond of union must, under the most favourable circumstances, be a very fragile one. The influence of this separation between the different parts of the State is, indeed, very visible at the present moment. An invasion of Ireland would be keenly felt, no doubt, in England, and there is hardly an English family which would not have an individual, as well as a national stake in the issue of the war. Still it would be a very different thing from an invasion of England itself.

Now Zealand, with respect to Jutland, or even to Fünen, occupies a very similar position to that which England would occupy towards Ireland, supposing the French landed in Galway, and supposing also it was absolutely impossible that they should cross St. George's Channel. Except under the most improbable contingency that the Austrian fleet should utterly demolish the Danish, and that the Germans should attempt to land an army in Zealand, the island, which contains the seat of government and the political centre of all Denmark, is as safe from the actual presence of war as Iceland itself.

I do not suppose that the contingency of an invasion of Zealand has ever even been contemplated by the Danish Government; it certainly has not been by the people of Copenhagen. In fact, except for the return of the dead and wounded soldiers, the Copenhageners know very little actually about the war. Though the enemy at the furthest point of his progress can be little over a hundred miles away from the capital, less is known about his movements than is known at New York about those of the Confederates in Texas.

I once came across a file of old newspapers published in the days when the Jacobite Army was marching down on the Midland shires of England. I should have thought beforehand that they would have contained much information as to the progress of the invading hosts, whose victorious march was only stopped in the county next to that in which the newsletter in question was published. I found, however, that the only intelligence given was in the form of an occasional report that a traveller, recently arrived in the town, stated that he had heard the rebels had been seen in some place or other in a neighbouring shire.

If you make allowance for the advance in the means of locomotion and communication during the last century, the Zealand Danes are hardly better informed about the position of the Germans than our forefathers were as to the advance of the Highland clans. Nobody here, for instance, can tell up to what point the Germans have penetrated in Jutland, or where the Danish cavalry, under General Hegerman, has taken refuge on the peninsula; whether the Austrians are preparing to cross the Belt from Fredericia, or whether the Prussians have as yet made any demonstration against Alsen.

The government, I think, has no wish to conceal the truth. Indeed, wherever news is known, it seems to me to be published with tolerable promptitude, and certainly with extreme candour. But the government itself is very imperfectly informed. Statements are published daily from the War Office that all is quiet in Als, or that nothing has happened before Middelfart in Fünen. But that is all. The private scraps of information given by the newspapers are very meagre. An announcement in today's papers that:

> An engagement took place on Saturday near Bold Wood, in Jutland, between the enemy and some of our troops; that particulars are not yet known, but that it is reported that, without any loss on our side, we took a score of prisoners.

. . . . .may be taken as a fine sample of the items of intelligence conveyed to the Copenhagen public by the press. The government acts perhaps wisely in concealing the movements of the Danish forces as much as possible; but yet it is strange that, though Fünen is only some five hours' journey from Copenhagen, nobody here not connected with the administration appears to have any idea what force there is at present collected in the island, or upon what point it is being concentrated.

May 5.

Let me endeavour to explain to you the general nature of the two parties which, for the last sixteen years, have swayed in turn the policy of Denmark.

It would be useless to enter into minute details, whose bearing on the question could only be explained by long disquisitions on the contemporary history of the country. What I wish to explain are the broad features of difference between the two parties which divide Denmark—the Eider-Danes and the Whole-State men, as they are called respectively. In Denmark—I am speaking now of Denmark proper, not of the Duchies—there is, as in England, no such thing as a foreign party.

No faction accuses or even suspects its opponents of being disloyal to the cause of Denmark, or of seeking any object, however mistakenly, except the welfare of the country. No party is supposed to favour Germany, or to seek any change in the dynastic succession. The questions on which the rival camps are at issue are those of domestic government and foreign policy. What renders the politics of Denmark so difficult of comprehension is, that, by a fortuitous combination of circumstances, the question of external policy is inseparably connected for the time with that of internal government. Ever since the accession of the late king, the relations of the Duchies to Denmark have been the absorbing issue of politics; and therefore the two parties have derived their names and their temporary character from the different views they took of the manner in which this issue should be dealt with.

Their real character, however, is derived from that divergence of opinion which separates Liberals and Conservatives in every free constitutional country. From the time the German unity movement came into active existence, it has been admitted by the Danes that Holstein and Lauenburg must, as German States and members of the Confederacy, follow the fortunes of the Fatherland. Granted this fact, the question arose how their relations to Denmark ought to be regulated. Speaking broadly, the Whole-State men advocated the view that such concessions should be made as would induce Holstein and Lauenburg to remain contented beneath the rule of Denmark.

On the other hand, the Eider-Danes asserted that no possible concession would ever effect the desired objects; that Holstein must be separated from the monarchy, or connected with it at most by such a bond as that which, up to the death of William IV., united Hanover to England; and that the other provinces of the kingdom north of the Eider must be consolidated into one homogeneous Danish country.

The difference in theory between the two factions was not unlike that between the advocates of State rights and centralised government under the American Union. The Whole-State party recommended the policy of separate local administrations for each of the four great divisions of the monarchy, Holstein, Schleswig, Jutland, and the islands, with a central government at Copenhagen, whose jurisdiction should extend only to matters of common national import.

The Eider-Danes wished to have one government only; and as Holstein could not possibly be comprehended in any arrangement of this kind, they proposed to detach it from the rest of the monarchy. Of course, in each party there were various sections who advocated these conflicting views with more or less obstinacy; and the modes by which each of them sought to carry out their opinions altered according to the circumstances of the day. Still, this divergence of sentiment was the mainspring of the policy which from 1818 downwards has directed the action of the Whole-State men and the Eider-Danes respectively. Looking on the question in the abstract, the views of the former party were the wisest and most statesmanlike; practically, however, there were many considerations which threw the power, not unreasonably, into the hands of their opponents.

The final cause, as metaphysicians would call it, of this war is, as I have always tried to impress upon my readers, not one of rival dynastic pretensions, or of internal government, or even directly of Prussian desires of aggrandisement, but of conflicting and hostile nationalities. The question which has agitated Europe so long comes, when you divest it of all accidental features, simply to this: Is the Cimbrian peninsula to belong to Germans or Danes?—is the ruling nationality in the peninsula to be Scandinavian or Teutonic?

Now, if no change had occurred in the course of events, there can be little question how this struggle would have ended. It would be entering on too wide a subject to consider the influences which operated in favour of the German party. But this much may be asserted without fear of contradiction, even from the Danes themselves, that up to the end of the last century Denmark was rapidly becoming Germanised. German was the language of all educated people, and in the Duchies was the official language of the country.

During the first quarter, however, of the present century, (19th), there was a national reaction in favour of Scandinavianism, owing partly to social, still more to political causes. The Germans tried to pull the apple off the tree before it was ripe, and the Danes awoke to the consciousness of the fact that the Teutonic tendency of their culture, society, and government was likely to prove fatal to their national existence. An attempt was made to undo the work of the past, and to re-establish the supremacy of the Danish element in the State. This attempt secured the support of all the energy, talent, and patriotism in the country, and the advance of Germanism, as it was styled, was retarded, if not checked. A new generation sprang up, imbued with Danish culture, ideas, traditions, and aspirations, and prepared to sacrifice almost anything to the maintenance of a distinct Danish nationality. The late king was perhaps the most ardent adherent of this movement, and he might well be taken as the representative man of the Scandinavian party.

It is not difficult to understand how this anti-German tendency worked in favour of the Eider-Dane policy. The only way to form a Whole-State was to allow something like autonomy to the Duchies. With such autonomy the Germanisation of Schleswig was a mere question of time. If Holstein, on the other hand, were separated from the monarchy, and Schleswig incorporated with the purely Danish provinces, it was at any rate conceivable that all Denmark, north of the Eider, might be made in course of time a purely Danish State. Thus arose the apparent anomaly that a party eminently patriotic, and whose sole *"raison d'être"* was the maintenance of the integrity of the country, based its policy upon the surrender of the richest and most important province of the monarchy. To draw a metaphor from a common proverb, I may say the Eider-Danes considered that half a loaf of purely Danish bread was better than a whole loaf of mixed Danish and German; and in this view they were supported by the united strength of the national reaction against Germanism.

The relations of the two parties were further complicated by the divergence of their wishes about internal government. Up to the death of Christian VIII., Denmark was ruled by an absolute government, despotic rather in name than in fact, and under which the different provinces enjoyed great local independence. When constitutional government was established in Denmark by Frederick VII., on his accession in 1848, there were naturally two domestic parties in the country.

The Liberals desired democratic institutions; the Conservatives wished to preserve as much as possible of the old despotic system. Now it so happened that Holstein and Schleswig were much more aristocratic in their institutions, sympathies, and tendencies than the provinces of Denmark proper. Any form of constitution, therefore, which was based upon the Whole-State system and preserved the local autonomy of the Duchies, must necessarily be much less democratic than a system based upon the principle of extending to all the States north of the Eider the same institutions as those desired by the island Danes, and more especially by the Copenhageners. In consequence, the aristocratic party and the adherents of the old absolutist system espoused the Whole-State policy, while the Liberals identified themselves with the Eider-Dane platform.

Thus it came to pass that the national aspirations of the Scandinavian party and the democratic movement of young Denmark both worked in favour of the Eider-Dane policy, which had also the support of the king himself; and, as a rule, this party has, up to the present time, directed the destinies of the country. But yet their victory is not so permanently secured as might be supposed at first sight. Constitutional government, it should be remembered, was given to the nation by the king, not wrung from the king by the nation.

There was no wide-spread national dissatisfaction with the old state of things, and the character of the movement which made Denmark a free country was not unlike that which established the short-lived constitutions of Germany in 1848. The chief leaders of the movement here, as in Germany, were the educated middle classes, the professors, and the officials. Fortunately, the country was so prosperous and contented that it contained little, if anything, of the revolutionary and socialistic element which ruined the cause of free government in the Fatherland; while the practical common-sense of the Danish people preserved them from the extravagances into which the German Liberals fell blindly. Moreover, the king, instead of working underhand against the new order of things, like his German brother sovereigns, sought loyally and honestly to carry out the system of constitutionalism.

The change has worked well; the country has made rapid progress in liberty and prosperity; and free institutions have steadily gained ground in Denmark. But still nations, like individuals, never value what has been given to them so much as what they have earned for themselves. An agricultural country, such as Denmark, occupied almost exclusively by small landed proprietors and peasants, is always conservative in its instincts; there exists undoubtedly, even in the purely Danish provinces, a good deal of jealousy against the preponderance which a centralised democratic government has given to Copenhagen and the islands on which it stands; and, until the hour of trial comes, it is difficult even for native politicians to say what amount of hold the constitutional form of government has acquired upon the rural districts.

From the causes which I have endeavoured to indicate as briefly as I could, the question of constitutional freedom is associated almost inextricably with the Eider-Dane policy, and its corollary, the maintenance of the November constitution. Now up to the present hour that policy has been a failure. The net result is, that the whole peninsula is occupied by Germany, that the Duchies seem almost irretrievably lost, that the army is well nigh destroyed, and that Fünen, if not Zealand, lies at the mercy of the invaders, Whether any other policy could have produced a different or a less disastrous result is a matter on which it is hard to form an opinion.

The result, however, is unfortunately patent, and the party to whose policy this result is immediately due bears, not unjustly, the responsibility of the failure. There is no doubt that the policy which dictated the declaration of war, and the gallant though hopeless resistance of the Danes, was the one which commanded the support of the vast majority of the nation. Still it is possible that public opinion may change, and the organs of the Eider-Dane party—the *Dagblad* and the *Faedreland*—appear to me nervously alarmed lest this should prove to be the case. The capture of Dybbol, with the practical loss of half the army, has produced an immense effect throughout the country; and the organs of the aristocratic and Conservative factions declare openly that the Eider-Dane policy has been the ruin of the country.

It is natural enough, therefore, the Danish Liberals should resent bitterly the imputation that the army was sacrificed to popular clamour; and the fact that the statement has too much truth in it renders it all the more offensive.

May 11.

The concluding chapters of a novel are always flat and wearisome. When you know the end, when even the least experienced of novel-readers can guess the "*dénouement*," you turn over the leaves impatiently. Whether the heroine dies broken-hearted, or terminates the romance of life by a happy union with the object of her affections, it makes no difference. The consummation is foreseen, and the details of the process can command but scanty interest. For the last three weeks my readers, as I have been painfully aware, have been perusing the last pages of the story it has been my duty to describe as narrator. If I have told my story intelligibly, those who read it must long ago have known what was to be the ending.

With the capture of Dybbol and the overwhelming calamity which befell the Danish arms on that fatal April morning, the unequal contest between Denmark and Germany was virtually ended. The crisis had come, and there could be no further question as to the termination. The spectacle of the period which has elapsed between the loss of Dybbol and the conclusion of the armistice has been a very painful one to all who cannot avoid sympathising with the heroism of a gallant people.

Further resistance was obviously impossible, and yet the Danes could not make up their minds to the fact that all was over. Everybody knew that the acceptance of an armistice on the terms dictated by the victorious enemy had become inevitable, and yet nobody liked to acknowledge the necessity. Men hoped against hope that the exorbitant character of the demands put forward by Germany might induce the neutral Powers to interfere actively on behalf of Denmark, and, faint as this hope was known to be, it was too precious to be abandoned. To be what I recollect hearing Garibaldi promised Italy should be, on the day when he addressed the crowd gathered to welcome him on his entry into Naples, *"padrone in casa sua"*—master of one's own destiny—is surely the greatest blessing that a nation can enjoy.

There may be advantages in the existence of small States; but nothing, I think, can compensate to their inhabitants for the dependence upon foreign Powers to which, however brave and heroic, they are virtually subjected. The bare possibility that England and France might go to war for her sake has protracted and embittered the agony of this gallant country. The Danes were afraid of owning to the world, or even to themselves, that the time had come to submit to force, for fear that such an admission might extinguish the last prospect of foreign aid. So they have gone on since the fall of Dybbol, to repeat an expression I have used before, drifting into peace. First they were confident—or I should rather say professed to be confident—that Fredericia would be defended to the last; then, that a stand would be made in North Jutland; and, finally, that the war by sea would be maintained at all hazards. Illusion after illusion has had to be abandoned, and at last the end has come.

The government has reflected faithfully enough the indecision of the people. I have never disguised my conviction that a suspension of hostilities had become unavoidable, and that, as the Germans would most certainly refuse to permit the continuance of the blockade while Fünen lay practically within their grasp, the blockade would have to be raised. I was assured on every side that such a proposition could not be entertained.

On this day week the official journal, the *Berlingske Tidende*, contained an assertion that no armistice could be accepted which involved the cessation of the blockade; and later in the week, this assertion, as I know, was confirmed verbally by the ministers themselves. On Monday, however, there were rumours current that the government had given way, and on that evening I learnt privately that the report was true.

Even then, however, disbelief in the conclusion of a truce was expressed in official circles. It was said the government had reason to know that Prussia was resolved on prosecuting the war, and that the only motive of Denmark's making these concessions was to place Germany more completely in the wrong in the probable event of fresh difficulties being raised. Whether this belief was seriously entertained, or whether it was merely put forward in order to break the suddenness of the change of policy, I cannot say.

This I know, that, in spite of these rumours, there was no expectation yesterday morning of the news which arrived in the afternoon. A despatch was received about noon at the Foreign Office, but it was so confused that its purport was doubtful. Later in the day, however, a private telegram was forwarded to the Exchange, and then it became known, by an official announcement, that the war was over and the defeat acknowledged.

Any fears that may have been entertained as to the manner in which the news would be received at Copenhagen have proved utterly groundless. Up to this afternoon there has been no public demonstration of any kind, and no manifestation whatever of popular feeling. Indeed, the predominant feeling for the moment is one of relief. It is a comfort, at any rate, to know the worst; and the blow struck at Dybbol is still too fresh in the remembrance of the people for any measure which stops the progress of the invasion to be absolutely unwelcome. Even the Opposition papers hardly question for the time the wisdom of the decision at which the Ministry has arrived.

When the urgency of the immediate necessity is forgotten, it is probable that a different state of feeling will set in. The terms of the armistice are bitterly mortifying to the Danes. It is believed that this is not a mere suspension, but a virtual abandonment, of the war. As the *Dagblag* of today remarks, with truth:

> The government will not be able to resist the extension of an armistice on the same terms as those on which it has consented to its conclusion; and the whole burden of these terms falls on Denmark.

In truth, with the one single exception that the island of Alsen is preserved under Danish rule, it is hard to see what the Danes gain beyond the broad fact of peace. Fredericia is taken, Jutland is occupied by German troops, and the pressure upon German commerce—the one weapon on whose ultimate efficacy Denmark relied confidently to the last—is thrown aside. Nothing can be better for the designs of Prussia than the maintenance of the *status quo*; hardly anything could be less favourable for the hopes of the Danes. The paramount object of securing an armistice was, doubtless, worth any sacrifice, but still the sacrifice made is a fearfully heavy one.

If the government could have consented to raise the blockade immediately upon the fall of Dybbol, it is probable that an armistice might have been obtained without the loss of Fredericia or the occupation of Jutland; and when the *Rigsraad* meets—supposing that ill-fated body is ever destined to assemble—the conduct of the Ministry is likely to be severely canvassed.

However, whether wisely or not, the bargain has been struck, and the Danes have set about fulfilling their share of the contract with their usual loyalty. Yesterday, as soon as the news arrived, a fast steamer was despatched to Jutland to stop the movements of General Hegerman, and this morning a decree has been published notifying that the blockade of the Prussian and Schleswig-Holstein ports will be raised tomorrow. In a day or two the whole line of communication between Kiel and Korsöer is to be re-established, and the Danish cruisers will be recalled as speedily as possible.

Happily, the last incident of the war has been one gratifying to the Danes, after a long series of mortifications. On the day on which the armistice was concluded, a naval engagement took place in the North Sea, within sight of Heligoland, between a Danish and Austrian squadron. As you will learn the details from Hamburg long before we know them in Copenhagen, it is no use my repeating the confused reports we have received here of the vessels engaged, and the amount of loss. The only thing which appears certain is that the Austrians were driven back, with one of their ships in flames, and that the victory was on the side of the Danes. The news of the battle and the armistice arrived here together, and the former somewhat broke the disappointment that the latter had caused.

LEONAUR

ALSO FROM LEONAUR
AVAILABLE IN SOFTCOVER OR HARDCOVER WITH DUST JACKET

THE FALL OF THE MOGHUL EMPIRE OF HINDUSTAN *by H. G. Keene*—By the beginning of the nineteenth century, as British and Indian armies under Lake and Wellesley dominated the scene, a little over half a century of conflict brought the Moghul Empire to its knees.

LADY SALE'S AFGHANISTAN *by Florentia Sale*—An Indomitable Victorian Lady's Account of the Retreat from Kabul During the First Afghan War.

THE CAMPAIGN OF MAGENTA AND SOLFERINO 1859 *by Harold Carmichael Wylly*—The Decisive Conflict for the Unification of Italy.

FRENCH'S CAVALRY CAMPAIGN *by J. G. Maydon*—A Special Correspondent's View of British Army Mounted Troops During the Boer War.

CAVALRY AT WATERLOO *by Sir Evelyn Wood*—British Mounted Troops During the Campaign of 1815.

THE SUBALTERN *by George Robert Gleig*—The Experiences of an Officer of the 85th Light Infantry During the Peninsular War.

NAPOLEON AT BAY, 1814 *by F. Loraine Petre*—The Campaigns to the Fall of the First Empire.

NAPOLEON AND THE CAMPAIGN OF 1806 *by Colonel Vachée*—The Napoleonic Method of Organisation and Command to the Battles of Jena & Auerstädt.

THE COMPLETE ADVENTURES IN THE CONNAUGHT RANGERS *by William Grattan*—The 88th Regiment during the Napoleonic Wars by a Serving Officer.

BUGLER AND OFFICER OF THE RIFLES *by William Green & Harry Smith*—With the 95th (Rifles) during the Peninsular & Waterloo Campaigns of the Napoleonic Wars.

NAPOLEONIC WAR STORIES *by Sir Arthur Quiller-Couch*—Tales of soldiers, spies, battles & sieges from the Peninsular & Waterloo campaigns.

CAPTAIN OF THE 95TH (RIFLES) *by Jonathan Leach*—An officer of Wellington's sharpshooters during the Peninsular, South of France and Waterloo campaigns of the Napoleonic wars.

RIFLEMAN COSTELLO *by Edward Costello*—The adventures of a soldier of the 95th (Rifles) in the Peninsular & Waterloo Campaigns of the Napoleonic wars.

LEONAUR

ALSO FROM LEONAUR

AVAILABLE IN SOFTCOVER OR HARDCOVER WITH DUST JACKET

THE 9TH—THE KING'S (LIVERPOOL REGIMENT) IN THE GREAT WAR 1914 - 1918 *by Enos H. G. Roberts*—Mersey to mud—war and Liverpool men.

THE GAMBARDIER *by Mark Severn*—The experiences of a battery of Heavy artillery on the Western Front during the First World War.

FROM MESSINES TO THIRD YPRES *by Thomas Floyd*—A personal account of the First World War on the Western front by a 2/5th Lancashire Fusilier.

THE IRISH GUARDS IN THE GREAT WAR - VOLUME 1 *by Rudyard Kipling*—Edited and Compiled from Their Diaries and Papers—The First Battalion.

THE IRISH GUARDS IN THE GREAT WAR - VOLUME 1 *by Rudyard Kipling*—Edited and Compiled from Their Diaries and Papers—The Second Battalion.

ARMOURED CARS IN EDEN *by K. Roosevelt*—An American President's son serving in Rolls Royce armoured cars with the British in Mesopatamia & with the American Artillery in France during the First World War.

CHASSEUR OF 1914 *by Marcel Dupont*—Experiences of the twilight of the French Light Cavalry by a young officer during the early battles of the great war in Europe.

TROOP HORSE & TRENCH *by R.A. Lloyd*—The experiences of a British Life-guardsman of the household cavalry fighting on the western front during the First World War 1914-18.

THE EAST AFRICAN MOUNTED RIFLES *by C.J. Wilson*—Experiences of the campaign in the East African bush during the First World War.

THE LONG PATROL *by George Berrie*—A Novel of Light Horsemen from Gallipoli to the Palestine campaign of the First World War.

THE FIGHTING CAMELIERS *by Frank Reid*—The exploits of the Imperial Camel Corps in the desert and Palestine campaigns of the First World War.

STEEL CHARIOTS IN THE DESERT *by S. C. Rolls*—The first world war experiences of a Rolls Royce armoured car driver with the Duke of Westminster in Libya and in Arabia with T.E. Lawrence.

WITH THE IMPERIAL CAMEL CORPS IN THE GREAT WAR *by Geoffrey Inchbald*—The story of a serving officer with the British 2nd battalion against the Senussi and during the Palestine campaign.

LEONAUR

ALSO FROM LEONAUR
AVAILABLE IN SOFTCOVER OR HARDCOVER WITH DUST JACKET

ESCAPE FROM THE FRENCH *by Edward Boys*—A Young Royal Navy Midshipman's Adventures During the Napoleonic War.

THE VOYAGE OF H.M.S. PANDORA *by Edward Edwards R. N. & George Hamilton, edited by Basil Thomson*—In Pursuit of the Mutineers of the Bounty in the South Seas—1790-1791.

MEDUSA *by J. B. Henry Savigny and Alexander Correard and Charlotte-Adélaïde Dard* —Narrative of a Voyage to Senegal in 1816 & The Sufferings of the Picard Family After the Shipwreck of the Medusa.

THE SEA WAR OF 1812 VOLUME 1 *by A. T. Mahan*—A History of the Maritime Conflict.

THE SEA WAR OF 1812 VOLUME 2 *by A. T. Mahan*—A History of the Maritime Conflict.

WETHERELL OF H. M. S. HUSSAR *by John Wetherell*—The Recollections of an Ordinary Seaman of the Royal Navy During the Napoleonic Wars.

THE NAVAL BRIGADE IN NATAL *by C. R. N. Burne*—With the Guns of H. M. S. Terrible & H. M. S. Tartar during the Boer War 1899-1900.

THE VOYAGE OF H. M. S. BOUNTY *by William Bligh*—The True Story of an 18th Century Voyage of Exploration and Mutiny.

SHIPWRECK! *by William Gilly*—The Royal Navy's Disasters at Sea 1793-1849.

KING'S CUTTERS AND SMUGGLERS: 1700-1855 *by E. Keble Chatterton*—A unique period of maritime history-from the beginning of the eighteenth to the middle of the nineteenth century when British seamen risked all to smuggle valuable goods from wool to tea and spirits from and to the Continent.

CONFEDERATE BLOCKADE RUNNER *by John Wilkinson*—The Personal Recollections of an Officer of the Confederate Navy.

NAVAL BATTLES OF THE NAPOLEONIC WARS *by W. H. Fitchett*—Cape St. Vincent, the Nile, Cadiz, Copenhagen, Trafalgar & Others.

PRISONERS OF THE RED DESERT *by R. S. Gwatkin-Williams*—The Adventures of the Crew of the Tara During the First World War.

U-BOAT WAR 1914-1918 *by James B. Connolly/Karl von Schenk*—Two Contrasting Accounts from Both Sides of the Conflict at Sea D uring the Great War.